WRITING THE WIND

A CELTIC RESURGENCE

WRITING THE WIND

A CELTIC RESURGENCE

THE NEW CELTIC POETRY

Welsh ▪ Breton ▪ Irish Gaelic
Scottish Gaelic ▪ Cornish ▪ Manx

Edited By Thomas Rain Crowe
with Gwendal Denez & Tom Hubbard

New Native Press
1997

The editors wish to thank the following for their support and assistance in this project: David Greenslade *(The Celtic Pen)*, Tom Johnstone (The Mercat Press/James Thin Booksellers & Publishers), Mark Owens *(Nexus)*, Keith Flynn *(Asheville Poetry Review)*, Peter Finch (Oriel Bookshop), The Scottish Poetry Library, Kenny's Bookshop & Gallery, Theo Dorgan (Poetry Ireland), Annaig Renault, Deirdre Davitt, Ian MacDonald, Wil Rees, Gabriel Fitzmaurice, Dillon Johnston, Pearce Hutchinson *(Cyphers)* and Peter Fallon (Gallery Books) early on, William Neill, and faithful correspondents Maureen Macnaughtan, Anne MacLeod, Dewi Stephen Jones and Stuart Reid.

Cover photos "Callanish Stones" by Rick Woods (EarthLight Photography).

Section title page photos: "Pentre Ifan" (Wales) by Nan Watkins; "The Rock Figure" (Brittany) by Alan Botrel; "Newgrange" (Ireland) by Thomas Crowe; "Callanish Stones" (Scotland) by Rick Woods; "Celtic Cross" (Cornwall) by Rick Woods; "Peel Castle" (Isle of Man) by Tony Lakin.

Cover and book design by Dana Irwin (Irwin Graphics).

Copy editing by Nan Watkins.

New Native books are published for Thomas Rain Crowe and New Native Press. Inquiries and book orders should be addressed to: New Native Press, P.O. Box 661, Cullowhee, NC 28723 USA.

Library of Congress Catalog Card #97-65729

ISBN 1-883197-12-0

99 98 97   6 5 4 3 2 1

Dedicated to
Sorley MacLean (1911-1996)

The editors and publisher wish to express their sincere gratitude to the following organizations whose support in solidarity not only lent the project a true Celtic community essence, but whose funding was essential to the publication of this book:

Skol-Uhel ar Vro (Institut Culturel de Bretagne)

The North Carolina Writers' Network

Bord na Gaeilge

The Arts Council of Wales

The Ireland Funds

Contents

Brittany / Breton

Ireland / Irish Gaelic

Scotland / Scottish Gaelic

Cornwall / Cornish

Isle of Man / Manx

A Celtic Resurgence: An Introduction

believe that the idea for this book began, consciously, during my years as a teenager when I began to wonder who the living literary progeny of poets like Robert Burns and James Joyce were, and unconsciously, as a much younger boy, with the rhymes of Robert Louis Stevenson, the songs of Burns and the tales of Sir Walter Scott that were whispered and softly sung in my ears by my mother at bedtime. Curious, and not being one to forget such deep-seated questions or recurring dreams, I continued to wonder about the identities and whereabouts of great contemporary Celtic poets and writers into my adolescent years as a writer myself when such literary figures as Yevtushenko, Vosnesensky and Solzenitsyn in Russia were rising out of the literary tundra of their country's contemporary history to plant their flags of influence on American shores. Other writers from around the world began making their way into the world of English translation, until, by the 1970s, there was a wealth of indigenous work which had been translated into English from every continent on the planet – Kenyatta and Achebe from Africa; Vallejo, Borges, Neruda and García Márquez from South America; Paz from Mexico; García Lorca, Machado, Hernández and Otero in Spain and new translations of Lautréamont, Artaud, Bachelard, and Alain-Fournier from France; Kundera and Milosz from the Eastern Bloc; Ritsos from Greece; Amichai and Adonis from the Middle East . . . all making their way into the literary subconscious of the English-speaking world.

As the translation boom extended and expanded into the 1980s and 1990s, there remained a large black hole in the field of translation of international literature – namely the vital new contemporary canon coming from the Celtic language countries. While it is true that by the mid to late 1980s, the names of a few non-Gaelic Irish writers had made the journey across the Atlantic to American shores, writers who were known as well in England and the U.K., there was little or nothing known of the wealth of indigenous language writers from Celtic countries until the "Irish invasion" led by the likes of Seamus Heaney, Eavan Boland, Paul Durcan, Brendan Kennelly, Ciaran Carson and Michael Hartnett, all of whom were writing in English. Soon the rip tide of the Irish invasion would bring new names from Ireland as well as drag along with it a few names from Scotland and Wales – names like R.S. Thomas and James Kelman. But, still there was a hushed silence from true Celts: the speaker/writers of Gaelic, Welsh, Breton, Cornish and Manx.

Partly out of frustration and partly as an appendage to a late-blooming interest in my Scottish family heritage, I made a first trip to Scotland in 1995 in search of not only my "roots," as it were, but of the "grail" of contemporary Celtic poetry. Having spent the summer of 1993 in Laugharne, Wales – the final home of Dylan Thomas – and having had an eye-opening and educational introduction to Welsh literary history during that visit, finding the gateway into the Celtic world of the twentieth century that had until then been a locked door, I entered Scotland for the first time armed with enthusiasm if not a dangerously small pocketful of knowledge.

During the year between my visits to the U.K. in 1993 and 1995, I had struck up a blazing correspondence with Welsh poet and language activist Bobi Jones in Aberystwyth. Through his plethoric knowledge and scholarship of things Welsh, I was able to get my foot in the door of the home of historic Arthurian legend *(The Mabinogion)* and its more contemporary offspring incarnated in such early twentieth-century Welsh literary luminaries as Waldo Williams, Euros Bowen, Saunders Lewis, R. Williams Parry begotten by the likes of earlier bards such as Ann Griffiths in the late eighteenth century, and a list of Llwyds and Llŷns and ap Gwilyms and Anonymous's going all the way back to Aneirin and Taliesin in the late sixth century. With this quick course in the Welsh-language literary tradition, I was armed with, if nothing else, an outsider's interest as I entered Scotland by train in the summer of 1995 headed for the western Highlands and the home of my Clan MacDhaibhidh forebears just north and west of Inverness.

In truth I was also on a "grail quest" to the home of Scotland national treasure Sorley MacLean on the Isle of Skye. At eighty-four years of age, Sorley MacLean was a living legend in the long history of Gaelic literature. "What Robert Frost and Carl Sandburg are to modern American letters, MacLean is to Scotland," I'd heard Gaelic translator and poet Pearce Hutchinson say to me only a few weeks earlier in Dublin. This was a superlative that I'd heard echoed in Edinburgh by Tessa Ransford and Aonghas MacNeacail at the Scottish Poetry Library only a few days earlier, and that I remembered as my train was making its way, sluggishly, through the terrain and blinding rain of the Highlands on its way to Skye.

As blinding as the rain that day was my faith. Going to meet one of the great Celtic writers of the twentieth century with no letter of introduction or advance warning given – impulsive and presumptuous perhaps, but my desire to meet this man had grown far greater than any sense of etiquette.

As luck would have it, I arrived in the community of Braes where Sorley MacLean lived just outside of the town of Portree on the Isle of Skye merely hours after he had left to go to Edinburgh. We literally had passed on the road, going in opposite directions.

Some would say that it is the journey, not the destination, that is most important. I had made the journey to Skye to the home of the Gaelic language's leading luminary, and instead of coming away with "the grail," I came away from Skye with a copy of a book that had been published in 1991 honoring the eightieth birthday of Sorley

MacLean – an anthology of sorts edited by Angus Peter Campbell and comprised of many of the Scottish-Gaelic language's most important contemporary poets which would be my gateway to contemporary Scottish-Gaelic literature and its history.

As I sat down to write the Introduction for this book, I received word from Scotland of Sorley MacLean's death. In phone conversations with Aonghus MacNeacail on the Isle of Skye and Tom Hubbard at home in Fife on the opposite coast of the country, and in letters from Anne MacLeod on the Black Isle just north of Inverness, and from others with whom I've become intimate through the mail during these past couple of years, comes the word of "an end of an era." So essential and important was the work of Sorley MacLean to twentieth-century Scottish literature and its modern tradition.

Since Sorley MacLean is seen universally as a cornerstone to modern Celtic language literary traditions, my co-editors Tom Hubbard and Gwendal Denez and I have unanimously agreed to dedicate this first comprehensive contemporary Celtic language in translation anthology to Sorley MacLean. His name and work have set the standard for what will come, as they have for what has transpired in the existing Celtic language communities, world-wide, for the better part of the entire century.

So, with my curiosity piqued and suitcase filled with names, addresses, and seminal books from Ireland, Wales and Scotland, I returned to the States in late August of 1995 convinced of the fact that this book needed to be done. Since that time, and after having edited the "Special Celtic Issue" of the *Asheville Poetry Review* in the spring of 1996, I have been single-minded in my attempts to give voice to the greater Celtic community of poets representing not only Wales and Scotland, but Ireland, Brittany, Cornwall and Isle of Man as well.

Soon after my return to the U.S. in 1995, I contacted Tom Hubbard in Scotland, who edited the important anthology of contemporary Scots language poets, *The New Makers,* and convinced him to join me in the editorial work of collecting the Gaelic contributions for this book from Scotland and Ireland. I did the same in writing to Gwendal Denez in Brittany – another anthologist of Breton poets and a poet himself – at the suggestion of Bobi Jones in Wales, who is a long-time friend of Gwendal's father Per Denez, one of Brittany's leading literary figures. Gwendal enthusiastically joined ranks with Tom Hubbard and myself volunteering to gather material from the Breton community as well as helping to establish contacts with poets in Cornwall and the Isle of Man. With the help of Bobi Jones and Menna Elfyn collecting material from Wales, we began the long and arduous process of soliciting work from poets in all six countries in order to, in the end, come up with a volume of Celtic language-based material that would stand as something of a touchstone or perchance a lightning rod for English-only readers to become acquainted with some of the Celtic world's most contemporary, prominent and promising poets. This, then, is how this book began.

By way of a bit of background for the many who may come to this subject and this book, as I did, as a newcomer to the basics of the Celtic literary traditions, a brief overview, here, to the history and heredity of Celtic languages and their subsequent literary traditions should provide an appropriate entry into these worlds.

The Celtic subfamily of languages is made up of three groups: the *Continental,* the Brythonic (also called *British*), and the Goidelic (also called *Gaelic*). Continental Celtic, which includes all Celtic idioms on the Continent with the exception of Breton, died out following the fall of the Western Roman Empire in the late 5th century AD. The Brythonic group includes Breton, Cornish and Welsh. These are all descendants of British, the Celtic language of the ancient Britons of Caesar's day. The emergence of Welsh, Cornish and Breton from British as separate languages probably took place during the 5th and 6th centuries AD and was the result of the Germanic invasions of Britain. Breton today reaches more than one million people in Brittany, most of whom are bilingual, also speaking French. In Wales there are around 500,000 people who speak the Welsh language as their primary language. The third group, or Goidelic subfamily, is the group to which Irish (also called Irish Gaelic) and Scottish Gaelic belong, as well as that of Manx-Gaelic indigenous only to the Isle of Man off Scotland's southern coast. All the modern Goidelic tongues are descendants of the ancient Celtic speech of Ireland from the pre-Christian days. Now the official language of Ireland, Irish is spoken by approximately 900,000 people in that country as well as some 50,000 more in Northern Ireland. Scottish Gaelic is the primary language of about 100,000 persons in the Highlands of Scotland. Most of these people also speak English as a second language. Gaelic speech began to reach Scotland in the late 5th century AD when it was brought by the Irish invaders to the Scottish Highlands. However, a truly distinctive Scottish Gaelic did not appear before the 13th century. The main difference between Scottish and Irish results from the substantial Norse influence on the Scottish dialects.

The Celts that made their way into Ireland, Scotland and Wales brought with them a bardic tradition that is still seen in many of the traditional literary forms today coming from certain Gaelic and Welsh writers. In those earlier centuries the bard was also, oftimes, a priest and philosopher, a physician and prophet, as well as a poet. Thus, the course of study for an Irish bard, or *fili*, included verse forms, composition and recitation of tales, the study of grammar, philosophy and law. The next seven years were filled with specialist studies and included the secret language of the poets. Then many more years of study would follow before the apprentice would emerge a bard, or a "man of learning." A far cry from today's American MFA poets, the poets of the ancient Celtic bardic traditions spent the better part of a lifetime in preparation for the role they would live for the remaining years of their lives. To be a "poet" in Celtic lands is, still, a serious and respected vocation. A lifelong preparation and commitment. To be a poet means a commitment to history as well as to craft. And in these traditions, that history has much to do with the memory of the Franco/English invasions and the plundering of their lands, languages, and cultures. And the memory of the Celtic bard is long.

When the tide of Franco/English conquest rolled in across western Europe, it left little of the Celtic language cultures intact. Not unlike the case in the last half of this millennium in North America of the European genocidal treatment of the native tribal cultures on this continent, so Celtic Europe became a forced community of homogeneity. When the tide ebbs, as we know it must by the very dictates of our observations of relative nature, we will see the Celtic tribes still standing and largely a result of the resilience of their writers, poets and bards.

At the end of the twentieth century, in Ireland, Scotland, Wales, Cornwall and the Isle of Man, the English still dominate (as do the French in Brittany) both the political and the literary landscape. The fact that we in America know little of the true descendants of the Celtic literary traditions, especially those who still write in their native Goidelic and Brythonic tongues, is proof of this monocultural myopia and forced subservience. As Celtic language writers are willing to be translated into English (such as Menna Elfyn in Wales, for instance, who, according to Welsh translator Tony Conran, is "the first Welsh [language] poet in fifteen hundred years to make a serious attempt to have her work known outside of Wales"), there is beginning to come a parcel of recognition. Only now, as the dominant drone of twentieth-century English literature begins to fade away, do we start to see what linguistic richness, what dialectical delicacies have been deprived us all these generations. In recent years, with bilingual and English language translation publications such as *Welsh Verse* by Tony Conran (Seren Books) in Wales, *The Penguin Book of Irish Verse* edited by Derek Mahon and Peter Fallon, and the *Faber Book of 20th Century Scottish Poetry* by Douglas Dunn, the silence has been finally broken. With the Breton writers following suit and the Cornish and Manx writers beginning to translate their own work into other languages, and now with subsequent bilingual books and this comprehensive Celtic volume, we can definitely say that the word is out.

For all the reasons above, as well as those more delicately detailed in each country section preface in this volume, we have subtitled this book "A Celtic Resurgence" to give the current international interest in things Celtic a fixed point of reference on the time line of this millennium coming to a close. And at the same time, to make something of a "declaration of independence" in behalf of the contemporary Celtic literary traditions represented here – if for no other reason than to honor the resiliency of those traditions which have faced overwhelming odds, and survived. And to honor the subversity in its struggle to survive. To honor all those (and they are many) who have put their careers and even their lives on the line for the sake of their language, and in turn, their culture.

For these, their written and activist work has been nothing short of an act of war. A war that in many cases was waged alone in one-man or one-woman acts of heroism against an enemy whose armies numbered in the millions. As Welsh poet Bobi Jones has said: "Just by the very existence of the Celts and the Celtic traditions that have survived, this is subversive!" And the fact that this volume is being released in 1997 – the 500th anniversary in Cornwall of the AnGov/Flamank Rebellion – is synchronistic confirmation, it would seem, of this book's subversiveness. Again, echoing Bobi Jones' words implying that by the very fact of the current existence of the Gaelic, Breton, Welsh, Cornish and Manx languages and by the considerable literary activity that has flourished into fruition in the last generation or so, we have good cause for celebration.

This particular "Celtic Resurgence" is largely a result of the activism of the past two generations of Celtic language speakers and their irrepressible single-mindedness to survive. This determination is coupled with a united front in the areas of the arts to quell the tide of a nostalgic romanticism perpetrated upon the Celtic world by big business, commercial advertising, politicians and opportunistic storytellers wanting to weave a web of some sort of "Celtic twilight" over the whole of actual Celtic culture and its unfortunate if not bloody historic past. This corporate myth-driven sentimentality and revisionism – "whose roots can be traced back to Tin Pan Alley and Broadway and London's West End," according to Fintan O'Toole who writes for the *Irish Times* – is seen by the contemporary Celtic language arts community as an anathema to its ultimate welfare. Or as the English bard might have so rightly written, had he been writing today: "A plague on all our houses!" And O'Toole goes on in the Culture section of the November 10, 1996 issue of the *Irish Times* to indict one of Ireland's leading literary icons, saying: "The whole of Irish culture was excised in favour of a rural and emerald-tinted ideal. W.B. Yeats [who along with Lady Gregory, was one of the spearheads of the back-to-our-mystical-roots movement] was very culpable in this. By involving himself in this Celtic revival business, he broadened his power base – and also set up a conflict between the culture of Romantic Ireland and the culture of the individual. All this has led Ireland [and therefore Scotland, Wales, Brittany, Cornwall and Isle of Man by proxy] to being regarded for years as a society that essentially slammed the door on the twentieth century."

But the fact of the big picture is, that dominant culture oppression of tribal European cultures (which in almost every case, mirrors the attempts at intentional annihilation of North American tribal communities during the second half of this millennium by Anglo-Saxon/European invaders) may have won the battle, but has certainly not won the war. The Celtic languages are alive and well, and kicking! The Welsh, Irish, Breton, Scottish, Cornish and Manx literary traditions are experiencing unprecedented growth in direct relationship with the growth in the number of Celtic language speakers in their respective countries. And while corrupting influences of the dominant monoglot cultures would, in some areas of modern daily life and sensibility, seem to be on the wane, so would be the literary pie-eyed nostalgia of a "Celtic Twilight," which, as Sorley MacLean puts it so aptly in his essay on the subject, "is harmless as long as ignorance and crassness are considered failings in criticism of poetry."

In making the selections of who and what would go into this book, the primary criterion, along with the quality of work, was that of perspective combined with sensibility. Not wanting in any way to contribute to the nurturing of the "Celtic twilight" myth or mentality, the editors were in unanimous agreement in deciding not to include poems or poets promoting that sort of fiction. Instead, we wanted this book to fully support the idea and introduction of "A New Celtic Poetry" as put forward in the book's subtitle. We wanted a collection of work that would truly represent the best contemporary voices of each of the Celtic tribes and traditions in the same sense that the Donald Allen anthology which appeared in the U.S. in 1960 did with its title *The New American Poetry,* which was a revelation if not a revolution in the eyes of the American literary establishment at the time. This book has gone on into more than twenty printings and has become both a cornerstone and a classic for students of modern twentieth-century American poetry. With the Allen book as something of a model for an essential addition to the standard academic fare in the U.S. at the time, we hope that this Pan-Celtic volume will rise to the occasion serving the same or at least a similar purpose for the English-speaking world literary community.

But perhaps the greatest hurdle this book had to face, beside the magnitude of the job of compiling such a volume, was the problem of defining – for the purposes of this book – just what was to be meant by the word "Celtic." Just how were we, the editors, to decide who and what was Celtic?

In an effort to democratize the process of coming to a definition and decision concerning this question, I wrote many letters to poets, scholars, anthologists and even booksellers to try and come up with some sort of consensus. The result of this attempt at a consensual definition upon which to base the selection process for the book was, of course, a potpourri of opinions inhabiting regions of far-reaching polar extremes. Responses received were everything from "those of us who use our indigenous Celtic languages on a daily basis and who use it exclusively in our writing," to "everyone who would, for whatever reasons, bloody or bloodless, consider themselves Celtic." With such a wide range of opinions we were forced to impose a legitimate ideal upon what we would accept as "Celtic." In the end, we all three felt that Celticness was best defined by the singular criterion of language. That language, better than any other gauge, most accurately created the kind of parameters between which the text of a cornerstone anthology of Celtic poetry would most comfortably fit. And so the decision was made to present a "Celtic" anthology based solely on Celtic language writers and their translators, letting the linguistic history of the Celtic language traditions, "by the fact of their very existence," define the volume as well as set the tone of the book's subversive element. And so, with this agreed-upon definition as our agenda, we pressed ahead.

But pressing ahead with this agenda meant having to exclude many poets writing in English or other dominant culture languages, whose work, by any other definition, would certainly have to be considered "Celtic." Poet-nationalists and language activists on the front lines of their respective country's struggles to establish or maintain cultural sovereignty would have to be excluded. Such prominent names as R.S. Thomas in Wales; Michael Hartnett and Ciaran Carson in Ireland; Michael Daugherty on the Isle of Man; representatives of the Scots language tradition (which it was determined was more Germanic than Celtic even though this language group is used by people of Celtic origin and contains some words of Gaelic) and such poets as Maureen Macnaughtan and W.N. Herbert; and great grand-niece of the legendary Scots bard, Elizabeth Burns, in Scotland; as well as any number of important poets native to Brittany, Cornwall and Isle of Man writing in French or in English. The decision not to include these writers, and others, was truly a gut-wrenching one, as in an expanded and more loosely defined book their addition would have been of huge benefit, not only to the book's overall quality of verse, but to the sharp edges of its subversive tone. In trying to achieve a true marriage between quality, comprehensiveness and right scholarship, the language line was drawn, and many of the Celtic world's strongest voices were omitted for the sake of clarity of vision. Yet we want to honor those English-language activists here, that their strong Celtic voices will join this volume in spirit, if not in actual manifestation of their work.

While I am on the subject of what might be missing from this book, I want to say that we have chosen not to include important work of any number of contemporary Celtic bards – singers, songwriters and musicians whose material, if not their language, is tuned to traditionally Celtic strings. For these are, perhaps, the more direct descendants of the ancient Celtic literary traditions before the time of Gutenberg and all that followed. Again, it was a matter of choice that we did not include them here, as a focus on the singular genre of book-poets seemed to be the order of the day. As for the bards – that is another book which needs to be done, the idea for which a seed has now been sewn. Yet we want to mention the names of a few of the more well-known musician/poets that their spirit, too, will reside here in the company of their colleagues of the unsung word. Such names as harpist and Breton traditional singer/songwriter Alan Stivel, Scottish balladeer Dougie MacLean and rock lyricist Calum MacDonald, and Welsh troubadour and instrumentalist Robin Williamson. All Celts. And all poets.

So, for all the "missing in action" here, I wish to offer as tribute the words of Scottish poet Elizabeth Burns from her poem "The Forbidden Language":

> In the slate-squeaking silence
> of the island's only classroom
> words spill out of a child's mouth
> like milk from a tipped churn . . . .

> . . . That night she dreams of empty heads
> anchoring her to the seabed
> pulling her down as swell fills her mouth
> and she spits out salt-

> She plots that when she's woman
> she'll dig up all the island's graves
> and hang a hundred clanking skulls
> about [the teacher's] gawky English-speaking neck

> and whispering at him every curse her language knows
> she'll drag him to the highest cliff
> pitch him into the rocks' pincers
> the gaping grin of the minch.

Because of the ever-increasing and impressive list of names now coming from the six countries represented here that are only recently finding their way into the journals of world literature, and because it would be impossible to put together a single issue that would even begin to include them all, the editors have made the selection they have for this anthology. A selection that, regrettably, due to the pressures of deadlines and the realities of difficulties of communication over great distances, made it impossible to include work, for instance, by three of the Irish Gaelic tradition's most important poets: Máire Mhac an tSaoi, Liam Ó Muirthile, and Seán Ó Curraoin. It is omissions like these, and others, that have made the editing job of this volume at times a painful one. Yet Tom Hubbard, Gwendal Denez and I remain positive about the inevitability of a Second Edition of this book and the hoped-for perception by its First Edition readers that what is found within these pages is inclusive of many of the bright stars of their countries' respective contemporary Celtic traditions.

Tracing the path of contemporary Celtic poetry through Ireland, Wales, Brittany, Scotland, Cornwall and the Isle of Man in an ordered fashion, we have organized the book into identifiable country sections, each prefaced by a short state-of-the-art address by one of its leading elder voices. This preface, then, is followed by the actual work of the poets, one by one in profile, representing that particular Celtic language. In each country, we begin, out of respect, with the elders – those who have carried the standard for the Gaelic, Welsh, Breton, Cornish and Manx languages the longest and most high. Using, in most cases, the facing original language versions of poems to begin their personal sections as if they were an identifying flag. In Scotland, we begin with Sorley MacLean; in Ireland we begin with Eithne Strong; in Wales with Bobi Jones; in Brittany with Anjela Duval; in Cornwall with Richard Gendall; and on Isle of Man that standard is set by Brian Stowell – in each case arguably that country's language's leading elder voice. With the succession of poets that follow, moving from older to younger in order to dramatize the direction of the wave of twentieth-century Celtic literature, country by country, language by language, from beginning to the present day. A continuity showing the advance from the early architects of the Modern tradition to the New Garde and even the Young Turks of each respective language community. The voices that have truly brought (in case there was any doubt) their respective literatures out of the mist of any would-be era of "Celtic twilight" and into the streets, flats, freeways and Internets of the post-industrial world. As Pound, echoing Rimbaud, said of what the best poetry should be: "truly modern." And these poets are, if nothing else, that: heralds announcing that Celtic literature is in league and every bit as "with it" as any existing traditions on the planet.

The poets in these pages come from traditions and countries, all, bordered by water. Bordered by water and westerly winds. Wind and rain. As a result, the essence of the poetry of these traditions is appreciably elemental. The Celtic poets are nursed by the weather, and learn at a young age to ride the gales of their cold, windy coastlines. In many cases they are weaned only by their own work – a creative process which, much like that of learning to survive in an unfriendly natural and cultural environment, must seem akin to a metaphor like "writing the wind." Riding, writing. The air as the green ink of their environment, or the red ink of their history's blood. Echoing the words of Gandhi who declared: "I will open my windows to the winds from all the countries of the world, but will refuse to be blown off my feet."

Finally, on behalf of Tom Hubbard, Gwendal Denez and myself, I wish to make meritorious mention of the work of the translators, too numerous to name, whose translations are truly the essence of this book's existence. In many cases, their last-minute work to meet deadlines was nothing short of heroic. This includes many of the authors represented here who took on the task of translating their own work, which in most cases turned out brilliantly (with the possible exceptions of a few poems, where a collaborative effort was found to be helpful—between poet and editors— in reaching the best possible versions of the work). Translation, as those of us who work in this trade know, is a much under-appreciated art. We cannot give enough credit to the translators of Gaelic, Welsh, Cornish, Breton and Manx who, in the end, were the only reason that this first comprehensive all-English volume is now available to a new and expanding audience.

While we are giving out laurels to those who have embraced this project as their own, and whose help has been invaluable to the process toward the birth of this book, let me add the names of Menna Elfyn, Bobi Jones, Dewi Morris Jones, Rhisiart Hincks, Lenora Timm, Padraig an Habask, Rene Galand, Richard G. Jenkin and Brian Stowell, here, to those of the three acknowledged editors as "honorary editors" for their monumental contributions.

Here, then, is a first look, for many, at what is going on in Celtic Europe with pen in hand. The work of "The New Celts," if you will. A book in honor of their literary histories and emergence. A resurgence. And a kind of note-in-a-bottle that with other collections surely to follow, will reach more than just America's shores.

—Thomas Rain Crowe
January 1, 1997

WRITING THE WIND

A CELTIC RESURGENCE

(Cymru)
WALES

WELSH

Welsh

London-watching can be entertaining. You just have to travel a few short miles to the west of the old imperial capital to notice how surreal it can get. I am reading this week's *Sunday Times* and am informed, that in that innocent little television series *Inspector Morse,* the sidekick for the main character, a Sergeant Lewis, was intended by the author to be Welsh. But the executives ordered him to be changed immediately to a civilised English person. No nonsense. Then again, when the writers of the successful drama-series *Bramwell* made a character Welsh, they again were quickly put in their place. What is uproarious to an assiduous London-watcher is how surprised the reporters of such tidbits seemed to get.

This has been going on for four and a half centuries. If you were to peruse the sister-paper of the *Sunday Times, The Times* for September 8, 1866, you would read, "The Welsh language is the curse of Wales. Its prevalence and the ignorance of English have excluded and even now exclude the Welsh people from the civilization, the improvement, and the material prosperity of their English neighbours ..." If, however, we read on to the end of this paragraph, we wonder what all the fuss is about, and how this "semi-barbarous language" can possibly be such a threat, as "For all purposes, Welsh is a dead language."

One could garner a crownful of such gems. They eventually derive from that happy Act of Union 1536 between England and Wales which ordered that "all sinister usages" such as the Welsh language be "expurgated" and "reduced."

Every now and again the parishioners of London as they stalk around Europe hit their feet against an odd stone. In Spain, or what should have been Spain, their awkward feet hit against Catalonia; in France, or what should have been France, they bounce off Brittany, and so on. Hundreds of these hidden phenomena. They're all over the place. The world's a more diverse situation than what they had thought. And they immediately catch the next train back to the comfort of the imperial capital.

Welsh literature is somehow such a subversive animal. It may – along with Irish – be the oldest living literature in Europe with an unbroken tradition from the sixth century to the present day. It may even have reached unusual heights with the prose *Mabinogion* and Arthurian legends, or with the astonishing poems by Dafydd ap Gwilym in the fourteenth century, or the mystic verse of the eighteenth. But all along the line, somehow it has been subversive and uncooperative.

Indeed, from the beginnings of defensive Welsh verse in the sixth century with Taliesin, on through Aneirin's remarkable epic in the early seventh and the long nationalistic poem of *Armes Prydain* in the ninth, yes on further through the patriotic protests of the thirteenth and fifteenth centuries in particular, right up to the present day, the verse has been inappropriately subversive. The language itself of course was always dying. It is difficult to think of a language that should have died more often.

Such literary aberrations should not be taken seriously by people who believe in uniformity. No-one should permit a world that tolerates such underground activities. Perhaps it really shouldn't be mentioned in mixed company.

And yet this same literature has been so enormously normal. Unquestionably, that is a part of the subversion. Love poems, religious meditations, praise of generous noblemen, nature lyrics, these have all been written on the edge of a precipice. Hanging perilously on to the last tuft of grass that has persistently somehow kept the language and literature alive and flourishing, excitingly if perversely flourishing, the poets have unaccommodatingly survived.

Of course, they must be at the same time dying, dying again and dying. Though they still survive. These repulsive creatures turn up in the oddest places, such as this rather subversive anthology.

Take Menna Elfyn for instance. At first glance, she should just be your token feminist, your run-of-the-mill radical, harping on about the civil rights of the sixties, sensibly supporting the obvious good causes. But it doesn't take a long time to recognize that she is doing something more than that.

Take again Iwan Llwyd. He is very susceptible to foreign fashion – as are all the ladies for their part too. He is inordinately fond of super-markets, a second-hand Ginsberg. The externals of modernism fascinate him. But scratch away at the surface, and you will find there is something else going on. Much more.

It is no less than a deep downright subversion. And this subversion takes the odd form of shaping an ancient imperilled civilisation at the core of a nuclear explosion. This civilisation has now shed some of its folk-dancing, its strange singing, its religious doctrines – but not all. Somehow, these things not only survive, but within an urban environment, on the shop-floor, on the television screen, in the next millennium, they are already not just defending a culture, but positively expressing its idiosyncratic flourishing and cultivation in the teeth of all common sense.

Perhaps the explanation is to be found in a particularly strange phenomenon.

In 1976 an unprecedented thing happened. A Society of some 1,000 members was established amongst the flood of Welsh cultural societies, dedicated to the rejuvenation of what had existed for well over 1,000 years, the ancient intricate metrics of Welsh verse, particularly as it had been developed in the thirteenth century. This, you might say, is not terribly unusual: antiquaries do such things. Yes; but well over three-quarters of the membership were young people, some scores of them had just emerged from jail for language activities.

The brightest light in a galaxy of talent was a twenty-eight year old, Alan Llwyd. He was surrounded by a shining crowd of very individual but deeply involved community poets like Gerallt Lloyd Owen and Dic Jones. They held bardic "contests," which for years now have provided the most popular show on the national radio. They publish a monthly journal, the second most flourishing poetry periodical in the United Kingdom, despite the reputed immense spread of English. The English know nothing about it. It was as if within that metric system they were dealing with, there was an energy that wouldn't let go. The power of something indomitable was moving in the grass.

What was this thing?

Let us examine just a few lines by one of the poets represented in this present selection – Alan Llwyd himself – and mention some characteristics of the metrics that energise his verse. Several of the poets never use any "technique" in any line other than this *cynghanedd* or harmony as it is called. Dewi Stephen Jones is an amazing example of a poet profoundly acquainted with international poetry on a broad scale, himself writing what at first sight seems a symbolically patterned verse with almost surrealist touches, yet still intricately formed, and a modernised development of this ancient craft.

Here, taking examples from Alan Llwyd's verse, are lines containing the four main types of *cynghanedd,* as the ancient Welsh metrical patterning is known. I will present each line and follow it with a simple analysis of the consonant chiming around the accent, although the form is even more subtle than this:

CROES type:

　　　yn sglein yr haul, na siglo'n rhwydd
　　　 n sgl　n　 r h' // n s gl　 n rh'
　　　roedd ôl y pridd ar ei ddwylo praff
　　　 r　 dd l　　 pr' // r　 dd l　　 pr'

Even these examples demonstrate that this technique is much more than conventional alliteration which is simply linked to the unity of repetition. The principle involved here is diversity within unity, both parts leading up to and being organised by the main accent.

TRAWS type:

> a chledrau'r ddwy mor grintachlyd â'r ddaear
>   chl dr   r dd' // (m r gr nt) chl d   r dd'
> diniweidrwydd mewn Eden o wydr
> d n'   dr   //   (m n) d n   'dr

This is a delayed-action echo. The repeat of the ordered diversity is held back as a few interfering consonants get in before the echo is heard. It involves the tension of suspense.

SAIN type:

> gerfydd   adenydd o   dân
>   YDD // d'n YDD // d'n
> esgeiriau a   charnau   chwyrn
>   AU // ch'rnAU // ch' rn

This has a three-part division as contrasted with the two-part hitherto noted. The first two parts rhyme simply, and the second two chime in the accepted manner around the accent.

LLUSG type:

> berffeithgan fy nghynghanedd
>   AN   //   AN
> wyt ffynnon wrth wraidd onnen
>   ON   //   ON

This is the simplest and the least common of the types of *cynghanedd,* where there is a rhyme at the caesura with the penultimate syllable of the last word.

Now all this may seem very abstruse. It is indeed a most complex metrical form, perhaps the most difficult in the world, although accomplished Welsh poets form such lines spontaneously at the drop of a hat. But what this tradition does, apart from providing an exceedingly mellifluous sound-patterning of great power (that was sometimes faintly borrowed by Gerard Manley Hopkins and more faintly by Dylan Thomas), it links the Welsh poets internally to a live heritage. It is an expression of history in the present, a militant survival, a symbol of renewal, a presence of an ancient muse provoking the ice-boxes, the computers and the satellites. The Celtic literatures, because of their state of perpetual crisis, are more obsessively conscious of the past in the present than are the more comfortable literatures. The poets wander in and out of history unconsciously. Being Celtic does not mean prancing around the countryside in druidic costumes as romantic foreigners tend to think, but it has everything to do with living dangerously.

The revival of intelligent interest in *cynghanedd* has been accompanied by a renewed respect and a green attitude towards what is known nowadays, usually derisively in fashionable circles, as "organic community." Pressures from outside Wales are not however altogether disadvantageous. They have brought thematic originality and a concern for social and cultural involvement independent of the topics that interest more widely spread cultures. They have also brought a passion and a seriousness that inevitably converge on crisis. From the Celtic perspective, there seems a fairly clean division in World Literature today. On the one hand, amongst the "big" powers, the fairly confident and stable cultures, a literature that is cosy. On the other hand in the third world, and until recently in Eastern Europe amongst poets like Milosz, Rocewicz, Herbert, Holan, poets in Israel and the Arab world, there is a literature of discomfort informing the normality. And it is to this latter band that the Celtic poets belong. Being Celtic means being as normal as impossible in an abnormal environment. This has significance for everyone.

– Bobi Jones

Bobi Jones
(1929 –)

Bobi Jones was born in Cardiff, Wales in 1929 and, as a poet, novelist, critic and scholar, is by far the most prolific and well-known Welsh writer of the later half of the twentieth century. Now a retired professor emeritus of the Welsh Department at the University College of Wales, Aberystwyth, his earlier publications such as *Y Gan Gyntaf* (1957) and *Ci Wrth y Drws (Dog At The Door)* had a similar effect on contemporary Welsh literature that Whitman's *Leaves of Grass* and Hart Crane's *The Bridge* had on American poetry. A major champion of Welsh heritage and the Welsh language in the tradition of such Welsh poets as Waldo Williams, Saunders Lewis and Euros Bowen, Jones is and has been a constant voice in the struggle for a Welsh cultural identity and for Welsh autonomy and self-rule. Of the many volumes of poetry, essays and scholarship he has written, he may be best known for his work concerning the subject of Welsh myth and mysticism as well as his magnum opus *Hunllef Arthur Cerdd (Arthur's Nightmare)* which is the longest sustained epic book-length verse poem in the Welsh language. He currently lives in Aberystwyth with his wife Beti while at work on a scholarly book on the subject of the Praise Tradition in Welsh literature.

Cymro Di-Gymraeg (A Welshless Welshman)

Yng nghegin gefn ei dŷ mae'n cadw cenedl,
Lletywr rhad na chyst ond lle i'w wely
Ac yn y parlwr ef ei hun sy'n byw, yn Sais ail-law
A'i ffenestri'n lled agored tua'r byd. Ba waeth
Os yw ei ben yn bwn, a chur y tu ôl
I'w glustiau? Y mae'r gwynt yn iach ysgubol,
Ac nid oes lysiau ar ôl i'w diwreiddio mwy
O'i ardd, dim ond cancr y llwybrau concrit.

Gwyn fyd yr alltud 'gaiff ymestyn mewn parlwr
A llygadu'r bydysawd maith o lwybrau llaethog –
Llwybrau llaeth a mêl.

Gallai, fe allai aros byth a syllu arnynt,
A llyfu diwylliant lleng heb feddu'r un,
Llwybrau llyfn. Pam mae ei wddf
Wedi ei nyddu ar un ochr i'w gwylied hwy
Fel pwped yn hongian ar hoel ar ôl y gyngerdd,
A'i geg ar lled, a lleufer yn y llygaid? Paham?

A Welshless Welshman

In the back kitchen of his house he keeps a nation,
A cheap lodger who costs no more than a place for his bed,
And he himself lives in the parlour, a second-hand Saxon,
His windows wide open to the world. What matter
If his head is a burden, and there is a throbbing
Behind his ears? The wind is brisk and sweeping,
And there are no plants left to be uprooted
From his garden, only the cancer of concrete paths.

Happy the exile who can stretch out in a parlour
And eye the vast universe of milky ways –
Ways of milk and honey.
Yes, he could stay gazing at them forever,
Licking a legion's culture without possessing it,
Smooth paths. Why is his neck
Twisted to one side to watch them
Like a puppet hanging on a nail after the performance,
Its mouth agape and a gleam in the eyes? Why?

– translated from Welsh by Joseph P. Clancy

A Poem of Praise

Here flowers stroll, and as they stroll they sing:
 Bees hurry like businessmen stuffing their bags
To the foxgloves that are prettier in party frocks
  Than chrysanthemum, than orchid, than old-man.
   In a field too green to be burrowed
    Far from the flesh's sty
   We too are adventuring
    In the hedge's caravans

Because here is our home. Isn't the evening morning
    When the moon's every breath is washing the moor?
Let's not go back to the civilisation like beer
    Boots have been left in over night.
        Here my eyes are storing up,
            Like magpies, your dear face,
        And my thick hands are sailing on
            The world's softest shoulders.

Our heads are tossed back to gulp July
    To the dregs. Getting drunk on the marvel of seeing its magic
And the minstrel-flies crooning in our hair and hissing like a kitchen
    And the wood-pigeons blowing blissfully through their noses.
        Around us a pasture rolls
            The laughter of its grass bellies
        And daisies are showing off
            Their white teeth in their smiles.

Here's the rainbow-happiness the Godhead moulded.
    It showers heavily in kisses on our hot foreheads.
Who would think such whitewashed walls could
    Shadow warmly such a sensible paradise?
        Lawns, sun, chairs,
            Desk, bed, noiseless hillside:
        On their well-grounded whetstone
            I lose something of my rust.

Here a house strolls, and as it strolls submits:
    You would wonder how the warmth bubbles together
Ungrudgingly and without ageing too much
    And creates, till it merits praise, a new world.
        Roof, floor, and wall were founded
            On cherishing the joy of song,
        The wealth of a hearth's minutes
            In a muddle of tiny flowers.

— translated from Welsh by Joseph P. Clancy

Racing Pigeons

The feet of the train,
    slowly
        but inexorably,
were leading them screeching, and bearing them,
dilly-dally,
staring stupid, out of their syntax –
heavy track's
click clack –
and battened in baskets,
further and further into a horizontal
pit.
      And they were evaporating
to the east,
        disenfranchised,
away through the frontier until their instincts'
sense of judgment was moaning, thundering
exile-wild
in their wings.
      There
they were, layers of them, having lost (and they cried aloud)
the instinctual sap of their rootworld's talons.
Anguish was scratching in their claws
and spraining their feathers and compressing the fettered dread's
lead in their spurious flight.
They were tangled, were torn from station to station in coursing
outside the witchcraft of their belonging.
          What miracles
could henceforth keep them from being bruised
deeper and deeper into the black orbit?

They were drawn there,
were drawn,
stains were stretched further. Oh! without fail, from their nets
of recognition
         Nary
one
    knew the true toll of its loss
or why a tail was plucked from its lair.
In the orphan lightning of their ridiculous

remoteness from their cosy roosts
they were becoming bankrupt of memory
and to an extent there was secret reaching all through their ear roots
aloft the terror language of their longing.

And yet,
    look, there's restraining:
        here comes their untangling,
look, there's the terminus of all concealing;
and they can
    be released,
        dispersed, to seek
the faith now of the sunny roads
of the slant breeze
with its silver
pavements.
    They sprinkle
their feebleness whirring high,
flip-flapping their tribulation in the home-patch of their twirling,
ceaseless, choiceless,
aloft in circled tomorrows, they chalk
back now,
    aiming
along them on the course of their lineage.
And ruled by their rapture,
leaping to magnets
and sailing back down sunshine,
from their need gladness they fashion
the pattern
    of pigeon mania's syntax.
And the pigeon-coop claims its pigeons.

* — translated from Welsh by Joseph P. Clancy*

from: **Land of Form**

How handy's Wales' death for us poets,
How nice tragedy on a spoon.
We collect deaths like children collecting stamps
And set each to a still sweeter tune.

A pocket-knife put through her heart,
Since blood's beauty, that is sublime.
We twist metrical ribbons to strangle her throat,
Bind her feet with our beads made of rhyme.

We eat valley decay for our breakfast,
Win a chair when we sit on her head.
She clinches so neatly the close of our poem
We sing over, and over, Amen.

Our lost nation's like a lost penny –
We've cried for a whole minute long.
Hope that the grief keeps us going until
We get to the end of this song.

. . .

You were a land too callow (or hollow)
To lose your feet (or foetus)
Your eyes were too sad
To raise reservoirs.
Now there's nothing left
But your false teeth.

I want to start out (or think of starting out)
And drive between your hedgerows
In an open charity,
Pulling out the blackbirds
Buried in your ear
As if it were a potter's field.

A thin breeze (or wheeze)
Has blown your mountains away.
Good grief, you're only
A baby of a language (or fact acknowledged)
In wool booties at the seashore

Wales

Hobb–ling learn–ing to walk
But the traces of your feet
In letters on the beach
Gradually vanish.

. . .

They say that lighting
    A candle in the gloom
Won't make the cherry-tree put forth leaves
    Nor even wake the thrushes up;
But I'm going to try it.

Extremism's the only moderate thing.
Polish my body, God, clear the vapour-haze
From my heart, till You see
Your face in me.

How can a single ant bend
    The buds on the tree-top,
Or two ants, or three, or four?
    But it's certain the entire tree will crack
When the ants come together,
If the ants come together.

It's been God's gift, the battle.

. . .

The visitors descend, a wolf-pack in T-shirts
tearing our flesh and picnicking on our ears.
There are hamburger scents on the heather. Porthcawl
is a bog where transistors
breed like mosquitoes. Sandwich wrappers
freeze the valley like snowflakes and close it
under their drifts so that Jack the Post
can't get through with his messages; plastic bags
like old abandoned thoughts, bits and pieces of brain
that will be kept safe in the soil with the Roman
pennies and the medieval dishes for the new
China's museums, and buzzes of portable radios
flying from flower to flower so that a butterfly

never has a chance to chirp, salmon-tins
near the brooks where there are sermon salmon
and where fields once lay in old-fashioned
sanctity. Pack the car, put the language
on top, and take her, take her
away.

• • •

When August comes it doesn't fly about our ears on gadfly wings
And it doesn't always come up our legs in the armpits of beetles;
Its tallow doesn't drip only along fox-gloves or clock-hands.

Not on empty faces either, and not only
On female backs on the beaches' griddle where their flesh was roasted:
It isn't in the day alone its face is important.

Not in the closed doors of schools, not in the hooray
Through the open window of the train. The shore isn't the only place
Where the insect stealthily spreads its web.

Not in our nostrils and our throats, when the air
Creeps inside. Not on our cheeks
And not only hidden in the refuge of our hearts is it encountered.

But rotting like a corpse, in the cottages empty
All winter long filled so cheerfully
When the innocent sun arrives, August is constant.

August's in a tank. Sometimes indeed it's
In secret bombs, and it hurls its army from its lair
And it darts its poisoned sting on summer-homes from its planes.

August's in a gun, in a prison, in a chain,
In the implacable police-force that descends on us like crows
In cultural uniforms. August's in London.

• • •

Young blood won't do the trick
at this point in time. It doesn't clot
in chalk, like the old, to make lipstick.
It isn't commercially viable.

Wales

It rusts the engines. Old blood's effective with varnish
on fingernails, but the young stays too runny.
It must be poured off. One could use
a drop or two, but it's bad to bring more. It
isn't much good on shoes either.
They say that with a little rice and onions
and toadstools in oil it makes a meal –
when it's all fried – that's acceptable in Chinese restaurants;
but that's racist nonsense . . .
We're confident however
that with time, the young will also
become adjusted

                         • • •

When I wear this language
    I'm black,
jet-black, and the visitors call me
    "boy,"
and I give black
    kisses.
A drum, the poem that echoes
    the proud
war of my mother Africa and my father
    shit.
I want to be a ghetto
    when
the labour-members say
    my mind's
the language of a back-yard sink,
    and I'm
a statistic, my blood black, black, black
    like my mouth;
and I give black
    kisses.
I'm someone who's always quite ready
    to come
out to dance if an anthropologist
    comes by,
or when London tries to make
    murder

look white as laver-bread in flour;
　　and I
give black kisses to my white-brother
　　Cain.
Only my bones are white
　　and they
bear their dose of harsh disgrace.
　　I'm nothing
but bread-and-butter in the end, say the
　　socialists;
but I give black
　　k!i!s!s!e!s.

　　　　　　　　　　• • •

Stand proudly, leek (they say), because of your stench,
With your smell more sour than a St. David's Day speech;
Stand on this dump of a world bold and virile
And launch your stink across the tepid daffodil.
You'll scarcely be more disgusting than the members
Of parliament, who aren't exactly flowers.
Show London it isn't the only trash-heap that farts
Into the weather from its pigeon-arse.
Why, old stalk, are you limp, spilled out all your vigour?
Your head shrivelled, your pod passionless, you quiver.
Your energy sold to a whore of a country,
You've spent the yearning in your balls pretty cheaply.
After you've worked with not so much as a thank-you till evening
And run pillar to post along a leg with no stocking,
"Stand in the gap," that's the patriot's chant,
When you've been standing until the urge to stand
Any longer's almost dead. Puny member,
Get up on your feet (they tell you) like a gorilla.
Lift up your head again, here they're exhorting
From the Eisteddfod, from Llangrannog, and from Glan-llyn.
For one bout, for one round, before London nullifies us,
All the moderate Welsh beseech you to rise;
And despite your purity, you'll stink once more like a cowshed,
And in your weakness, you'll get it up like a lighthouse.

— translated from Welsh by Joseph P. Clancy

R. Gerallt Jones
(1934 –)

R. Gerallt Jones, along with Bobi Jones, is one of Wales' most prolific contemporary writers. While still a student in University College of North Wales, he launched the literary magazine *Yr Arloeswr*. He has published several volumes of poetry, including *Ymysg y Drain* and *Cwlwm;* and he published *Poetry of Wales 1930-70* which he edited. Two of his five novels have won the Prose Medal at the National Eisteddfod. In 1982 he was elected Chairman of the Welsh section of Yr Academi Gymreig. He was, until recently, Warden for the Gregynog Cultural Center, home of the acclaimed Gregynog Press. His *Collected Poems* recently won the Welsh Arts Council Poetry Prize. He currently lives in West Wales, not far from Aberystwyth.

A Funeral In Llŷn

From the Garn's summit
a pattern is visible.

Small fields, gorse hedgerows,
a tidy topographic quilt,
and the ffridd of bilberry and fern
assenting, if reluctantly,
in the conspiracy.

And so with our society.
Every relationship was patterned,
the fruit of interwoven years
of careful pruning and hedging and closing gaps,
of knowing the nature of each gateway,
of knowing, as the need arose,
when to lock the gates.

Then death came,
the volcano of human topography.
We can only watch the lava flowing,

its primitive shapelessness penetrating,
civilised hedgerows laid waste,
everything sharp-cornered,
today as it was at the beginning,
before order was established.

It is now that we stand naked
staring wildly at each other;
no gates to close,
one man's land in another man's field,
so uncompromising the indiscriminate sea
that flooded in.

Tomorrow, the hedges will be rebuilt,
the gaps closed,
and the day after a new safe
pattern;
we shall again walk seemly through the appropriate gateway,
but today a volcano erupted
and we stare
    into each other's eyes
naked.

– translated from Welsh by Joseph P. Clancy

For Ewan McLachlan

(A memorial to the Gaelic poet stands in a graveyard in Fort William, Scotland. He was buried, according to the inscription in English and Gaelic, in Ardgour.)

Ewan McLachlan, the rickety footbridge
between us and your singing is long down;
it's Ewan now, not Eóbhan, even in Welsh
for the remnant who speak it.

You lie, so it says, in Ardgour.
But what is left now that is yours
in Ardgour, or here in Duncan's town
or anywhere? Where are the poet's songs?

Nearby a girl sits on a tombstone
reading verse; she and her dog and I

own the tipsy graveyard, thighdeep, thistled.
She reads verse, but Eóbhan, not yours.

Has she heard that your bones and the bones
of all civilised living lie in treeless Ardgour,
watched by the sentry hillsides? No.
Not a word. Not a grieving word ever.

The chasm yawns uncrossed, not between us
so much, the Welsh, and the Gael,
but between this grey tomb and every yesterday,
between this dark afternoon and mornings of simpler light.

Words, words remain; ruins of houses squat on Mull;
ghosts of Eóbhan Maclachlan, your father's father
and MacDonnell of Keppoch, fierce at Culloden,
walk where each sunset weeps on Ardgour, nightly raw and red.

– translated from Welsh by Joseph P. Clancy

The Preacher

(on seeing a Victorian photograph of an open-air preaching meeting in Llŷn)

A bobbing sea of bowlers, fields are filled,
and with gardens of blinker bonnets; straw
hats, once white, dark sepia now; old hands, raw
from black-leading, hold up a child, foam-frilled,
to see the preacher's face and she, self-willed,
kicks out above the crowd. He, trance-like, law,
Tablets from God, in his clenched fist, saw,
did he, angels dwell in the fields they tilled?

It died, that summer's day, as all days die,
bowlers to feed the moths on wardrobe shelves,
he to earth, they to their graves in due time.

But here, burnt brown, he preaches, hands flung high,
and hundreds clamber out of their dead selves,
thronging a holy field with solemn mime.

– translated from Welsh by the author

Shetland

From leaflight windblown islander, sun-dappled,
young waves, blue-green, blue-white, white
excite, entwine over the lonely sand.

Singularity prevails.
One herring-gull, its tribal greed
at one remove, approaches elegance,
one hopscotch trace of bird's trefoil
validates the shore's virginity.

Later, touchdown achieved, galetorn on Jarlshof,
the centre shifts, norms are abnormal.
Whalebacked, spray-wracked, Fair Isle lies southerly –
compass unhinged, North's South, mind's almanac tipsy.

Viking burrows pockmark the headland, wringing out
earth's warmth, suns shining in old legends
soothe the rain's whiplash.

Walk then at evening on Burra,
day dying furious, aflame over Foula,
cross unsheared gorse,
look seaward where the icepack gathers –
grey chords vibrate along the wires.

Survival of self is all.
Sea-maidens moan from the deep
all winter long, naked torches march,
great boats, aglare, flare out against the moon,
brave embers yield at last to the cold sea's grasp.

– translated from Welsh by the author

Offeiriad Gwlad (Country Parson)

Eisteddai yn ei gadair
a'i ben llew yn llonydd
a'i lygaid ymhell.

Eisteddai yn y tŷ mawr hwnnw
yn yr ystafell wag
a'r te'n oer yn y cwpan
ac arswyd ei swydd amdano.

Eisteddai'r oriau hir yn ei gadair,
wedi i'r brain glwydo,
a'i lygaid yn gwrando,
ond ni ddaeth un llais i'w gysuro
na thaw ar y mudandod mawr.

Country Parson

He sat in his chair
his lion head still
his eyes distant

He sat in that vast house
in the empty room
the tea cold in its cup
his awful calling wrapped around him

He sat long hours in his chair
after the crows had slept
his eyes listening
but no voice came to comfort him
nor any end to the great silence

— translated from Welsh by the author

Dewi Stephen Jones
(1940 -)

Dewi Stephen Jones, considered one of Wales' most disciplined and meditative poets, was born in 1940 in Ponciau, part of the mining village of Rhosllannerchrugog which lies near the Welsh border in North-East Wales. Almost half of its eight thousand inhabitants speak the Welsh language. His education includes the Ruabon Grammar School and a degree from the University College of Wales, Aberystwyth. One of the foremost writers carrying on the ancient Welsh literary *cynghanedd* form, he has contributed many critical essays on poets to *Barddas, Taliesin, Barn* and other Welsh, English and American publications. A first volume of poetry, *Hen Ddawns* (Old Dance), was published in 1993 and received the G.J. Williams Memorial Prize by the Welsh Academy of Arts in 1995 for the best first publication by an author in any category. At present he is living back in the town of his childhood, Ponciau, in the "Borders" region of East-Wales and has just completed a book on the early poems of the Welsh poet Bobi Jones.

Ffenest Olaf (Last Window)

Yn dy lofft dlawd
(un gadarn ei chysgodion)
cyn trimio gwanc, cyn y trymaf gwsg,
yn noeth, symetrig,
(heb lesni brigau)
o boen y ffrâm
nid o'i baenau ffraeth,
y gras a ddaw
o wawr
y groes ddu.

Last Window

In a frail loft
(a fortress of shadows)
before desire is trimmed,
before the soundest sleep,
stark and symmetrical,
(without the freshness of twigs)
of the sorrows of the frame
not the hubbub in its glass,
grace comes
from the dawn
of a black cross.

— translated from Welsh by the author

'Tew Oleuni' (A Density Of Light)

Y dŵr a'i rafft o bowdrau'r haf.
Gro
     a gwas y neidr
am agor ei gŵys o hen wydrau.

A Density Of Light

The raft of summer powders rides the stream.
Death's gravel bed
     and a dragonfly
about to plough its furrow of old stained glass.

— translated from Welsh by the author

In Weakness . . . .

In weakness, as cumbersome as
the resurrection of a creature from its winter sleep,
slowly, with the palm of my hand, I make
a window in the steamed-up pane

And O - the shape of it -
the same bright wonder
as the mouth which took the very first swig
of winter's chill.

— translated from Welsh by the author

The Balance

The gleam of blood and a charge
in the steep eye,
it trembles above an acre of wheat
and then swings away
to where the sky meets memory;
searching–searching
returning
to hover above grasses
and the summer pollen on its toes.

— translated from Welsh by the author

The Elder Tree

An insignificant one catches
the eye. I make its entanglements
a song from the heart
to widen my window and not to darken it.
It wedges between my words, kept
from storm-winds and axe.

But in the pith beyond the ritual flowers
lies time's quiet bomb-shell,
felt but not known until
the beads of blood within the tree
impair the sight in that season of their wine
like lamps of mist shining at noon.
The old sun's colour
is of change
        and farewells.

This knot of earth and air,
a shelter in coldest March,
is uprooted piecemeal
from the sky, leaf by leaf from the land
and when the sun is broken
I whisper,
        I whisper.

Withered the place but ripe is the moon,
and the chorus of the earth's song is the sound
of death's wave as it ploughs.

— translated from Welsh by the author

The Coat

With no tear-marks between the shoulders,
why! you're almost as new,
without frostbite tingling the sleeve,
without a pocket ravelling,
but somewhat hunched, perhaps,
like the curve of the hill.

Between one pace and another, somewhere,
a button was lost, the colour
of horn or the tallow candle
(now burnt-out)
leaving its black wick
like scorched stubble in one corner of the field.

Thread by thread
the loosening,
like the leaves of the forest in the stillness:
one by one
each glowing lamp is darkened,
the taste,
the sight.

Coming closer,
from the holes of a ruin
I hear the sea
call the foamrags of all rivers

home.

— translated from Welsh by the author

Nesta Wyn Jones
(1946 -)

Nesta Wyn Jones was born in Dolgellau in 1946 and got her early education at Ysgol Rhydygorlan. She went on to attend the Dr. Williams School and then to Bangor University College where she graduated in 1970. Right out of school, she worked with the Welsh Theatre Company (1969, 1970) and then with the Welsh Schools Council Project on a team led by Dr. Emrys Parry preparing school books in Welsh for children. From 1974-1980 she was an author's assistant for the Welsh Books Council in Aberystwyth. In 1987 she moved to the country and took up farming with her husband and child, and lives in the Meirionnydd District of Wales still.

Nesta Wyn Jones has been a member of the Welsh Academy of Writers since 1970, and in 1994 was elected its chairman. She is a member of the Gorsedd Y Beirdd (Eisteddfod's Bardic Circle), having judged crown competition four times and has taken part in the Welsh Arts Council's "Authors In The Schools" program.

As a writer who has had her work published in various magazines throughout Wales, as well as having work appear on radio and television, she has three books of poetry to her credit published by Gomer Press (*Cannwyll Yn Olau, Ffenest Ddu,* and *Rhwng Chwerthin a Chrio*) as well as a memoir (*Dyddiadur Israel*) and a children's book (*Cyfri Pryfed*). She has won the Welsh Arts Council Prize in 1976 and 1991 as well as an Arts Council Prize for her book *Rhwng Chwerthin a Chrio*. She won the G.J. Williams and Welsh Arts Council Prizes for *Cannwyll yn Olau*. As a Welsh-language poet, she is considered to be one of the premiere 60s generation voices in all of Wales.

Lleisiau (Voices)

Ie, hwn yw fy llais,
Llais ymadroddi deheuig,
Yn ymateb i gwlwm llygaid
A rhethreg dwylo.
Cadwyn o eiriau llafar
Gan lais

Wales

Sy'n haeru hyn a'r llall.
Hwn yw fy llais.

Ond mewn distawrwydd,
Pan dywylla fy llygaid,
Fe glywaf lais sydd daerach.
Llais a ddirdynna holl dannau f'ymennydd
A'i fin fel seiren ganol nos
Yn dryllio tywyllwch fy mod.

Llais unig
Y tu hwnt i fynegiant,
Yn flaidd sy'n udo'i wae parhaus ar leuad y diffeithwch,
Llais sy'n mynnu bwhwman drwy gelloedd gweddw fy nghof
Yn anesmwythyd i gyd.

Mor arswydus yw sylwi, toc,
Na chlywaist ti gyni hwn,
Y llais fu'n lliwio'r distawrwydd â'i sgrech,
Fy llais mud.

Voices

Yes, this is my voice –
Voice of deft speech
Responding to eyes' knot
And rhetoric of hands.
A chain of words spoken –
Voice that asserts
One thing or the other.
This is my voice.

But, in a silence
When my eyes go dark,
Another, more importunate
Voice I hear –
A voice torturing every wire in my brain,
Lipped like a hooter at midnight
To shatter the dark of my being.

It's a voice lonely
Beyond expression
Where a wolf moans for ever its grief
At the wilderness moon –
A voice that would pace up and down
The solitary cells of my memory
In utter lack of rest.

O then, how terrible to look up and notice
You did not hear this agony –
The voice that stains silence with its shriek:
My dumb voice.

– translated from Welsh by Joseph P. Clancy

Poppies

August, in Brittany,
And in the breeze sways and pirouettes
A red ballerina.

Brittany
As if someone
Had thrown tiny pieces of red
Tissue paper
Over the hedges
And they'd all unfolded
Flaming
In the sun.

August
And my hand longed to gather them,
But I knew, if I did,
There'd only be the stain
Of red
On my fingers
When the dew lifted.

Twilight, August in Brittany.
Into the dark staring and staring

Wales

I see their purple bruises
In every corner
Quaking
To the rumpus of crickets.

    Here,
    There's a wreath of plastic in the rain . . .
    It's not that flower that's plaited in it.

— translated from Welsh by Joseph P. Clancy

Shadows

The two World Wars — no, we never saw those days.
We were born when the dust was clearing
From the remains of slaughter and burning.
Our voices had no reason to crack
As we prayed for "daily bread."
Our dear ones did not vanish
So that we never knew
The when or the how
Precisely . . .

    We'd come at a soft time
Into a world middling blest.
But sometimes a savour of guilt
Will maybe start
In the harsh wake of shock
When we see, when we hear
Fragments of what was
In the dark days —
Fragments searing into our consciousness,
Experiences too alien to comprehend.

    That woman once, in Belsen,
Her sanity in ribbons in the shambles around her,
Who still insisted on nursing
        on the memory of an arm
Her dead child.

That body, so amusingly contorted,
Like a scarecrow that's finished its work
On the barbed wire . . .
A skull, all teeth, under a steel helmet.

The tenacious multitudes, dead, dead,
Ribs like washboards,
Stomachs empty troughs –
The terrible remainders
Of the gas ovens.

The orderly rows of white crosses
Fiendishly quiet, and so numerous
We cannot credit
That such a huge reckoning
Lies there.

No, we know nothing of those days
– Only we sometimes hear
Of incidents, before our time,
Beyond our understanding.
But as, from the slaughter and the burning
Slowly the dust rises,
Maybe we do feel a tightness,
An echo of a scream,
As the old, never-satisfied eagle
To the horizon flies,
The shadow of his wing
Perishing us with cold
For a moment
Before it passes.

– translated from Welsh by Tony Conran

A Field of Wheat

Today,
The blue sky leaned
On the bushes' drowsy stillness.
Tasting blackberries
On a patch of smooth new grass,
I watched, beneath my hand,
A small child toddling
To pry in the picnic basket.
    I had a feeling
If I believed you were on the far side,
The blue of your eye shining,
I too would walk,
I would dance like a butterfly
Above the bent heads of the wheat field's fullness
Not disturbing the snugness of the mice below
Safely to reach you.
    But with you so far,
This afternoon,
I must be content
To relax in the heat,
And gaze at the day's wheat-ear
Wilting in the palm of my hand.
I will keep it, nonetheless,
To show you.

— translated from Welsh by Joseph P. Clancy

Alan Llwyd
(1948 –)

Alan Llwyd was born in 1948 and brought up on a farm at Cilan on the Llŷn peninsula. After graduating in Welsh at the University of Wales, Bangor, he made a career in Welsh publishing and has lived in the Swansea area since 1976. He mastered the art of strict-metre poetry as a schoolboy, and first achieved fame by winning both Chair and Crown at the National Eisteddfod in 1973, a feat which he repeated in 1976. His first collection of poetry was published in 1971 (under his original name, Alan Lloyd Roberts), and since then he has produced a steady flow of volumes, culminating in his first complete collection in 1990, which have established him as the most dedicated and accomplished exponent of *cynghanedd,* both in the strict *englyn* and *cywydd* forms and in free verse. His work draws inspiration from his upbringing in a rural monoglot Welsh community in Llŷn, and from his close family life with his wife Janice and their two sons, but also responds to his urban environment and the barbarities of the twentieth century.

Alan Llwyd was one of the founding members of the Welsh Poetry Society, "Cymdeithas Cerdd Dafod," in 1976, and he has been editor of its monthly magazine, *Barddas,* from its inception. Since 1983 he has been employed full-time as the Society's organizer, and has developed it into the major publisher of Welsh poetry, establishing a series of anthologies, chronological and thematic, several of which he has edited himself. As poet, critic and editor he has been a central figure in Welsh poetry for the last twenty years, and has done a great deal to raise standards and encourage new talents. The poetry of the First World War has been one of his particular interests, and led him to branch out into a new field when he scripted the Welsh-language film "Hedd Wyn," which was nominated for a Hollywood Oscar in 1994.

The Place

I don't know where I had started from
to reach it, nor which direction
I then took as I departed
from the place without a name.
I remember that there was an impulsive
river flowing opposite
the church, and, as it rolled onwards,
it carried with its flow the trees and the sky,
like scenery
rushing past in a ribbon
through a train's window.
Perhaps there were houses there, but I did not notice
any houses in the summer's haze,
but there was a bell, groaning
audibly from a church steeple:
a steel bird
swaying to and fro on its perch in a cage of stone,
its voice following its leap.

The bell submerged its notes
in the water
before hanging its handkerchief of tinkling
to wave in the wind. I do not remember
anything else, only
the sound of the bell mingling with the blue water
of that frightened river,
and the crystal tinkle of its pebbles
echoing the undulating notes
of the bell above its flow.

One day, I shall go to look
for the nameless place:
I shall search for the bell which made
the sky pale with its peals, swelling the water
with its bubbles of notes,
that bell which slurred its slow sigh
above the land and the water below,
echoing its own echo.

I will never find it.

— translated from Welsh by the author

48

Memory

Shatter the military memorials
to dust; throw into the fire
the books in which our century's history is told.
Tear out the pages which contain the images of murder,
and delete the rage from each age;
let the maggots completely devour the remains,
the maggots in the corpse of our century,
and the images will cease to exist.

    Not so. Who could scrub the scream
    completely from the walls of our nightmares,
    or wash the earth clean of the dust of Jews
    so as to erase the images –
        the torture, the blood, the pile of shoes,
        the mound of scraggy skeletons,
        the hair in glass cages?
    The dead will drag their bones through our sleep,
    and in our nightmares mad hounds, slobbering saliva,
    will gnaw through their chains.
    Even if we erased all the images
    of that horror, we would still possess
    the negatives in black and white.

– translated from Welsh by the author

Llŷn Peninsula

By now, a place in the mind: Hell's Mouth was near,
but Porth Ceiriad was nearer, with the sea rolling the beach
all day, every day; all night, every night: the hissing
from the rocky shore filling my ears. I would listen to the hoarse
call of the gull, as it glided widely through my dreams;
the screech of the owl rubbing against the night;
Bardsey's lighthouse hiccupping light across Hell's Mouth
like a candle in the wind spitting against a wall,
and the foam of the sea was like melted wax
around the base of the rock's candlestick,
and seagulls were caught like moths in the blinding light;

a frowning willow like a fountain in a frozen gush,
and the cows, heavy with sleep, swaying clumsily from the moor,
and a curlew gargling my name in its throat, in the days
of my childhood, before the years stole those days
from me, leaving Llŷn to remain only in the mind.

— translated from Welsh by the author

The Horizon-Gazer

(a tribute to R.S. Thomas on his eightieth birthday)

Old horizon-gazer, you tread
On the shores of our anxiety,
And see, above the waves,
Ancient blood and ancient dreams.

The summer sky of the centuries bloodstained
By the heroism of the ages;
In the distance you see our old valour,
The old valour of our extinction.

The sky of our identity, yesterday's sky
On fire with our desire,
And the heavy blood of each ancient Cátraeth
On the horizon of our heroism.

But the horizon's line is now so distant,
The line tamed by the alien tide
That claims us, outcasts,
And, wave by wave, claims the land.

The tide did not delete our dignity
Nor obliterate our community;
The ebb did not wash away our lineage
Nor the waves our kinship.

Now the slow tide with its brine
Erases our last vestiges,
Leaving only the trace of summer's children
On the shores of our extreme cowardice.

Under such a bruiseless, hazy sky
There remains on the shores
Only the footprints of sandalled feet
And the flotsam of our brittle Welshness.

Old horizon-gazer
Is it not the blush of the heart's shame
That you see, and not the traces
Of yesterday's bravery staining the waves?

— translated from Welsh by the author

Y Gymraeg (The Welsh Language)

Saf uwch y dibyn serth, a rho waedd yn yr hollt:
hi yw'r daran yn y distawrwydd, y trwst yn y gwacter oer;
er cydio o'r ffoaduriaid yn eu rhaffau dellt
hi yw'r un a'n ceidw rhag cwympo i'r mudandod mawr.

Hi yw'r glaw sy'n ireiddio'r ddaear, hi yw'r rhuddem hardd;
awel cynhaeaf, a'i threigl yn y gwenith a'r ŷd:
glain y goleuni yw hon, hi yw'r emrallt yn y gwellt gwyrdd,
hi yw siffrwd yr haidd ar y maes, hi yw'r saffir drud.

Hi a geidw rhag myned ar ddisberod urddas y bobl,
hi yw'r gaer rhag pob gwarchae, hi a'n gwerchyd rhag yr erchwyn mud;
hi yw'r rhaff uwch yr affwys rhwth, a rhag anhrefn ein hendref nobl,
hi yw'r did a'n deil, hi a eilw'i gwehelyth ynghyd.

Os tyr y ddolen yn chwilfriw, pa ryw ddinistr a ddaw? —
Y mae'r rhaff fesul cainc yn ymddatod ar y dibyn draw.

The Welsh Language

Stand above the abyss, and shout into the cleft:
she's the thunder in the silence, the sound in the cold emptiness;
although fugitives grope for their splintered ropes on the cliff,
she's the one who prevents our fall into the great muteness.

She's the rain that refreshes the earth, the ruby's sheen,
the harvest breeze, rolling in the corn and the wheat;
the precious sapphire, the emerald in the grass that is green,
the restless rustling of barley, the bright gleam of light.

She protects from the mute edge, the fort that keeps enemies at bay,
and above the gaping abyss she is our tether;
she preserves our dignity, our home against all disarray,
the knot that unites; she gathers her people together.

Should the link shatter and break, what would be amiss?
Knot by knot the rope now opens above the abyss.

– translated from Welsh by the author

Menna Elfyn
(1951 –)

On the eve of Menna Elfyn's 1995 publication of her book *Eucalyptus*, Welsh writer and critic Tony Conran heralded her as "the first Welsh [language] poet in fifteen hundred years to make a serious attempt to have her work known outside Wales." Writing of her 1996 collection *Cell Angel*, M. Wynn Thomas has called her "one of the most significant poets currently writing in Wales. Her conspicuous moral and political commitments, international in scope, are always underwritten by her prior commitment to language."

Born in 1951, Menna Elfyn was educated at the University Colleges of Wales with a degree in Welsh. Consequently, she has been a part-time lecturer at University College Lampeter (where she became a Writing Fellow in 1984) and Swansea, is holder of two Welsh Arts Council bursaries for writing, and the recipient of a travel grant to complete a children's novel about the street children of Mexico.

Having always written in the Welsh language, she has published six highly acclaimed collections – some of which have been translated into other languages – two of which have been winners of the Welsh Arts Council Award for best volume of the year. Author of six plays, her verse plays have been screened on television as well as performed on stage. Her last project was a television documentary of Vietnam which was aired by BBC Wales in 1996. Her previous collections include: *Mwyara* (Blackberrying), *Stafelloedd Aros* (Waiting Rooms), *Tro'r Haul arno* (Turn the Sun On), *Mynd Lawr In Nefoedd* (Going Down To Heaven), *Aderyn bach mewn Llaw* (A Bird In Hand), *Eucalyptus* (a bilingual edition), and most recently (1996) *Cell Angel* – which focuses, in part, on young people trapped in a world of violence as well as poems composed while spending time in prison as an activist (she has been imprisoned twice and arrested over twenty times in relation to language and peace demonstrations). She currently lives in Llandysul, in West Wales.

Cwfaint (Nunnery)

Mae cwfaint a charchar yn un. Lleian mewn lloc
a morynion gwynion dros dro'n magu dwylo,
eu didoli nis gallwn. Diystyr cyfri bysedd mewn byd

mor ddiamser. Fe ŵyr un beth yw trybini y llall,
bu yn ei bydew yn ymrafael â'r llygod ffyrnig,
dioddefaint yn sail i'w dyddiau,

mae cariad ar oledd y mur' croes rhwng troseddwyr
a gafodd. Cell rhyngddynt a'u manion croesau,
yn llawn seibiannau mawr. Pa Dad

a'i gadawodd mewn lle mor anial, llygad ychen drws
ei unig wrthdrawiad. A holodd hwy am fechnïaeth-
am brynu amser? Galw arno am drugaredd?

Lleianod cadwedig ydym yma. Wedi'r swpera
awn yn ôl i fyd ein myfyr. Yr un a wna rai'n sypynnau
heb gnawd. Yma, ni yw'r ysbrydol anwirfoddol,

yn dal y groes a'r troseddwyr rhwng ein gobennydd
yn gyndyn mewn aberth, yn dyheu am adenydd.

Nunnery

All one, a nunnery and a prison. The nun in her cell
and those temporary virgins wrapped in their own arms.
You can't tell them apart. No use counting your fingers in a world

so timeless. Each knows the other's sorrow,
has been in the pit fighting the rats,
grief the ground of her days,

love askew on the wall, a cross between two thieves,
only a cell between them and their petty hurt,
their deep occasional sighs. What kind of Father

abandoned him in such a godforsaken place, the ox-eyed door
the only quickening? Did he ask about bail,
about buying time, cry out for mercy?

We are anchorites. After supper
we turn to thought. We make fleshless
bundles. Like it or not we're spiritual

bearing our little crosses under our pillows,
stubborn in sacrifice, waiting for wings.

– translated from Welsh by Gillian Clarke

Double Bed

I never understood the tyranny of the double bed.
Sleeping limbs are single, on the move

unpartnered, in territory held
staunch beneath the duvet, uncolonised by the nation-state's

pillage of fruitful land. Coalition
sometimes, other times wormwood on the tongue

struggling to free a leg or to slip the straits of the mattress.
How sound is the deepest sleep, though passion unites us, after

we keep our distance. Avoid the flying elbow,
the sharp shoulder-blade. Overlap is the hard part

of belonging. Left with nothing but a corner. Yet, you away,
I find no self in bed. It's too big to gather

our identity. On my pillow I'm half afraid
the trespasser won't come back to the restless feathers

and the bed without your body is a wooden
scabbard. I'm left dreaming

of the articulate flesh, desire's needling,
the perfect disarray beneath the sheets.

– translated from Welsh by the author and Gillian Clarke

Cell Angel

Grey cells either side of him
keep safe the bones that hide
for a second their weight of pain

yet weren't the angels mortal,
Greek and Persian soil joyous with vengeance,
the Bible quick with quarrels?

He led me from his cell, this angel, to the hall,
him and me and a grand piano,
the door-keys restless in my hand.

Locked, he began a concert for his patron –
twinkle, twinkle, then one violent tone –
before failing to ascend the black slopes

an angel on the road, homeless, lost
and the sky drowned in the piano's depths.
How I wonder what you are.

The pause ends the solo. Keys locked sharp
in the black fist of the piano. Discord
an unplayed instrument in his face. Descending

angel and his passionate concerto
turn suddenly to notes reverberating
through this musicless place. To reach for one fine string.

• • •

I would give quotas on angels,
ban seraphic sopranos
from high-church places where stars play

their easy flutes in gilded choirs
of angelic boys, their voices clean as glass
between the marble and the echoes. God's no more there

than here, in the angel cell
where chords ring without descant
where I rise to my feet of clay to applaud.

Encore to the dream of a cell angel
that he might fly bodiless
through walls, without shadow, light

winged to the great cathedral.
But behind this door the boy-gangs box
laughing through a chink in the brow of glass.

And for every Michael, Gabriel, Raphael,
there's a cell to keep him fallen
and the keeper of the keys
is only a love song. A god without power to unlock.

– translated from Welsh by Gillian Clarke

Wild Flowers

Behind bars, the lay judges hold court. Before them,
I flower as bravely as campion, although
I'm truly the weakest of vessels.
But I can't pretend. They can see,
although I look like nightshade
I am the most shrinking violet.
The bittersweet climbs toward me. A harebell leans over me
and knows that I never was torn, never plucked from the hedge.
I never felt man's hand like a blade at the back of my neck.
I've dwelt among untrodden ways.

They give judgement swiftly, together. I am
not brave, but stupid. And blind. A woman who'd be scared
if a butterfly followed her. What sort of girl would forgo
the random, nectarish Saturdays of youth,
the pleasures of the hedge? They pity

my sober sepals, these scarlet pimpernels.
My arms bear no needle-scars. I suck no stub to ward off pain.
I am unmanacled. I've had a shady hollow
among petals which have seen hurricanes and cruel reapings.

The time has come to testify –
to graffiti, on the *tabula rasa* of the wall,
three long-stemmed poppies in paradise –
here's the red poppy on parade, triumphing death
though the meadows still run with the stain of blood,
here's the white one I wear as a bone of peace
each November, defying war's pieties;

and here am I, the Welsh poppy, head bent –
our spinelessness a yellow fever.

The judges left, smiling at a humble poppy
on the crest of her anger. A stalk bending in the wind.

– translated from Welsh by Elin ap Hywel

After The Court Case

(Blaen-plwyf, 1978)

While you were in prison
the banks of the Teifi froze
in civil disobedience,
and the salmon died
of broken hearts!

While you were in prison
all the birds of creation
migrated from lack of welcome,
and the stray cats of the parish
had an attack of existential insecurity.

And while you were in prison
the snow held pickets
in fear that the sun would
steal the rights of the earth's mint,
and the rain sulked
for lack of attention.

While you were in prison
two hundred sorrows were scalded
in a pitcher of song,
the postman claimed overtime
in the Swansea area,
and Basildon Bond became scarce
in all shops.

And while you were in prison
twelve jurors
went home to an open fire.

– translated from Welsh by Elin ap Hywel

Eucalyptus

(I heard how the scent of the tree filled Baghdad during the Gulf War, its oil being used to cook with in the absence of electricity).

Before I saw it in Lisboa
it was only a name to me—
the best medicine for a cold,
a pretend sweet
to free the chest
of chirping.

But today, those petals are banners:
they give the same
festival to everyone—
genial trees, that favour
no one people or land.

Warmth rises from their roots—
oil lighting the world,
grease in a bowl
and a family fed.

The golden eucalyptus
spluttered, and did not fail.
Though all round hell exploded
it still compassed food,
creating a table of blessedness.

And isn't it for this we go on living
from ready meal to love-feast—
rhythms of water to our throat,
metres of nourishment on each lip?

Drops that once were released
as a kindly fate
for the unfortunate,
spread their odour—
richer in the giving,
and in every share of it, giving enough.

In a night cold as a corpse

it's the eucalyptus
that they smell, those hide-outs
and gathered fellowships
amid rape and rubble.

The simple oil
once kept me breathing,
now over blackened lives
shines like light.

— translated from Welsh by Tony Conran

Chinese Lanterns

(in memory of Beijing, 1989)

February: under the lash
the lanterns totter
to their end.
I lift them up,
I give their twopence-coloured faces
their dignity
at the window.

Under the east wind's lash
lanterns from China brighten
like a picture on the mind's lintel
of one who is holding a banner out
to a tank

daring the forehead of Goliath
– a gesture of the young,
full of love

as he kindles a fire of endurance—
an early hint of springtime
in the impudence of the heart.

— translated from Welsh by Tony Conran

Message

(at a moment of weakness)

Welsh people . . . please listen.
Let us vanish
off the Earth's crust
with the dignity of people
and the tongue of a human race,
not whimpering like waifs
with our backs to the wall.
Let us sing in melody
while holding on to the dark
before falling asleep
pillowed on *Y Gymraeg*
grateful for one last pull
at the teat of history.

As people we had the death wish
in us, life's zest coming
to us as a nation
at second-hand.

And if we were
to die voluntarily
I daresay it would be
the last sweetener of an item
on "News at Ten",
an announcer's jovial remark
before the Close Down.

— translated from Welsh by R.S. Thomas

Iwan Llwyd
(1957 -)

Iwan Llwyd was born in Carno, mid-Wales in 1957, but has spent most of his life in Bangor, North Wales. He is married and currently works for Cennad Quadrant, a PR firm based in Caernarfon and lives in Talybont, near Bangor. Iwan is an MA graduate of the University of Wales, Aberystwyth. His MA thesis was on the Patrons of the Welsh Poets in Medieval Caernarfonshire. Iwan has been writing poetry for over 20 years and published his first work *Sonedau Bore Sadwrn* (Saturday Morning Sonnets) in 1983. His two other published works are *Dan Anesthetig* (Under Anaesthetic), 1987, and *Dan fy Ngwynt* (Under My Breath), 1992. After winning bardic chairs at the University of Aberystwyth and the Urdd Youth Eisteddfod in 1980, Iwan won the National Eisteddfod of Wales Crown in 1990 for a highly acclaimed series of poems, *Gwreichion* (Sparks), commenting on the political and social upheavals in Wales during the 1980s and paying tribute to the Welsh underground movement, Meibion Glyndŵr (Sons of Glendower).

Since the mid-80s Iwan has been part of a group of younger poets who have been actively taking their poetry out into the community, and took part in the "Fel yr Hed y Frân" (As the Crow Flies) and "Cicio Ciwcymbars" (Kicking Cucumbers) poetry tours. A series of poems by Iwan formed part of the Camre Cain dance project, *Comisiwn* (Commission), performed at the Builth National Eisteddfod in 1993. More recently, Iwan has produced two works for television. *Dan Ddylanwad* (Under the Influence) is a poetic portrait of America. *Dan Draed* (Under Foot) is a similar contemporary portrait of Wales. Both have been broadcast on S4C, the Welsh language television station, and Iwan is working on a volume of poems written for these two series. As well as writing poetry, Iwan has written a television play, *Paradwys Ffŵl* (Fools Paradise); a stage play, *Hud ar Ddyfed* (Spell on Dyfed); and he is the bass guitarist with two leading Welsh bands, Steve Eaves a'i Driawd and Geraint Lovgreen a'r Enw Da. A new CD has recently been released by the Steve Eaves trio, *Y Canol Llonydd Distaw* (The Still Quiet Center). He is also a member of the Welsh Academy and has recently been appointed on the Welsh Arts Council Literature Board.

Gadael Tir (Leaving Land)

(i Jean François Saliou)

Fe wyddwn fod y môr yn agos,
roedd ei flas ar y gwynt:
wrth inni brysuro ar draws y twyni

a thorri gair byrwyntog,
torrai fflachiadau'r tonnau ar greigiau pell,
mor gyson â phelydr goleudy Aber Wrach:

roedd dy olwg gwantan dithau
ar y môr fel ag erioed;
pob tro y deuai pryderon

a dydd o brysur bwyso
deuet yn ôl at y môr,
at y gorwel a'r gwymon,

a lynai'n wydn a chyndyn yn y graig:
ac ar fore o Basg
a dim ond ambell bererin pell yn cregynna

yn dynn ar sodlau'r trai,
gwelwn dristwch yn dychwelyd
i darfu ar dy orwelion

fel rhimyn o olew ar y llanw,
ac yn fratiog, ailieithog
clywn hen iaith dy deulu yn gadael tir,

yr hen eiriau ac ymadroddion
a'n clymai'n gefndryd agos yn ymbellhau,
eto yno ger y môr ym mhen pella'r byd,

yn Gymro a Llydawr
medrem gyd-flasu'r heli
fel garlleg ar y gwynt.

Leaving Land

(for Jean François Saliou)

I knew that the sea was near,
I could taste it on the wind:
as we hurried across the sand dunes

and swapped out-of-breath words,
the flash of waves broke on distant rocks,
as regularly as the beams of Aber Wrac'h lighthouse:

you kept your eyes
on the sea;
every time fears rose

and the tide came in
you went back to the sea,
the horizon and the seaweed

clinging firmly and stubbornly to the rock:
and on an Easter morning
with only a lonely girl in the distance

collecting shells close to the shore,
I saw a sadness return
like the ebbing tide

like the rim of oil in the waves,
and in a broken second tongue
I heard your family's old language leaving the land,

the old words and phrases
that tied us close-cousins disappearing,
and yet by the sea on the far edge of the world,

a Welshman and a Breton,
we could both taste the salt water
like garlic on the wind.

— translated from Welsh by the author
version by TRC

Aneirin

With your camera and your helmet
you climbed down from the helicopter,
just a mile from the fighting,

then legged it bent double
for the nearest shelter, the shots
exploding around you in smithereens:

past the burning skeletons of tanks
and the ash of empty bodies, the empty men
and raw meat that fed the crows,

tripped and fell through the mud,
getting up to take a colour picture
of a man killing

in black and white.
In Catraeth and Kampuchea,
the Somme and the Six Counties,

you bred magic with mystery,
and they flocked to answer your questions,
to follow with their eyes the rush of the lens:

you gave them fame that outlived the war
and a glimpse of forever
in the biased poetry of unknown words.

– translated from Welsh by the author
version by TRC

Weather

A weather of mice and thieves,
cold as an unloved man
driving through rain across country:

a weather of regret
dripping, and the wiper keeping
the car's regular heartbeat:

a weather of farewell and feuding
turning the heavy rain's bouquet
to alcohol, like a knot:

a weather of the season's end,
with the taste of dirt on the road's surface
deep in remembrance,

a weather on the lorry's tail,
and an old terror driving me
too close for comfort.

— translated from Welsh by the author

As Long . . .

As long as we exist the Welsh language will be a hard bargain,
a stubborn layer of rock,
a promise on the pillow, a lie between husband and wife,
restless sleep, a drunken chorus at New Year,
a barrier to keep the tide at bay,
the beer talking, a cradle rocking,
smashed glasses, a beach at ebb tide,
foolish brawling, a woman crying,
a journey south on a May morning,
a street at day's awakening,
cruel money, raw iron,
a mist enveloping backroads,
the sound of a guitar in the moonlight,
the laughter of children on a cold hearth,
fireworks and hair-pulling,
the crack of cynghanedd and fire-lighting,
happy smiles and sour grapes,
the final prayer of old men,
the last hymn by the grave-side,
blood on a palm, a rusty sword,
a slippery slope, a salty waterfall,
a shining spring in a wooded glen,
Zion on the hill, an asylum in the valley,
a wheelchair on the edge of the precipice,
sunshine through showers, snow melting,
five o'clock on a Friday evening,
a locked cell, an ending, a bondage,
the chill of winter, a marriage also,
a heartbeat under the tips of clay,
an etched love under the chapel pews:
as long as we exist, we will be dependent, I fear
on taking a drag of her, year by year.

— translated from Welsh by the author

Gwyneth Lewis
(1959 -)

Gwyneth Lewis was born in 1959 in Cardiff and writes in both Welsh, her first language, and in English. She went to a bilingual comprehensive school in Pontypridd and studied English at Cambridge before going to America as a Harkness Fellow–studying at Harvard and Columbia and working in New York as a freelance journalist. She returned to the UK, doing research at Oxford on literary forgeries, and now works as a television producer in Cardiff.

With humor, both sardonic and direct, and above all, commitment to human feeling, her Welsh/English pendulum swings warmly across worlds as separate as the rural communities of Wales and the academic palisades of Britain and America. Or, as Joseph Brodsky said of her work: "Felicitous, urbane, heartbreaking, her poems form a universe whose planets use language for oxygen and thus are inhabitable."

Her first Welsh language collection, *Sonedau Redsa,* came out in 1990 by Gwasg Comer. She also won a major Gregory Award in 1988, and was featured in New Women Poets in 1990. In 1996, she toured the U.S. reading from her much heralded book *Parables & Faxes.*

Hanner (Half)

Mae gan berson cyflawn bedair coes,
deugain o fysedd (gan gynnwys y traed),
dau ben, dau ymennydd i reoli gwaith
ffatrïoedd y mêr a labordai'r gwaed
ac mae hiraeth ofnadwy yn llenwi'r rhai
sy'n sengl, ond heb hanner eu henaid.

Priodas yw dinas yr haneri coll
sy'n chwilio ymhlith y ffracsiynau di-ri
am fathemateg a all asio dau
a'u lluosogi i fod yn dri,
gan ddymchwel holl onglau bod ar wahân
ac ailosod y 'rheiny' yn rhan o'r 'ni'.

Pob clod i gyfanrwydd y bodau llawn
ac aml-lygeidiog sy'n mynd yn hen
wrth gau ar ei gilydd fel llyfrau trwm,
eu cloriau'n cenhedlu clasuron ein llên
a dalennau eu caru fel glöyn byw
yn llosg mewn cusanau, yn llachar mewn gwên.

Half

A person who's whole possesses four legs,
has forty fingers (that's counting all toes),
two heads and two brains to supervise
the marrow's factory inside the bones.
But a terrible longing fills those who know
that the soul is in half when it lives alone.

Love is a city of misplaced halves
who turn among fractions endlessly
in search of a mathematics where two
and two together always make three,
confounding all angles of being apart
and changing "those others" into a "we".

All praise to those beings to dare to live whole,
who close on each other like heavy tomes
time after time, till their pages compose
private stories for each others' eyes,
classics which flower into public flames
which burn like exotic butterflies.

— translated from Welsh by the author

from: Links

1.

Here Scripture begins with a man in a jungle:
thorns encircle
his flesh, a spiral
of monkish letters spun from gold; here's a miracle

of divinity, here's talent's alpha
and knowing's end;

here the world comes round
again in scarlet ink with the stigmata

of man on scripture's cross; here's the Word's
fate in words' thicket;
here's God in the net
of his own sentence; here's wax's wounds

on parchment-skin; here's the apex
of eloquence because,
in crude blood, the grammar of grace
fashions the clauses in pain's syntax

and the hooks are life, not annihilation,
for the soul's a knot
and the links of fate
the most beautiful, weightiest decoration.

2.

We've heard about Alexandria
and her libraries. DNA

is more stuffed with lore.
Forget all books. It's an acid store

in which the monks of the blood-cell
copy humanity and re-tell

the gene's mythos, a narrative
much greater than any one person could live –

a story of plains, of men in a wood,
of hands and arms, of growing food

and cathedral churches, a story of learning
to split the atom and catching the chatter

of light with itself. The helix is our being
and heart – the scholarly mutter

of chromosomes; our bodies are its subject-matter
and every mutation's a new plague's sting,

the end of some period. This chain
outpowers the intelligentsia's brain:

its links eternally climb a stair
to a structure in praise of a designer

who works without paper, in syllable-flesh:
and dying is this essay's text.

3.

Six years of age and the tongue's a bait
that follows the pen on its journey through "a"
till the voice recognises it, mouths it, eats it,
while "g" in a row of monkeys' tails

on a branch of the line gossips away
with the vowels below, denizens
in a zoo of curious smells. In the next pen
a pair of "o"s like the eyes of an owl

cold and dangerous, understand
more of the custom of copying than
the child himself. It's conjuring. At last
the red-letter day: links are grasped,

words seized one by one and put on a page
like the plan of a street, each word a cottage,
and the driven pen goes lickety-split
down roads to unfamiliar districts . . .

4.

In the archivist's landscape-scheme
there are many categories of green:
emerald lawn, laurel, beeches,
every one with its shadows. Winter's

formal and unflattered by leaves;
ice is a light, its glitter survives
in the stumps of the tree's shadows
till afternoon's heat hits the meadows.

What grammar could be more perfect than this?
Cattle are black words on white and the silver
question-mark of the river
winds through the valley's parentheses

with the commas of birds for punctuation
throughout – crows on the wires,
claws tightly curled round conversation
long-distance . . . words . . . sighs.

5.

(In memory of Louisa Maud Evans, aged 14, who died when she fell from a balloon in 1896.)

Venturesome? I was, if you think of the time
and the limitations placed on the kind

of thrill thought suitable for girls. My dream
was rising. I dressed the cunning

lines linking basket and balloon
like a virgin's gown; then breathed in,

full of lightness. Below, the earth
turned into a map, Somerset

into a composition. I was the knot
in the ropes of the men; to the God

of traffic an offering, seed of a white
and short-lived fruit; I was the weight

that fell. My grave's an anchor preventing me
from sinking into the earth more deeply.

Read the words. Men's promises
are frail, their obligations grass.

I'm proof of this assertion.
But the privilege of the fall was mine –

lungs bursting, air a knife,
my blood like electricity, and I so very light

between the frail basket and the steady state
of graveyard roots and arrival's weight.

6. Rapunzel

To the witch
the hair
is a staircase.
To the girl
the tresses
are a golden chain,
a burden, heavy as death.

The prince perceives
the magic of both:
the girl in the tower
and the land locked
in a forest of illusions.

Something must alter.
Who can free
the girl from the tower,
the witch from the girl
and the prince from enchantment?

Scissors are sharp,
can sever the tangle
of links that yoked together
three heads of hair
in a fairy-tale.
They know from experience,
now their world's lost,
that trimming the lovely tresses costs –
but keeping them's your neck on the block.

7.

The Family of Birds*

Every lie buys time.
I'm leaning here on the gable-end,
watching the corn growing,
among the golden stalks my darling
lingers to make love to me
if I can hinder my father till summer
and stop him harvesting.

The sound of my lover hid in the meadow's
the corn's rustle and sigh as it grows,
the birds of the wind twittering
and a thousand ears listening.

If I buy another day in the name
of the crows and the sparrows
I can swallow its fulness again
and drink from peace the barbaric
smell of his earth and his barley's hiss
and defeat the scythe's arc
with the song of turtle-dove and heron.

Between night and the marriage-feast
the electricity of birds; the harvest
strengthens with their song
and the crop's their conversation.
But I'll fail. My father will come and scatter
the frail body along with the seed
in a scribble of blood and gold and fire –
his sickle's prudent sentence.

Our kin's history starts here:
the scarlet blade and the links that sear.

– translated from Welsh by Richard Poole

*According to the legend, The Family of Birds received its name when a girl fell in love with a man who was unacceptable to her father. He hid in a cornfield on the family's land. When harvest time came she won time to court her beloved by begging her father not to reap yet, since the song of the birds in the corn afforded her so much pleasure.

Elin ap Hywel
(1962 –)

Elin ap Hywel is a Welsh-language poet, translator and editor of *Honno* (Welsh Women's Press), the author of two volumes of poetry, *Cyfaddawdu* and *Pethau Brau*. She was educated at Queen's College, Cambridge, and University College of Wales, Aberystwyth, where she graduated with a joint honours degree in Welsh and Irish. She has spent three years researching Irish political discourse and the concept of femaleness in the years leading up to the Easter Rising. She lives in Aberystwyth.

Gold

They used to say that underneath our fields
were the bones of heathen queens, tricked out
for some terrible wedding. They said that every spring
the plough would throw up lozenges of gold,
delicate as tree-bark or a baby's thumbnail.

Arkady scoffed. But at our marriage feast
his grandmother broke bread above my lap,
wishing us wine and wealth and many children.
The night was sluttish with stars. My bridal veil
let in their light in tiny, glittering points.

I got the wine, all right. It roared
out of Arkady's mouth on market days
when he'd bartered the goat and kid away for drink.
And as his palm
was franking my legs with bruises, dull as florins
it sang a song of gold, of striking lucky.

Well, I've grown old
waiting for Arkady to bring home the bacon.
But he never did get round
to the salt and necessary coin of everyday.

And now they say it was there all the time,
that even the field-mice wove it into their nests,
spangling their darkness with a little glory.

Such richness. I like to think of it like this:
year after year
unravelling ligatures, letting leather rot,
freeing the lunulae of frozen metal.

Then there is nothing left but a pattern,
the shape of a woman picked out in earth and light.

– translated from Welsh by the author

In My Mother's House

In my mother's house there are many mansions,
parlours all full of air and light
where the table is set for afternoon tea
and the shutters always open outwards
to a view of the sea without ships; dark-brown passages
which go on for miles, hot and airless,
ending in sculleries where the crockery totters
and something major's gone wrong with the plumbing.
Staircases which spiral down down down
past family photographs on flock-papered walls
(– look, there's my grandmother. There's a weasel on her shoulder!)
till they get to the bad place
that cellar that's full of charcoaled bones,
of children's skulls thin as blown eggs.

Tonight I'm trying to get to the bathroom,
a tiny Antarctic of marble and glass.
I've been here before once. I played with the soap,
I loved the way it shot through my fingers,
leaving a snail's trail of tears behind
and I thought
if I could stick my head under the tap
the water might make me feel better.

I've been coming here each night since the funeral.
I've walked, danced, and wandered through the rooms of this house,
whose geography changes

quick as an hour-glass. I love the back kitchen,
the dresser carved from a hunk of bog-oak,
solid and black, more fruitcake than furniture,
with my uncle's initials gouged in its side.
The Staffordshire china dogs
stand guard over the willow-patterned plates,
their eyes as small and jealous as sloes.
Sometimes, if I'm lucky, they'll talk to me:
She went thataway. You only just missed her. She's in the corridor! —
and I'll catch a glimpse of the hem of her skirt.

Once, I'll never forget it, I went in
and there she was, in an armchair by the fire.
She stretched out her hands to me, her fingers
harpists' fingers, slender and white.
I laced my fingers in hers. We said nothing,
each of us embarrassed that we'd been caught out,
fraternising, as it were, the wrong side of the curtain.
I can't remember now how I got out of that room.
I look for it every time I go back.
Sometimes it's there, sometimes it isn't.
Sometimes her cup still sits in its saucer
Sometimes the fire is cold, cold ashes.

— translated from Welsh by the author

Adroddiad (Owl Report)

Erbyn hyn, mae'n falch gen i ddeud,
mae'r cyfan yn dechrau dod i drefn;
'rwy'n dechrau ymgynefino
ag adareiddrwydd.
('Rwy'n teimlo'n awr, ers rhyw ganrif neu ddwy,
fod hedfan yn dod yn haws. Mae'r cydbwysedd
rhwng yr adain dde a'r chwith wedi gwella
a'r broses o lanio yn esmwythach o lawer.
Aerodynamig. Dyna'r gair.)

Mae'n gam mawr, edrych yn ôl.
Weithiau, bydd y gorffennol
yn gwasgu yn gas ar fy nghylla,
yn fwled drom sy'n llawn esgyrn a blew,

yn enwedig ar nosweithiau o haf —
ar yr eiliad honno, rhwng cyfnos a gwyll

pan fo'r byd yn rhuthr o rwysg adenydd
a bywyd mor fyrh â cho' llygoden,
yn wich fechan rhwng dau dywyllwch.

Ond bryd hynny mi fydda-i'n cofio:
'doeddwn i ddim yn leicio'r ffordd
y byddai'r gynau sidan pob-lliw
yn glynu wrth fy ystlys yn y gwres
ar y prynhawniau tragwyddol hynny
pan ddodai Llew ei law ar fy nglin.

Ydyn, mae plu yn well o lawer,
yn sych ac ysgafn, fel dail neu flodau:
'dydyn nhw ddim yn dangos y gwaed.
Maen nhw'n haws o lawer i'w cadw yn lân.

Owl Report

I'm glad to report that by now
things are starting to make some sense;
I'm beginning to get used to
birdishness.
(I've been feeling now, for a century or two,
that flying is getting easier. Co-ordination
between the right wing and the left has improved
and landing has become much, much smoother.
Aerodynamic. Yes, that's the word.)

It's a big step, looking back.
Sometimes, the past gets me by the gullet,
weighing down heavy,
a hard pellet, full of hair and bones,

especially on summer nights –
at that second, somewhere between twilight and dusk
when the world's a rush of wings in glory
and life's as short as a mouse's memory-span,
a little squeak between one darkness and the next.

It's at times like these I remember:
I never did like the way

those multi-coloured silk gowns
used to stick to my sides in the heat
on those eternal afternoons
when Llew used to put his hand on my knee.

Feathers are really much better for you,
they're dry and light, like leaves or flowers:
they don't show the blood so much.
They're much, much easier to keep clean.

— translated from Welsh by the author

Silence

She sees them moiling down by the gate,
jerking their heads like children asking questions,
their greed for maize
pulling at her grubby hem like hands.
They're forever hustling for something,
their anxiety a hoarse edge to the voice,
like a sudden punch in the pit of her stomach
as she fills her apron. Then again
it's a hot, knowing tongue which probes
every nook and crevice of her memory.
Yet their rush for grain
is a stitch which catches up the afternoon's long slack.

She's feeding her poultry on no-man's-land,
sowing a magic circle of corn around herself.
She throws her golden fistful to buy forgetting,
a forfeit scattered to the four winds,
like a woman in a folk tale. Or a refugee.

Sometimes she thinks
that their beaks are rather cruel, like the bayonets,
and their claws could tear through flesh, and then she dreams
that she steals towards their perches, like a vixen
one moonlight night, at the hour
when hens are slumbering, like dark cushions;
then her long-suffering jaws
silence the sound of their snoring
on a wave of feathers and blood,

and then, hearing their cock's stern call,
she wakes, in her warm bed,
to another dawn on a foreign farmyard.

— translated from Welsh by the author

Blue

(in memory of Derek Jarman)

There's a tortoise-man on TV. His skin
is so old, it's ancient, eternal, as if
seared to a husk by a sierra wind,
a peel without zest or sap.
A tortoise-man without a shell, whose head
jerks, incontinent, towards the camera
— looking to see if the world's still there.

I want to touch him —
to reach, somehow, inside the TV,
my thumb longing
to smooth out the hollows under his eyes,
I want to place one finger on his papyrus cheek
and say thanks, silently

— for the gleam of silk, for glamour,
for powder and paint, for pain,
for gemstones, for candlelight,
for grapes, for strawberries, for wine,
for velvet, for a warm breath,
for excess. For elation. For gilding
the black and white screen with a rainbow's eye —

colour by colour they fade and run
and there's only blue left, a blue
that's as true as the sky or the sea,
like the smoke rising from the morning's first cigarette
like petrol on a rained-on road,
a blue like the twist of salt in a packet of chips —

blue, too, like a cardboard file, a nurse's skirt,
a surgical gown, an artery,
a knife's edge, a fading bruise,
like small grit sucked on by the tide
like the colour between the living and the dead
like the hard screen that's between you and me.

— translated from Welsh by the author

Elinor Wyn Reynolds
(1970 –)

Elinor Wyn Reynolds was born in Bridgend in 1970, moved to Treorchy and was brought up in Carmarthen, West Wales. She read Welsh at University College of Wales, Aberystwyth and Jesus College, Oxford. She has published two volumes of poetry, *O'r Iawn Ryw* (Honno, 1991) and *Dal Clêr* (Hughes a'i Fab, 1993). She was one of four poets selected for the *Dal Clêr* tour of Wales in 1993. She has published numerous poems and short stories in magazines such as *Barn, Golwg, Tu Chwith*, etc., and does frequent radio broadcasts for the BBC in Welsh and English. She loves pantomimes, patchwork and laughing, and says she wishes that she could combine them in her poetry. She lives in the Gwynedd region of Northwest Wales in Llanystumdwy.

Cwpwloleg (Coupleology)

Yn y caffi
dwi'n eistedd yn flêr
fel slyg wedi arllwys ei berfedd
drwy hollt yn ei groen
ar ddiwrnod poeth,
yn llysnafedd a stecs ffiaidd.
Rwyf' yma ar fy mhen fy hun
yn llygadu'r cyplau yn llyffant-heriol.

Yn y theatr,
yn llawn dewrder,
wedi prynu tocyn i un,
diolchaf i'r nefoedd am ddramâu un act.

Coupleology

In the café
I sit in a heap
like a slug having poured its innards
through a slit in its skin
on a hot day,
all scum and gross stickiness.
I am here on my own
challenging the couples, with my bulging toady eyes.

In the theatre,
full of bravado,
having bought a ticket for one,
I thank heaven for one act plays.

— translated from Welsh by the author

The Sun's Flowers

She was carrying sunshine in her bag
that woman on the train,
I know because I saw
one shaft of sun fall out
and light up the whole cabin
before being shoved back
behind the closed mouth of a zipper.
Everybody smiled,
and all the tiredness of travel rubbed from every eye,
it was like a sunset
at the end of the day we had never seen.
As the bag closed
everybody frowned
and the unfamiliar cold blew through the cabin,
again
through the knowing woman's lips.

— translated from Welsh by the author
version by TRC

Dŵr (Water)

Yr haf yma, aeth pethau'n ormod
i'r pibau dŵr dan yr heol;
rhoesant y gorau i bwmpio,
a chwydu'u cynnwys ar hyd y ffordd
yn fôr o wrthryfel a rhialtwch.
Mae'n haf! Mwynhewch!
Daeth gwahoddiad i ddawnsio yn y dyfroedd,
i roi'r gorau i'r car om ychydig o hwyl,
tynnu'r esgidiau a sblashio.
Ond mae'n rhaid mai dim ond fi glywodd,
a thra 'mod i'n troelli a hercian
yn y pyllau
roedd ceir yn dal i fynd heibio'n araf
a wynebau lliw uwd llipa'r gyrwyr
yn goleuo am eiliad wrth weld y ffŵl yn y dŵr.

Water

This summer, things got too much
for the water pipes under the street
they gave up pumping
and spewed their contents all over the road
a sea of rebellion and ribaldry.
It's summer! Enjoy it!
The invitation to dance in the depths came;
to abandon the car for a little fun.
Pull off your shoes and splash!
But I must have been the only one to hear
and whilst I windmilled and hopped
in the pools
the cars still drove past as slow as hearses
porridge coloured flabby faces
lighting up for a moment
looking at a fool in water.

— translated from Welsh by the author

(Breizh)
BRITTANY

BRETON

Breton

There is something of a miracle in the very fact that we can today boast of a poetry of some value. We have enough Middle-Breton poems to rest assured that a Breton poetical school kept alive the technique of the old Britto-Welsh tradition. But what riches was our heirloom? The libraries of all our monasteries were destroyed at the time of the French Revolution, castles were sold and ransacked and "sorting-out committees" were appointed to go through all collections of books and documents. As an example, we may cite the Committee for Rennes which, going through the archives of the district, cleaned out 3777 files out of 4152. It may be that Breton language documents were rather scarce in Rennes and around. But the same screening operations were carried in the Breton-speaking area, and one may easily imagine what fate befell Breton manuscripts and books when the destruction of all non-French languages on the territory of the Republic had become the order of the day. Sung poetry was very much alive among the Breton folk, but the work of collecting it began only in the mid-1800's, when the Breton community was in the process of being broken up and a relentless war was waged against the language by the schools and the other State institutions.

One might wonder how a people thrown for centuries into a minority status can find time for poetry. But literary expression is as much essential to a language as using it for bargaining on the market-square. And so, through thick and thin, a poetry we did have and we do have.

Our beautiful old poems were essentially concerned with the joys, and still more, the pains of the other world. Our folk poetry strikes a fuller note when it deals with the drama of life rather than when it tries to express its happy moments. The XIXth century written poetry is more quiet, more subdued, empty of all unwise love, and sad, as become the verses of people who are just passengers on earth, even if passengers to Paradise . . .

The Gwalarn school, with Roparz Hemon as an avenue opener, from 1925 onwards made Breton poetry fully human - no make-believe anymore, love was love, and the place to live it was this world of ours. The struggle for the language was for the poet a matter of life and death. His enthusiasm was that of the fighter.

In the second half of this century, the confident freshness in tomorrow's victory had disappeared. It was replaced by a darker appreciation of the endless struggle which had to be waged. And then, there came along this technical revolution: that the human voice could be kept, and stored, and reproduced as easily as his writings. A new generation of poets was thus born, who sang, as the bards of old, their poems to their audiences. I am thinking of Glenmor, the great awakener and of Youenn Gwernig, that master of verse and guitar. The poet is challenging not only the French power, but a destructive way-of-life as well (or should we say "way-of-death"?).

The XIXth century poets wrote in an easily flowing language, in which sound was more important than meaning. Not so now. Research in words and research in forms are at their highest. There are lovers of the old Britto-Welsh metrics, and devotees of the free verse. This new poetry indeed has pushed a step further the care that Gwalarn took with the language. Our poetry today is unsmiling, quietly harsh, relentlessly rough, as the very struggle of the Breton people.

— Per Denez

Anjela Duval
(1905 - 1981)

Anjela Duval was born in North Brittany (Ar C'hozh-Varc'had) in the region known as the Trégor. She is a towering figure among the ranks of Breton poets of the 20th century, though she herself was self-effacing about her craft, claiming first and foremost to identify with the life she had been born into—that of a small land-owning peasant family whose homestead and lifestyle she maintained through the decades until her own demise in 1981. She left school early and worked with her parents on the family farm (Traoñ an Dour). Duval came late to poetry, in her 50s, only after the death of her parents. She began writing poetry in Breton first, publishing in the Breton literary journals *Barr-Heol* and *Al Liamm*, and later writing memoirs. Between the rounds of agricultural activities – carried out *à la ancienne mode* with a horse as her engine – and the demands of barnyard and domestic chores, Duval found time to generate hundreds of poems, some written in haste on the back of a used envelope or scrap of butcher paper. Her fame in Brittany is the result of her authentic voice – of a *bretonnante* living a lifestyle that, in many, evoked a nostalgia for the old days. Among her published work one can cite such titles as *Kan an Douar* (poetry, 1973), *Traoñ an Dour* (poetry, 1982), *Tad-kozh Roperzh* (memories, 1982), and *Me, Añjela* (memories, 1986) as among the favorites of the Breton-speaking people.

Karantez-Vro (Love For A Country)

E korn va c'halon 'zo ur gleizenn
'Baoe va yaouankiz he dougan
Rak siwazh, an hini a garen
Ne gare ket pezh a garen
Eñ na gare nemet ar c'hêriou
Ar moriou don, ar broiou pell
Ha ne garen 'met ar maeziou
Maeziou ken kaer va Breizh-Izel

Brittany

Ret 'voe dibab 'tre div garantez
Karantez-Vro, karantez den
D'am bro am eus gouestlet va buhez
Ha lest da vont 'n hini' garen
Biskoazh abaoe n'em eus e welet
Biskoazh klevet keloù outañ
Ar gleizenn em c'halon 'zo chomet
Pa gare ket pezh a garan.

Pep den a dle heuilh e Donkadur
Honnezh eo lezenn ar Bed-mañ
Gwasket 'voe va c'halon a dra sur
Met' gare ket pezh a garan
Dezhañ pinvidigezh, enorioù
Din-me paourentez ha dispriz
Met' drokfen ket evit teñzorioù
Va Bro, va Yezh ha va Frankiz.

Love For A Country

In a corner of my heart there's a scar
That I have borne since I was young
For, alas, the one I cared for
Didn't love what I loved
He only loved cities
Distant countries, deep seas
And I only loved the fields
The fair fields of my Brittany

Forced to choose between two affections
Love for a Country, love for a man
I've given my life to my nation
And let go of the one I loved
I never saw him again later
Heard nothing of his life's course
The scar in my heart stays there
For he didn't love what I love.

Every man must follow his Destiny
In this World that's the law
My heart's crushed most certainly
But he didn't love what I love

For him riches, honors
For me disdain and poverty
But I'd not exchange for treasures
My Country, my Language and my Liberty.

− translated from Breton by Lenora A. Timm

Thank You!

Thanks to you God the Creator!
To have destined me to be a farmer.
Oh Master of Nature
You have given me the Happiness
To work in your company.
You give the Earth, the rain and the heat.
I fertilize, sow, weed, harvest.
And is there in this World
A nobler profession?
The disdain of city-folk makes me laugh
When they take the farmer for a poor leper
Yet he owns a thousand gold things,
And his silver shines
On dewy mornings
On the tip of each grassblade in his green meadows.
Seas of grain shafts wave on his terrain
Ponds of emeralds where his livestock wander,
And amethyst paths among his fields.
To him the wholesome perfumes and the pure songs
Of birds and flowers.
To him the buzzing of the bees,
The rustling of the leaves.
To him the howling and humming of the wind,
And the infinite vault of a star-studded sky.
O yes! Thanks to you Lord
To have destined me to be a farmer.

− translated from Breton by Lenora A. Timm

My Poems

If I write by the light of my lamp
Disorderly and empty verses
Uncertainly with this small stub in my tired hand
If I write at night on the back of envelopes
Insignificant poems: poor merchandise
In which are found only wildflowers . . .
And a crumb of love,
All this I do for those I love.

Yet I do write, other poems
Not by the light of the lamp.
But by the rays of the Sun
Not on the back of envelopes
But on the bare breast of the One I love,
On the bare skin of the Country I love.
I don't write them with a pencil stub
But with steel tools . . .
– Don't think of a lance or sword,
My tools are tools of peace and of existence –

I don't write verses of twelve feet
In counting on my fingers,
But of twelve-by-twenty paces . . . and more.
My verses are written swath by swath
With the sharp steel of my scythe
  on the yellow hair of my country
The Sun turns them into fragrant poems
That my cows scatter for me during winter nights.

My verses are written with the blade of my plow
On the living flesh of my Brittany, furrow after furrow
– In which I hide grains of gold –
Springtime turns them into poems
Emerald seas waving in the breeze.
Summer turns them into lovely lakes of shafts
The Harvest-Wind sets them to music
And the clanging of the thresher sings them to me
During the hot days of the eighth month
During days of pain and dust and sweat
My poems sacred and . . . disdained!

– translated from Breton by Lenora A. Timm

Imprison

Ah yes! Be proud
Superman of the atomic age
Be proud! You're the victor . . .
You're the master. For shame! Such work . . .
You've imprisoned Fire
And tamed Electricity!
Imprisoned Water!
Imprisoned speech and music
In the cage of the Radio.
Imprisoned shadow and color
Behind the glass of the Television.
Imprisoned numbers
In the case of the Computer.
Imprisoned enlightenment
Behind walls of libraries.
Planted your banner on the Moon.
And your opponent in jail.
And put God in your pocket.
Yes then you are a superman
Be proud!
    While you may . . .

* — translated from Breton by Lenora A. Timm*

Humming

I would rather hear
Things than people.
The sound of the fire hissing
The gander honking
In a howling wind,
Water gurgling in the stream
And the sluice-gate rumbling.
Far away I hear their humming
Like an echo coming
From the depths of centuries
The voices of my ancestors.

* — translated from Breton by Lenora A. Timm*

Boud (Humming)

Selaou kentoc'h a ran
An traoù eget an dud.
Trouz an tan o c'hwezhañ
Ar c'harz o tifronkañ
Dindan an avel yud,
Dour ar stêr o ruilhal
Hag ar skluz o krozal.
A dreuz o boud, me 'glev
O tont 'vel un heklev
Eus don ar c'hantvedoù
Mouezhioù va hendadoù.

The Old Mare

"Gentle in the stable,
Good in harness."
(Advertising in Le Paysan Breton *for a mare for sale.)*

The old mare is tired from being too exploited,
too poorly-nourished, to brutalized.

She's tired from hearing talk more often of "Getty-up!"
than of oats!

Never a kind word, never a caress.
Nor a gesture in recognition of her loyal service.

She's the best mare! She's going to resist, to
fight, to protest, to rise up.

She was used too much, and her blood is bitter.

"BRITTANY" is the name of that mare . . .

— translated from Breton by Lenora A. Timm

The Dismantling Of Brittany

– Do I write poems? – Yes, I write poems.
But it does not please me at all to be called a poet!
My occupation has always been cutting worms.
And I talk to my animals as if they were people . . .
I have always liked my occupation,
As the fish likes: the water.

But there are things that I don't like,
And I need to say it:
I don't like seeing the fields of my Country
Lying fallow and harboring wild animals.
I don't like seeing the buildings of my Country
Passing into hands of foreigners for a handful of paper.
I don't at all like,
Seeing the hedges of my Country – the framework of the Celtic
Countries –

Razed pitilessly and thoughtlessly,
And the youth of my Country running to the cities
To sell their energy and life's freedom
To the oppressor who mocks them.
I don't like to see the old people of my Country
In the city death-houses weeping at their lost effort
Or young mothers of my Country
Speaking the oppressor's language to their little children.

It is a crime to break the Chain
It is a crime to contaminate the Race
And no one raises a word in opposition.
No one! Or so few!

That's why I write poems – It isn't my occupation –
To hide my pain in them
To hide in them as in a drawer
The pearls of my tears . . . And then,
Where to keep the last seed
If not in the garden of the Poet.

– translated from Breton by Lenora A. Timm

The Conquerors

They fell on our territory,
Like a flock of crows
On the battleground after the attack,
The conquerors!

For a fistful of French paper
And a signature on a document
They had the right to own our land.
The conquerors!

Old mills in peaceful valleys
Are now their possessions.
Castles and manors will soon be theirs,
The conquerors!

They will scour our countryside,
To tempt, with money, the poor man,
Who will sell the clock and bed of his father,
To the conquerors!

They will mount the walls of our Sanctuaries,
And enthrone in their living rooms
Old statues of Breton Saints carved in wood,
Houses of the conquerors!

Foreigners yesterday in our Country,
Tomorrow they will be our masters.
And in the valley their web constantly expands,
The conquerors!

But are we a meek race, then?
And a laissez-faire people!
If we let our Country's treasure go to the band
Of Conquerors!

You, Bretons dispersed in the World,
I'm asking you,
You, Compatriots asleep in your Country,
I'm rousing you.

You, on whom Fate has smiled,
I'm entreating you,
Have pity on our Country, hurry to combat
The conquerors.

A poor Patriot:
Anjela Duval.

— *translated from Breton by Lenora A. Timm*

Elves

A people of elves
A degenerate people
A genocidal people
Drowned in red wine
Drowned in French pom-pom
And in the political slogans
A people resembling Elves
Playfully amusing themselves
In the abandoned heath
Dancing among the megaliths
To the sound of the toads
To the mysterious music
Of the wind and the sea
The lament of the streams
The rustling of the woods

And the enchantment of the Harp
And the bagpipe of the night-Festivals
Elves crouch in their hole
As soon as the Masters roar
As soon as the Frenchman's roosters crow
A defeated people, drowned
Like the City of Ys in the ocean★

Some complain in the dark night
About their lost Liberties
While dancing like Elves
On the dried ground of the warren
And kneel every morning

Brittany

Before the French-God.
Do back-breaking work,
During the day, during the week,
For the Country that sucks them . . .

Ah! People disintegrated
Turned to elves!
What miracle will be needed
To awaken you?

— translated from Breton by Lenora A. Timm

A legendary city submerged in the sea due to the wickedness of its people.

Per Denez
(1921 –)

Born in Roazhon (Rennes) in a family from the country, Per Denez learned Breton when he was a teenager. He graduated in English and spent a year in Aberdeen (Scotland) before being appointed as a teacher in Périgueux (Southwest France), Kemper (Quimper, West Brittany) and Douarnenez (West Brittany), his wife's hometown. He takes part in many struggles and actions to renew the Breton language. In 1954 he created the linguistics periodical *Hor Yezh* with the linguist Arzel Even. He founded the political magazine *Ar Vro* in the late fifties. He entered the University of Rennes to teach Breton in 1969. He became Head of the Department of Breton and Celtic studies a few years later. His State Doctorate (1978) deals with Breton modern linguistics. He has published a great number of works: studies and surveys on Breton linguistics, poetry, novels, short stories, dictionaries, teaching methods as well as a number of translations (from Welsh and English mainly). His literary works are mostly novels and short stories: *Diougan Gwenc'hlan* (1979), *Glas evel daoulagad c'hlas* (1980, translated into English in 1993), *Hiroc'h eo an amzer eget ar vuhez* (1981), *Eus un amzer zo bet* (1992), *En tu all d'an douar ha d'an neñv* (1993), *Kenavo ar c'hentañ joaioù* (1994), etc. Per Denez is now retired and lives in Douarnenez.

Negro Song

(e doare Langston Hughes)

Me zo Breizhad.

Me zo bet sklav.
> *Galeour ez on bet e bagoù ar Roue Loeiz.*
> *Toullet em eus hentoù, douget va samm a vein.*
> *Savet em eus, en o c'hêrbenn, o falezioù.*

Me zo bet soudard.
> *Va obidoù em eus kanet e lannegi Plañwour*
> *Breinet em eus en erc'hegi Rusia.*

Breinet em eus e rizegi Hanoi,
Tufet va gwad e fozioù pri Verdun.
Lazhet em eus ar re zu
Ha distrujet an doueed a azeulent.

Me zo bet mevel.
Mousc'hoarzh ar re faezhet em eus bet o servij.
Desket em eus d'an dud komz evel va mistri.
Ruzet em eus va zreid war bavezioù Pariz
Ha graet 'm eus dezho c'hoarzhin
Rak me zo bet farouell.

Me zo bet merzher.

Negro Song

(to Langston Hughes)

I am a Breton.

I have been a slave.
I have pulled the oars on the galleys of King Louis.
I have opened roads, carried my load of stones.
I have built their palaces in their capital.

I have been a soldier.
I have sung my funeral on the moors of Planwour.
I have rotted on the snowy plains of Russia.
I have rotted in the rice fields of Hanoi.
I have spat blood in the muddy trenches of Verdun.
I have killed black people
And destroyed the gods they worshipped.

I have been a servant.
I have performed my duties with the smile of the vanquished.
I have taught people to speak the language of my masters.
I have shuffled along the pavements of Paris
And I made them laugh
For I have been a fool.

I have been a martyr.

— translated from Breton by Gwendal Denez and Natalie Franz

Ian Palach

They have smashed your tombstone
trying to wipe out the place
where your remains lie.
Soon they will exhume your body
so that people can't reach you anymore.
You, Ian Palach, who are in and through your death
such a big danger for them,
you must be definitely destroyed.
Your tombstone will be used for paving roads
your ashes will be scattered in the wind.
Your name will be erased from any official memory.
They will have to do much more though:
to eradicate from your language
the letters that shape your name,
and create a new language without an I, without an A,
without an N.
They will have to root out that language
for it keeps alive the memory of the generations
and children must not hear these sounds
nor gather them together
in order to shape and call your name.
They will have to drown your songs and your poems,
and crush your History, the memory of your people . . .
They will have to . . . What else!
In order to get rid of your name and of your memory
they will have to clear out of your homeland
with their armoured tanks, their machine-guns, their cops
and their servants, and find shelter where they were born.
They are the ones who made of your name a call
that will re-echo in spite of them
in the heart of their prisons.
And then, Ian Palach,
right in the middle of their Red Square,
your light will shine anew
and it will be acknowledged
as the red flower of Freedom.

— translated from Breton by Gwendal Denez

Songs In Springtime

It's on a night like this that I will choose to die,
When earth and heath are peaceful and calm
As they are today on the banks of the summer river
In whose limpid shallows the trees are gleaming.

There will be neither star nor moon over me
And I won't turn my gaze towards the sky;
Just as on this evening I will keep my thoughts on the earth,
On the sea whose murmur I will hear in the distance.

I will live again the trouble of our night
When I could feel the warm weight of your shoulder upon my arm
And you shall hear from far away, stronger than the laughter of joy
The call of my soul so deeply moved for ever.

— translated from Breton by Gwendal Denez and Natalie Franz

Kanoù En Nevez-Hañv (Songs In Springtime)

En un noz 'vel houmañ e tibabin mervel,
Pa vezo tir ha lann ken habask he ken sioul
Ha ma vezont hiziv war c'hlann ar stêr hañvel
A velezour ar gwez en he donderioù boull.

Ne vezo a-us din na steredenn na loar
Ha ne droin va sell etrezek an neñvoù;
'Vel henozh e stago va soñj ouzh an douar,
Ouzh ar mor a glevin er pellder e voubou.

Bevañ 'rin adarre trefu hon nozvezhiad
Pa santen war va brec'h ho skoaz o pouezañ tomm;
Ha c'hwi pell a glevo dreist da c'hoarzh an eurvad,
Galvadenn va ene, ken don atav e from.

Going Past My Youth

The peaceful smile of my mother
in the pale meadows
hot in the Autumn sun.
Ravens hopping
and trampling lightly
on the newly-harrowed earth
ready to be sown.
Further is the long cart-track we used to walk on
when there were cowslips along its edges
and bluebells in the fields.
But where is the ancient Roman way
that led to Baragon moors?
It has become a wheat-growing land,
nothing can hold out against a bulldozer.
And where is the honeysuckle road,
its chestnut-trees and its wild-cherry-trees
and the long brambles weaving garlands
around the holly-tree hiding a robin nest,
the road we loved to walk on
in the youth of age and of summer,
where is it?
It has become a memory
of a memory.
My mother's smile,
where is it gone?
Perhaps the weeds could tell,
or the ravens,
but I am in mourning for it.

For it and for her.

— translated from Breton by Gwendal Denez

A-Ruilh E-Biou D'ar Yaouankiz (Going Past My Youth)

Mousc'hoarzh sioul va mamm
er pradeier sklaer
ha tomm gant heol an diskar-hañv.
Brini o pilpasat,
gorrek o c'hammedoù,
an douar nevez-ogedet,
prest evit an had.
Du-hont an hent hir a raemp
pa oa roz-amann a-hed ar wrimenn
ha bleunioù-koukoug er bradenn.
Met an hent roman kozh
a gase da lanneier Bagaron,
pelec'h emañ?
Douar gwinizh eo deut da vezañ,
netra ne bad ouzh an diskraperez.
Ha gwenodenn he gwezvoud,
he gwez-kistin ha kerez-med
hag he drez hir o plezhennañ garlantezioù
da wenn-gelenn he neizh draouennig,
ar wenodenn ma karemp bale enni
e yaouankiz hon oad hag an hañv,
pelec'h 'ta emañ?
N'eus diouti ken nemet
eñvor un eñvor.
Mousc'hoarzh va mamm,
da belec'h eo aet?
Marteze e oar ar geot,
marteze e oar ar brini,
me avat dioutañ a chom e kañv;

Dioutañ ha diouti.

Naig Rozmor
(1923 –)

Naig Rozmor was born in Kastell-Pol (St. Pol-de-Léon, North Brittany) into a peasant farming family. She grew up in a solidly Breton-speaking milieu and did not acquire French until she went off to school. Her father was in fact a Breton-language militant, for he had been punished as a child (with the classic "symbole" hung around his neck) for speaking Breton instead of French at school. Thus, family members took it as a point of pride to speak Breton among themselves. Her real name is Anne Bian-Corre. As a native Breton speaker, she began writing in the 1950s – short stories, plays, and poetry coming later in the 1970s. As only one of a tiny handful of women poets publishing in the Breton language, Rozmor is well known to the Breton-reading public, and much admired for the grace, simplicity and honesty of her poetic style. She is perhaps the only one to have published poems on erotic themes. Her work possesses a keen historical consciousness about the cultural, economic and political oppression suffered by the Breton people under the dominion of the French-controlled state. Rozmor was a founding member of the now immensely popular Strollad ar Vro-Bagan, a traveling acting troupe that performs principally in Breton; she both writes for and acts in this grass-roots theatrical company. Her play *Sacré Tanguy Bihan*, about the expropriation of a peasant family from its lands in the northwestern region of Brittany (Léon), is based in part on her own family's experience of this tragic upheaval during the 1930s. As a young woman, Rozmor was greatly attracted to and influenced by Oriental philosophy, particularly that of India. She was attracted to the writings of Rabindranath Tagore, the Nobel Prize-winning Indian poet and writer whose works had been translated into French by André Gide. She was awarded the Breton Writers Prize in 1977 for *Karantez ha Karantez*, and the Imram Prize in 1989. She is currently involved as an actress in television and theatre, where she is mostly interested in women's issues of identity in Breton society and literature, as well as social changes in rural society as her play *Ar Mestr* witnesses. She lives in Rosko (Roscoff, North Brittany).

If I Could Write

If I could write when you make love to me,
I would disclose pearled arches,
Swaying seas,
Flaming lighthouses and hidden fountains . . .
If I could write when you make love to me!

If I could write when you make love to me,
I would sing strange psalms,
Fevered moanings,
A wild wind and the howling of wolves . . .
If I could write when you make love to me!

If I could write when you make love to me,
I would reveal wild crowds,
Abandoned abysses,
Red wounds and often pain . . .
If I could write when you make love to me!

If I could write when you make love to me,
I would tell of the earth's joy
Under the hot kisses of the sun
And the great trembling of the earth
Receiving her first waters . . .
But I can't write when you make love to me!

— translated from Breton by Lenora A. Timm

Pity

My eyes are too tender
To look at guns
My ears are too tender
To hear gunshots
My heart is too tender
To suffer moaning . . .
Much too tender in truth!

Oh how cruel to be alive, at the time of the hunt
When one is so tender as I am!

Hunter! Excuse me
I would like it if
The rabbits were swifter
The foxes were craftier
And . . . your gun were empty!

— translated from Breton by Lenora A. Timm

Alleluia

How many times have we two communed
In the depths of the feather-bed?
How many bonfires has our love ignited in it?
How many nights have we burned in that way,
How many chains have we broken together?
How many alleluias have you drawn from my liberated body?

Only the hearth beetles could answer me
For they are the guardians of the fire.

— translated from Breton by Lenora A. Timm

Affliction

Will you know how to read my eyes
When they flower for you like southern flax?

Will you hear my heart's hammer pounding
To ask entry to the door of your heart?

Will you understand the language of my cavorting?
And the cries of my enflamed body
Will you leave them waiting a long time for you?

Oh yes, my beloved, I am confident
For I see above the sunset,
The red star of love
Already ascended to lead the night.

— translated from Breton by Lenora A. Timm

My Father's Hands

Tears come to my eyes
When I think of my father's hands!
The hands of a peasant, red and cracked
Like the soil when it's parched
By the bitter north wind.

They were wide like paddles
Spread by hard labor
But when they cut our bread,
Like those of the priest at the Host,
My father's hands dispersed graces.

— translated from Breton by Lenora A. Timm

Reun ar C'halan
René Galand
(1923 –)

Born in 1923, in the small town of Kastellnevez-ar-Fao, in the heart of Brittany, Reun ar C'halan studied at the *lycées* of Brest and Rennes, and at the University of Rennes, where he received a baccalaureate degree in mathematics (1941), another in philosophy (1942), and the *Licence ès Lettres* (1944). In 1942, he made contact with the *Résistance* against the German occupants, and, at the time of the Normandy landings, he fought with his underground group to prevent German troops stationed in Brittany from reaching the landing beaches. After the liberation of France, he was admitted to the French Officers' School of Saint-Cyr, then relocated in Cherchell (Algeria). He served with the French Occupation Forces in Germany until the fall of 1946. After resigning his commission in the army, he rejoined his parents and his sister in the United States in 1947, and entered Yale University as a doctoral candidate in French Literature, completing his doctorate in the fall of 1951, then joining the faculty of Wellesley College, where he served as Professor of French (1951-1993), serving as Chair of the French Department from 1968 to 1972.

At Wellesley, he taught mostly courses in 19th and 20th Century French Literature. His publications in this field include several books: *L'Ame celtique de Renan* (1959), *Baudelaire: poétiques et poésie* (1969), *Saint-John Perse* (1972), *Canevas: Études sur la poésie française de Baudelaire à l'Oulipo* (1986), *Stratégie de la lecture* (1990), contributions to collective works: *Baudelaire as a Love Poet and Other Essays* (1969), *A Critical Bibliography of French Literature* (1980), *The Binding of Proteus* (1980), *The New Princeton Encyclopedia of Poetry and Poetics* (1993). He was made a *Chevalier* in the Order of the "Palmes Académiques" for his contributions to the study of French literature and culture.

A native speaker of Breton, he has also written extensively about the languages and literatures of the Celts. His essays, poems, and short stories have appeared in *Proceedings of the Harvard Celtic Colloquium, Al Liamm,* as well as in other journals and in anthologies. He is the author of three volumes of poetry: *Levr ar Blanedenn* (1981), *Klemmgan Breizh* (1985), and *Lorc'h ar Rouaned* (1989), which all appeared under the Breton form of his name, Reun ar C'halan. He was the recipient of the Xavier de Langlais Prize in Breton Literature.

Gouestl Ar Goañv (The Vow Of Winter)

Bez' ez eus deizioù boull zoken e-kreiz ar goañv
Diouzh ar mintin e strak ar prad dindan ar rev
Ar riv en em sil betek kalon start ar mein
An iliav war ar voger a zo chomet glas
An etev diwezhañ a zev war an oaled
Ur fulenn a bik he diamant war al ludu
Pa vez steuziet pep dremm diouzh ar melezourioù
E teu kraoñenn an noz da darzhañ gant ar skorn
Teñval e vez an ti n'en deus na tan na toenn
Na teñval ar bed en ti hep tan na gwele
Pa zeu al linad da c'holeiñ an dismantroù
E park hon hendadoù n'eus manet den ebet
Deomp e vo an noz e-lec'h ma red an tangwall

The Vow Of Winter

There are limpid days in the heart of winter
In the morning the meadow crushes under the sleet
Slowly the cold has crept into the stone
The ivy still lives, clinging to the walls
On the hearth the last log crumbles into ashes
On the soot a spark pins a final diamond
When all the mirrors have forgotten all the faces
The frost cracks the kernel of night
Dark is the house without fire or roof
Dark is the house without fire or bed
When thorns and nettles have covered up the ruins
No one is left in our fathers' fields
We will take back the night where the fire still burns.

– translated from Breton by the author

The Ghost Of Liberty

How could we have forgotten?
All the bridges have been cut
Our daughters wore their chains of tears
Our days were candles by a death bed
But the nights roared like mountain torrents
As we slept on the worn stones of churchyards
Who could seek shelter outside of time?
Pleasure curdled within our hearts
A ghost vanished into the dusk
Paler than the phantom of freedom
And his voice faded away
When would the dead open their mystery
The Tír-n-an-Óg of heroes and saints?

— translated from Breton by the author

The Dream Flower

The gods then were so close to us
They placed in our hands the golden herb of dreams
The earth sang to us through the mouths of fountains
Roses bloomed under each of our steps
The grass was as soft as a woman's hair
And the trees offered their fruit
The sun waddled in the water
And our eyes laughed at its flame
Far away, the sea kept shining like a mirage
Each star whispered its name in our ears
The bee of wisdom hummed around our brows
And we sang hymns to the night
The night so soft with its velvet sighs

— translated from Breton by the author

Song Of Exile

Long ago, during the night
The daughters of the rain
Would fly to our cradles
Their hair blowing in the wind.
We heard their sweet voices
In the meadow by the brook
As the clouds brought from the sky
Their heavenly blessing.
Where have they gone,
The daughters of the rain?
The rushing brook tells only lies.
In the ancient wood of the fay,
Pigs burrow with their snouts.
The milt of toads
Poisons the silvery springs,
And the dregs of seasons
Have soiled our hearts.
We will not see again
The green woods: they are stained
With the victims' blood.
We will not taste again
The bread of innocence.
Who cast this evil spell
Over the ancient kingdom
Of the white ermine?

Note: The ermine is the traditional emblem of Brittany.

— translated from Breton by the author

Youenn Gwernig
(1925 –)

Youenn Gwernig, born in Skaer (Central Brittany) in 1925, emigrated quite early to the United States where he spent many years in New York working as a sculptor in a furniture plant. During his stay in the States he met Jack Kerouac and they became friends. As a result there is a definite influence of the Beats and the Beat Generation on Gwernig's work. Having returned to Brittany from the States in 1969, today, as one of Brittany's most admired living poets and much admired by the younger generation of Breton readers and writers, Gwernig lives in Berrien, France where he is also a folk singer and writer for radio and television. A poet whose work has been published and translated into many languages, he has recorded records and published volumes of short stories. Some of his most well known titles include *An toull en nor* (1972), *An diri dir* (1976), *La grande tribu* (1982). Loneliness, Breton identity, love and revolt are his major themes.

125th Street

There is something there, man, something you can feel
there's something blowing in the wind there, man,
of long awaited spring
I ain't singin no blues, man,
and keep your alleluias
caterpillars can roam
the cold and barren streets
but spring is here, man,
spring is here
budding cracking blowing
and you shall never eat up, man,
you shall never eat up
my green.

— translated from Breton by the author

The Bridge

This is the bridge you've got to cross and go
where? nobody knows and I don't care
if only I could stand the howling of that train
empty parade of a thousand windows
beaming in a dazzling sun
and the useless deafening silent call
of the rooms with their lights
on;

the huge and naked bridge I met years ago
with that man wearing a wavy beard
on his white shirt
I can find nowhere the song of his words
nor the quiet fire of his eyes
there's only some of his breath left in the wind
and little of his warmth waning on the cold floor
of the bridge.

– translated from Breton by the author

Identity

They had forgotten where they were born
was it a castle, a cottage or a stable
to be born was their own masterpiece
to feel the wind of the spring
on their nostrils and the beating of the blood
in their chest
pick pick pick the stone cutter won't stop
just to be alive was their own masterpiece

building blocks heaped stonework
round the garden's wild flowers
there's no wall you cannot beat
there's no wall without a hole
and who cares where a man was born
slates are alike on any roof
and the smoke mingling with the dreamy cloud
– better brush up your knowledge –
carries only the message
of a dying firewood.

– translated from Breton by the author

Brittany

from: **Stairs Of Steel**

I

Nobody me going down the stairs of steel
along with a herd of nobodies
up there the train's rolling its thunder
with hate and speed to yet another load
of ghosts live hungry and dirty ghosts
endlessly going down the stairs of steel
each one
     in his heaven
         in his hell
all alone

shrieking voice of a crazied wild Black woman
a Black woman yelling
"my kingdom is not of this world"
nobody listens
a little old man only laughing a toothless laugh

ten steps and a stop – too narrow that door downstairs –
hot smell of human bodies
smells of sweat
smell of cheap perfumes
this one hasn't washed her hair
for three months maybe
smells of labor

huge bulk of a belly panting in my back
front of me the little ass of a lean dark girl
lamblike hair tickling my chin
a girl half crushed on my left
my right side crushed against beams of steel
the Black woman screaming
"it's not of this world but of a world to come"
nobody listens
down down the endless staircase
nobody me along with
    a herd of nobodies
        dirty and hungry
going half crushed
down down to that too narrow door.

III

According to legend, the boys of my hometown had been given a most
bothersome gift: to become invisible. A good reason for women from my
hometown to go to bed in complete harness. They undressed their headdress,
their collar, their socks, and that was all. Of course, it was only a legend, a fairy
tale, grandmother's nonsense.

> Well, now the girl is at her door
> noise of the key and opens it
>
> only one letter in the box
> a letter from her loved one
>
> and then upstairs she is rushing
> her simple heart jumping jumping
>
> to the little room by the roof
> to her relaxing paradise

as usual the girl turns on the radio
hangs her coat and in front of the mirror
starts to unscrew her earrings,
with a searching look
– strange music hammering tonight over the radio
funny enough and relaxing –

she takes off her sweater
and then her skirt
then her very shirt
and

they could see a Celtic warrior, a real giant, dancing a war dance in front of the
Roman army; he was holding a sword in each hand, wearing a shield upon his left
arm; he was stark naked but for a necklace round his neck and rings round his
wrists.

In front of the mirror
the girl's looking at her body
young and healthy
perfect

her breasts she caresses
– so sweet now the music: violins –

burst
    and tender yet
        of the brass
raising her arms now
with no haste and happy she turns
her left foot first
    and starts to dance

under the cold glasseyed Moumoute
she turns and turns around the room
drowned in the devil of music
    burst
        BURST
            BURST of the blaring brass

here they are all of them beasts animals
swarming
their hides their furs and worse the smell
of their desires

but they're tame as tame as Moumoute
so the goddess dances in her heaven
owner of sun and moon
owner of earth
owner of men on earth
owner of all Moumoutes on earth . . .

music's over
a voice now saying
what kind of weather we'll get tomorrow

Nini opens a can of beer and
lying on the couch she starts
to read the letter from her lover.

V

He came in very quietly and was standing
shy in the doorway and he so small
rain water dripping from his long hair
Sal shouting
    "get out ye crap-yeller"
him asking
    "got empty bottles please Sir"

Sal howling
      "get out ye fuckin thief"
and him
      "empty bottles . . ."
a child knows how to wait
when he is poor

and I told Sal to shut his mouth
and tried to smile to the little guy
his big beautiful guileless eyes
looking at me
with no sunshine in their black velvet
"got empty bottles please Sir"

and we looked around the place
for empty bottles
"thank you Sir"
and then
"what's your name Sonny"
"Pablo"
"good boy Pablo hasta mañana"
"thank you hasta mañana Sir"

and I am feeling very sad tonight
remembering Pablo
with no sunshine in his eyes.

(New York 1966)

– translated from Breton by the author

Two Short Tales For A May Day

The Lord Mayor is happy
his lousy parishioners went to Paris
to get
their rear-end
clean

the Lord Mayor is happy
cows won't shit anymore
on the quiet roads

Brittany

of the parish
and so
unharmed
shall walk
the peaceful army
of our civilized tourists

The Lord Mayor is happy
for the land
is going to be sold
to strangers
casting a right ballot.

          •

People around, my country people
and things growing
things
good only to be eaten
to be
crushed and cut and left
to die
people and things around
and spring has come at last
people throwing up their wine
others are happy
with no bellyache at all, happy
with their pension
with their scorched soul
and some others
buying smoked sausages
for the baptism dinner
of the little one . . .

Lots of fields around here
good land fat land
plenty of things growing here
things and people

they're growing sprouted
green
from our land

and the sun won't care
people and things sprouted
green
weeded out blindly
for the good
of the State,

for the Bretons are
– more than shortsighted –
very obedient.

An old crippled woman bent
under her pains
walking the old road
she's got a son – the elder –
became a man got a blue coat
plexiglass too over his face
she's got a son – the other –
stayed home
to work
the land
the old woman will never know
her two sons met once
face to face
one evening in Guingamp

and who cares
this coming summer
the two sons will have
to speak Breton at home
for the old lady can't understand
any other
language.

– translated from Breton by the author

Annaig Renault
(1946 –)

Annaig Renault was born in Neuilly (near Paris), where she spent most of her youth. She presently works in the Breton Cultural Institute in Rennes. She has already published several works, including: *Barzhonegoù*, poems (1985), *Planedennoù*, short stories (1989), *Dec'h zo re bell dija,* a novel (1996), which was awarded the Per-Roy Prize. Some of her short stories published in various magazines have been translated into Welsh. She has published a collection of studies and surveys about literature dealing with the Breton poetess *Benead* (1994) and women writers in Breton literature: *Skritur ar maouezed abaoe mare Gwalarn*. At present, she is completing a thesis about the Breton poet Maodez Glanndour, *La pensée religieuse et philosophique dans l'oeuvre poétique de Glanndour*.

Who Will Take Away From Me

Who will take away from me
the fear of the long nights?
Secrets are hidden no more
from the one who reads
the mysteries of the world in the stars.

My path will plough
a furrow into the distorted quietness of truth.
That school has been deserted
since Hiroshima and Auschwitz.
Who would be crazy enough now
to lean on an insane science
and dare to teach the world?

We are waiting for prophets!
We shout in the darkness,
but they are already among us,
one can see them
in the laughter of children.

Where secrets are no longer hidden
from the one who reads
the mysteries of the world in stars.

— translated from Breton by Gwendal Denez / TRC

Follentez (Madness)

Roget he doa he yaouankiz
a-hed an noz da evañ glizh.
Adkroget 'doa bep noz ha deiz
war ribl he soñj da goll he meiz . . .
N'he doa ket lakaet, evel Bizmeud,
meinigoù gwenn en he chakod.
Kollet he deus penn he buhez
pa save just ar goulou-deiz.

Madness

She ripped apart her youth
drinking dew all night long.
She did it again every night and every day
on the verge of thoughts till she went mad . . .
She didn't have, like Tom Thumb,
those little white stones in her pocket.
And she lost her way
right at the break of day.

— translated from Breton by Gwendal Denez / TRC

Chagall

He has coloured the emptiness of the canvas
with the pain of his heart,
and nailed all the animals
to the endless skies of his soul.

He will always write
forever searching
the dim path of my desire.
He explains
when the hours of daylight get heavy
that sad joys exist

Brittany

lit up by the eyes
of an angel who unveils
a thousand glints of truth.

On all fours in the white-wash of the sky:
a donkey-goat.
Me?
You?
The Wandering Jew?

His Vitebsk is my unconsciousness . . .

I have been given Chagall
as a mirror into another world.

— translated from Breton by Gwendal Denez / TRC

I Walked About . . .

I walked about your city
secretly.
I drank the air
that feeds you.
Theft.

Pale corn.
Dark night.
Effects of paradise.

To be
a cat licking itself
in a patch of sunlight.

— translated from Breton by Gwendal Denez

Question

In your eyes
I pecked at
specks of dust . . .
Desire?
Do these thoughts belong in your house
or in mine?

The hours unwind.

— translated from Breton by Gwendal Denez / TRC

Goulenn (Question)

Ez taoulagad
em eus greunataet
poultrennoù an deiz . . .
Goulennoù ur c'hoant
– ar c'hoantadenn? –
Annez piv da soñjoù?

Dibunañ 'ra an eurvezhioù.

Bernez Tangi
(1949 –)

Bernez Tangi was born in Karanteg (North Brittany) and is a native Breton speaker. After completing his studies he decided to travel around the world before settling in Berrien (Central Brittany) where he lives now. He is a poet, a short story writer, as well as a well-known singer of both traditional ("kan ha diskan") and rock music, and was a lead singer with the rock band Storlok before going on a solo career. As a soloist, he released an album in 1990, *Kest al lec'h*, which is the title of one of his poems. His collection of poems *Fulennoù an Tantad* (1987) was awarded the Imram Prize.

Kuzh-Heol Rous (Red Sunset)

Kentañ tro
'm oa graet en avel-dro
ma zreid staget-mat ouzh ar stur
hep gouzout sur
dre beseurt hent 'z ae ar vag
ma fenn nemetken oa distag
ur speurenn etre korf ha spered
boued al livenn-gein a zivere ba'n dour-red
tennañ ar c'hartoù a rae Marjelina
bet eo bet priñsez e pleg-mor Akaba
skoachet e oan er gwele-kloz
dall da viken 'vit kan a boz
c'hwitell a rae Mestr Meur ar chas
war al leur-gêr e c'hoarzhe glas
treuzet em eus ar c'huzh-heol rous
kuzhet dindan pluñv al lapous

Red Sunset

First time
I swirled up
my feet stuck to the helm
without knowing for sure
which route the ship was heading
only my head was loose
a wall between body and mind
the food of my spine was dripping
into the undertow
Marjelina used to read cards
when she was a princess in Akaba Bay
I was hiding in a wardrobe
blinded forever with a sing-song
the Almighty Master of the hounds whistled
on the town square and he sneered
as I went through the red sunset
hidden in the feathers of a bird

— translated from Breton by Gwendal Denez

Near Ti Mizeria (The House Of Destitution)

I am not that man
who was by my side
on the day when the girl
dropped the dog on
the seashore . . .
    Who saw
        the child
close to
       PONT AR GORED?
a pig broke up
the black river
and the poor people
did cry all night long
all night
on the shore
    I am not the one
    I am not the one
I remember now

Brittany

I had the feeling that
the sea
was dizzy
on that day
dizzy like the dog
thrown by the girl
on the sand
I was then able
to hear
the eyes
of the wretched dog
grinding
like the stone
     of SAN GREGORIO MILL
rich were the lights of heaven
over
the roof of the world.

I am not the one
no
I am not the one
     – and I am getting tired
     of talking all the time
     all the time
getting tired of people
getting tired of uttering
words words words

Walking through the woods
it is a long time since I last heard
the green-haired girl
singing
on the oak-tree
standing near
TI MIZERIA where last year
Soazig Penvenn's son died
during the war
     – that was centuries ago –

Foreigners had planted
that oak-tree
in order to warn people

"THE CENTURIES TO COME WILL BE
DARK, COVERED WITH CLOUDS."

— translated from Breton by Daniel Madeg

Song For Anna

Jazz
    Jazz
    howling
And   inside my body
    me   two eyes
       in the weight   like
          of my body two persons
              gnawing
              my voice
ANNA   stubbing out
              my tears
              a dog
              (rotting)
              in my fist
              (clenched)
          and that music
          still wailing
        inside my body (curling up)
Louis is still alive
    I said   – two months ago
I can now
    see
    the title of the film
       that didn't end

Tonight
    I remember – two months later
       Louis is still alive
    and is a clown
    Listen
       Anna
    the scent of the weeds
    the scent of the fern
    the smell of your body

Brittany

       between
       the nettle and the wall-flower
  our night
       Anna
  our night
       so wonderful
  so wonderful
And   me
  after that communion
  alone
  again
Anna the weight of the world
  is
  on my eyes
       the warmth of your skin
       gnaws something
       deep inside me
  but today
       in the evening
  I was a bear
  a holly leaf
  in my hand
  spurting air
  out of my nostrils
       like a mad horse
  don't want to be heart-broken
  by you no more Anna
  from Landevenneg
       on the shore

  I'm waiting
       for August
          in the sky
the wind doesn't know where it is
it pulls the trees to pieces
as in a cold winter
and I don't know either
where I am
       I am waiting near the shore of the bay
       for red sails to be set

Anna
    your name is black
I was like Mad Salaun
    riding
    my motorbike
DRUNK
    I laugh now
    at this grotesque image
Khoudafes
    do widzenia
       Anna
    (my broken glass is on the floor)
THERE ARE FIGHTS AT THE LIVING BEING'S HOME
THERE ARE LIGHTS AT THE DEAD BEING'S HOME
IS THE RIVER AON A STYX, perhaps?
I have seen   red sails
    on the sea
    and PEACE has been disturbed again
Anna
    your name is black
    your name is black
       the warmth of your skin
       doesn't worry me any longer
    in the twilight   one can hear in the distance
PEOPLE   the laughters
ROCKS   of the women
TREES
FIRES
SPRINGS
ANIMALS   "The world is objective"
    the poet says

– translated from Breton by Gwendal Denez

Mikael Madeg
(1950 –)

Mikael Madeg was born not far from Paris of a Breton-speaking family. Says Madeg: "I have always had a fascination with languages. I learned French, English, Greek and Latin at school; Breton, Welsh and Scots-Gaelic out of school on my own. I hold two doctorates of Celtic Studies and have specialized in names – place names and nicknames in particular. I live in the Breton countryside where I am and have been a language teacher of both English and Breton. We speak only Breton at home."

The author of some fifty books of short stories, novels and literary scholarship, Mikael Madeg is also author of several books of poetry (and "some 200 poems in Breton," he says), although he completely stopped writing poetry from 1980 to 1992. Some of the titles of his books include *O Breiz Va Bro!* (O, Brittany My Country!), *Arvoriz* (Sea-Side People), *Tra Ma Vo Mor* (As Long As The Sea Exists), *Gweltas An Inizi* (Gweltas of the Isles), and *Ar Vougou* (The Cavern).

"I suppose love is the main theme in my poems," says Madeg. "That and life lived; and womankind in what they are and what they can symbolize. However, these days this kind of romanticism can get one in trouble, and has."

Mikael Madeg's most recent book is titled *Barzaz*, which he has declared his last book of poetry as a statement of militancy in the face of the "unacceptable" language conditions in Brittany.

Wherefrom

Wherefrom comes
    This voice
    That tells us
There are too many of us
That sends us into far exile
    To die for it

Maybe it
Does the killing
And brings here instead
Businessmen
Soldiers
Policemen and tourists
To make us leave
Our land
And on the threshold of our soul
Asks us
To get rid of
The live mud of our memory
Is this how
It'll have to end
This land
That used to be ours

— translated from Breton by the author

Goulennig (Small Question)

Rit ket biloù
Pa vezo prest pep tra
Kit oll en ho kourvez
Tremen a rin war-lerh
Da glenka ar gerioù
Niverenna an eskern
Liva e gwenn kement a zo
Distaga eun orezonig vrezoneg
Plega ar bed 'barz va godell
Nemed dilasteza an ti da genta
Prizacha ar voestig freuzet
M'ema ho c'horiellou
Ha gedal eur pennadig
A-raog laha ar goulou
Nemed e rafen eur fazi
Rag c'hwi marteze a raio.

Small Question

>   Don't you mind
> When everything's ready
>   Just lie down   all of you
>   I'll make a last round
>   To put the words in order
>   To number the bones
>   To paint everything white
> And say a short Breton prayer
> I'll fold up the world into my pocket
> But I'll clean the house up first ·
> Give you an estimate of the broken up box
>   Where your toys are
>   And wait a little bit longer
>   Before turning out the lights.

— translated from Breton by the author

Poltred War Gimiad (Portrait For The Leaving)

Kemend all a heriou
Souchet em fenn
Aner
Pa 'n-eus
Skouarn ebed
Er bed war gleo
Ouz o gortoz
Ha koz
'Teuan
Krignet a basianted
En amzer
Dener
M'on dezi
Boued fri
Debret a uhelegez
Euz streviadenn
Souezadenn
Pennadig
Eur gwechall
Mall warnañ
Mond da get.

Portrait For The Leaving

Such a host of words
Crouching in my head
    Useless
    Since there is
    No ear
Listening in the world
    Waiting for them
    And I grow
    Old
Gnawed by patience
    In the tender
    Time
    For which I am
    Nose-picking
Eaten out by uppishness
    A sneeze
    Surprise
    Short moment
    Of a gone past
    Very busily
    Disappearing

— translated from Breton by the author

Poem Trying To Understand

In the dispossessed mountains
Of heat beaded water
    There is a blade of grass
    City-born though I am
    I loved it
    There's one
    Actually two
But when there are two
    A sort of double
    Makes me close to
    Voiceless
    The grass with a secret

Brittany

Its beauty has a quivering in it
        When watched
From my cold-ridden eyes
From heavy-worded years
Though brittle, I wonder
Could it grow? Should it
Be taken out of there
        Or die
Unless I'd love it fearlessly
        How can I know
Ironically long-traveled are
        In me the crumbs
                Of my spirit
Could there be healing for the small
        Wound I opened
To feed it on my blood
Which seems so dried up

It was so close to me that I
Spoke no word about its soul

— translated from Breton by the author

Civilisation

(in memory of Motovato's Cheyennes and the "battle" of Sand Creek)

        Raped and badly soiled
Knifed, a thousand times crippled
        Their brains as dirt
On the boots of the civilised man
        To be cleaned with a joke
Their blood wherewith is written out
The commercial greatness of their land
        Wherefrom they are eradicated
                Turned white and polite
Cleanly mustered the dumb bones
        In the grey silence of the pages
                Blinded children
From the exploded womb of their disembowelled mother
        Thrown in the middle of eternal pains

Self-justified humanity
The decision of a stroke of pen
Without owner, comfortably registering
The doing away of millions
Which means one and one and one
Slowly born, harshly so
Fed and gradually becoming
Adults provided
Invaders aren't educated enough
To turn them into savages
Massacred, horror devoured
Carelessly thrown the heart of their race
As a red red banner
Of remorse
Which will never bring back to life the smile
Sourly redrawn by worms
Nor whoever understood it
They are a very short moment in my mind
And in front of the ashes
That overfeed my stomach
And clothe my mind
I only have my poem
To call their names
Bring them? Give them meaning?
My human breathing
Unknown to me everything they were
Torn alive and blindfolded
In the words that pretend to pray
Their content of future forgetfulness

Is it civilised enough that red little spot
Reddening
Into nothingness
Deep in my mind?

— translated from Breton by the author

Hail . . .

Pure its wool, and white
    the snow, and shy
on the virgin mountain road
Emotion and stream and fragrance
    sowing in you
The light wedding of fingers
      My kisses on your breast
        Harvest-time flakes
    without head nor tail
      My infant love
of the blue navel
a treat and an ease of mind
    is life when it's fearless
      for now, don't
I know your name, Mary

* — translated from Breton by the author*

How Obedient And Shy You Are

How obedient and shy you are
    Live earth of my country
    That crumbles the eyes
      Full of you
      Young virgin girl
      Slightly gazing, merry
      Snow fancies
Cold, so cold and soul-less
    The terrible oak-shirt
    Where lies a fiery idea
    It was an original sin
      Without remedy
To lose sight of your eyes
In the harsh stream of a dance
      Open eyes
    In you, earth
    Cold, so cold
For those of your sons
    That are dead

* — translated from Breton by the author*

Lan Tangi
(1951 –)

Lan Tangi, born in 1951 in Karanteg (West Brittany), grew up with his grandparents in a Breton-speaking village in the Are Mountains. A student in Rennes in 1970-71, he was involved in the political and cultural revival of the seventies in Brittany, gave up his studies to go traveling all over the world for 15 years while doing all manner of jobs. Back at the university in 1990 for Celtic studies, he began to teach Breton to adults. Along with three others, he recently founded the first Cooperative Breton Language and Cultural Centre located in An Uhelgoad (Are Mountains). He writes poems and short stories, collaborating with many different magazines. His first book of poems will be published this year.

If Man Is Descended Of Monkeys

If man is descended of monkeys
Woman is born of birds
He dropped down from the tree
She flew down from the sky
Look at her
Fixed in her flight
Memories of wings in her open arms
Hers is the leap of the gazelle
Yours, the weight of the draught horse
Hands earn your living
Fingers and wind for her
Your hands in the dirt

Now take the path to the mountain stream
To quench your thirst
She will meet you there and teach you
The taste of water

— translated from Breton by the author
version by TRC

East

How beautiful is the dirt of the world
The good smell of the burning gas
Cheap petrol
Sheep grease spilling
Bowls of curd
Dust and urine
And in dirty papers
The cymbals of the circus blow

The capital of Croatia
Is not what you think
East doesn't begin in Zagreb
But further on the other side of Belgrade
In the souk
On the market place near the highway
Down by the lanky buildings
Square heads climbing to the sky –

Europe
I'm fed up with your poodles
I have to leave you
Travel on the dirt road
Far from rich, neat towns
Disgusting cakes on silver plates
Too much cream and sugar
It is wild animals that I want to see

Let's go farther than Niš
Let's drive by Skopje
Go to the bigger Balkans
Full of tribes and
Far away
Everywhere in the world is the same old trap
Break your window: it was a mirror
Seven years bad luck
Your own image reflecting there inside
Outside there is free earth
Is there a heart?
Or is it only an ass hole?

You don't care
You have crossed the bridge at Nantes and
Tomorrow you'll be on the other side

– translated from Breton by the author / TRC

Mousafir

This time I saw holy men
And in the Kulu Valley all along the night
A pink monk sang
A stupid scholar shaking his bells
Be quiet, useless talker
And go to the river
Naked
Through the coldness of the white country
Or go down the valley
Mumbler
Two days walk
Down by the cliff of Aut
You'll find a man sitting
In a mud hut
With bright white hair
Three feet long
Dressed in red flames
Bones for a body
Leather for skin
In front of the fire
In the middle of the hut
Above a hole in the roof
He will show you
The root of a magic plant
Or a man's head maybe?
Five times reduced

The holy men walk at my side laughing
Beggars on the road to coldness
Their foreheads coloured with ashes
Monks of ice-fields
God hunters
Through mountains abounding in game

I stopped listening to the monk
The white knives of night were stuck to my ribs
And the silver hammer of hunger, too
I lie down in the temple
Like a mummy
Waiting for the door of morning
To open

Brittany

With the sweet voice of a girl
Singing her prayers
Decorating the penis of a god
With garland flowers
As she confesses her sins
With long tanned legs
And pours milk on his member
Which drips into my mouth
Waiting there to kiss the sky

All over the world
I have seen beautiful flowers
But there is nothing like
This girl's perfume

I'm on the road again
With a song in my head
And no clouds in the sky

All this time I have been a man
And holy.

— translated from Breton by the author / TRC

Gwendal Denez
(1951 –)

Gwendal Denez was born in Kemper (Quimper), West Brittany. He is a native Breton speaker, graduating from university in English and linguistics, holding a State Doctorate in Breton and Celtic studies in 1989. His thesis was about the Breton writer Fanch Elies-Abeozen. He has taught at Rennes University (Department of Breton) since 1992. He founded with others, the magazine *Al Lanv* in 1981. Among his books are: *C'hamsin* (1989) and *Blues komzet* (1990), a collection of poems which was awarded the Imram Prize. He is the editor of the anthology *Skrid*. He has published a study about the fishermen in his hometown *Pesketourien Douarnenez* (1979), as well as various other works about World War I and the Breton writers. He has also published a number of translations from English and into English. He lives in Rennes and is co-editor of this anthology.

dienez (misery)

kala-goañv
ur spontailh kolo o vreinañ
e-barzh ur park toullgofet
ur jak diempret o treiñ
goustad da ludu
tanioù kafunet
e-mesk atredoù kailharek
ouzh troad an tiez
o tislonkañ
ur vag o sankañ
un tammig bemdez
e-barzh lec'hid ar porzh
hag o verglañ
tremen ra ur bugel noazh
dirak mogerioù ruz kêr
ha santout ran pouez
ur yev war ma choug
pa gomzan brezhoneg

misery

early november
straw scarecrow rotting off
in a wrecked field
dismembered dummy slowly
crumbling into dust
fires banked up
among muddy scrap-heaps
in front of derelict tenements
boat sinking
day after day
into the silt of a harbor
and rusting
a naked child walks
along the red walls of a city
and I can feel
my neck bending under
the burden of a yoke
when I speak breton

— translated from Breton by the author

The Poor Man's Share

the homeless man walks
along the roads of the world
a smothered porter
looking for his soul
his heart cold from the chill winds of death
speechless ghost of the setting sun
the homeless man
whose shadow quakes
upon the cracked walls
is waiting for the wind to wail
the clouds to invade the sky
the thunder to crash
the lightning to whirl above the sea
the hurricane to bring forth
a fog to choke the horizon
he is waiting for something

to intensify the dusk
and there is only a blue-grey moon
among the pale stars
the lapping of the waves against the rocks
giving rhythm to the nightfall's calm
and the silhouette of the ankou in the distance
returning from his rounds
I am the homeless man
I am looking for my soul
lost long ago
in the crooked mornings of winter
I have built this world with my mother's hands
yet I have only the right
to remain silent
to remain silent and servile
and to die

— translated from Breton by the author / Natalie Franz / TRC

The Ankou's★ Garrote

the night was tamed by neon
years ago
when there was still fire and water
fog and mist
and life in the world
now that light disappears
dying from weariness
distance draws nearer
attracted by the disappearance of time

waiting
waiting for someone
listening for a sound
watching for a sign
and nothing
nothing at all
beneath the ugly moonlight
only the sinewy silence
locking up time
I turn my back

Brittany

on the grey engulfed rivers
on the dark burned seas
on the flooded cities of legend
and I am alone
the ankou's garrotte
tightening at my throat.

– translated from Breton by the author / Natalie Franz / TRC

*the ankou is death personified in Breton

Your Eyes

your eyes are these oceans
that hide the virginity of daring seamen
whose pricks are flaccid and flabby
their guts churning up diarrhea
their fright foaming with sperm
your eyes are death
rotting all ultimate desires
your eyes are the pus
from burst boils
your eyes are the breathless souls of a hurricane
jerking off
side-faced drifting shadows
two stones thrown on the fine sand
your eyes are a flood-gate
in which love melts away meanly
your eyes are the thorns of that love
scratching my heart
your eyes are a hell of rage
your eyes are these fields of wheat
burnt off before harvest by eastern winds
through which white horses run
mad horses blind horses
fleeing the fire
your eyes
your eyes are two cockroaches
trying to die

– translated from Breton by the author / Natalie Franz / TRC

I Remember

it was Shrove Tuesday
the yellowed halo of the moon shone
among the stars
the wind maimed the abandoned beaches
winter was arriving with the hurricane

I remember
the vermin were astray in my head
together with crushed crabs
it was the crabs who sucked my brains
when I was a child

I remember
they found a decaying polecat
at the bottom of the empty well
one day
the smell of spearmint
the fragrance of burnt heath
filled my ears and eyes
the stench of mire filled my nose
when they lifted the polecat from the bottom of the well

I remember winter was approaching
and death rose up in the heart of man

— translated from Breton by the author / Natalie Franz / TRC

The Devil Of Paralysis

I want to die in front of the sea
in the warped calm
of an afternoon running dry
when the sun sets
between Raz and Pennaroz

I shall lie down on the damp sand
and let the droning of the sea
slip the devil of paralysis into me
I shall hear the shriek of the gull
fading away in the wind

Brittany

the cold
will transfix me
numbing my blood
petrifying my body
the fire in my head
blackening my withered laments
I shall close my eyes
and slide out effortlessly
with
the arid coldness
of those who have lost
battles
and the bitter melancholy
of those who have loved uselessly
inside my heart

— translated from Breton by the author and Natalie Franz

Alan Botrel
(1954 –)

Born in Ploue (South Brittany), Alan Botrel spent most of his life in Paris before returning and settling down in Rennes where he now lives. He was graduated in philosophy, linguistics and Celtic philology in Paris, and earned a Ph.D. in Celtic studies in Rennes. Botrel has, since, specialized in middle-Breton and modern literature and teaches Breton in Rennes University. He has published poems, short stories and translations and book reviews from English, Spanish, French and modern Greek. Among his books, one might mention: *Pa sav an tenval* (1976), *Barzhonegoù* (1983), *Bues santes anna* (1985), and translations *Teir barzhoneg kuzh* (from Seferis) and *Ma beajou-me* (from C'himonas). At present he is preparing a collection of short stories (*Orea*) and translations from the Greek poet Kavafis.

IRHAEMA / INRI (In The Glory Lies The King)

Komz an dar a tav ar bez.
Pe henour ennañ o c'hourvez?
Skeud na roud na hirvoud hez.

Tra ne van e kleuz an arc'h
eus kedern un hen diernac'h
nag a'r rin, n'e veli arc'h.

Pe da goun, ar gerioù noazh,
'vel dargan yezh wan hon annoazh?
Kavell. Bac'h. Ha bez arc'hoazh.

C'hwezh an netra, gleb, er c'havell;

hun an hoal en teñval trell.
Ned eus heklev 'met en tevel.

Brittany

In The Glory Lies The King

Words of stone lie in the silence of the grave
Which chieftain lies there in rest?
With no shadow, no trace, no peaceful breath.

There is nothing left in the empty ark
of the old warrior's lineage
of their king
or of his power.

What memory is there in those naked words,
announcing the poor language of our agony?
Cradle. Prison. And tomorrow's grave.

Nothingness breathes, damp, in the cradle.
Time sleeps in dazed obscurity.
There is no echo, except silence.

— translated from Breton by the author / TRC

Dark Nudity

So silent, each skeleton . . .
Nothing matters to its cold bones,
neither happy girl, nor rosy cheek,
and the slight breath of its night-time mystery
still dreams around its rest,
soothed by the knowledge it will age no more.

Like the wind, it is an echo
that lived long in our silence,
in the cave haunted by mystery:
already hovering. Light and thin
is the dream of silence in the corpse
that at the dust of our nothingness shall bring cool relief.

Ah, the naked laugh of a cruel tomorrow!
Our anguish . . . Obvious and
faced with the disdain of mockery, that disinherits . . .

Such a frame. Without further pain of
man or beast, when will it be yours?
There's no hope.
You will not hear a word.

— translated from Breton by the author / TRC

Lanv (High Tide)

Kan ar c'hro zo maro trumm – dan ludu

louet al lano tuzum;
n'eus ken spoum edan ar brum
ma stran hen donnoù distumm.

Na brell e ve gant brulu – liv ruz don

o ruzañ a bep tu,
diniver evel ul lu
o kanañ reuz an droug du.

War hun houl an eoul lor – e lar euzh

al loar ez eo ar mor
koun ur rezid dic'houdor,
ur rezid mui na lidor.

(High) Tide

The song of the shore suddenly died – under the grey
      ashes of the heavy tide;
   there's no more foam beneath the mist
   where old shapeless waves are wandering.

How strange it would be with foxgloves – dark red,
      drifting all around,
   innumerable as an army
   singing the disaster of the black evil.

On the dormant swell of the murky oil – the dreadful
      moon says that the sea is nothing
   but the memory of a stark liberty,
   a liberty that cannot be maintained.

– translated from Breton by the author

One More Time

I'll bury my silence
under the earth of a poor century
– I swear it's my pledge tonight –
and my cruel laughter, already this old
will protect me against evil or pain.

To sleep long under a fertile land,
heart free from trouble,
to escape the forgetful hold
of the dry roots of the burnt yews,
humming in a treacherous future.

Old crow, singer,
croak as much as you like;
I am a lean corpse without regret,
with no friend under this clay,
every mystery gnawed by roots.

And my last poems? Upon my grave,
the rustling of the mourning trees . . .
Their words, one more time,
will conquer, respectful, the silence of space,
the dazzled laziness of a quiet land.

– translated from Breton by the author / TRC

(Éire)
IRELAND

IRISH GAELIC

Irish Gaelic

In the early part of this century, poetry in Irish was in poor shape. The Irish language revivalists, whose mission was to revive Irish as the spoken language of Ireland, knew that literature would play an important part in that revival. But, bogged down in tradition, they produced a poetry that looked backwards instead of to the future. Alas, many of these revivalists were no more than Victorians in kilts. There was no revolution. The best of these poets was Patrick Pearse, later an executed leader of the 1916 "Easter Rising," who, at his best, wrote an impassioned poetry in Irish and English.

After the Second World War, three major figures emerged: Máirtín Ó Direáin (1910-1988), an Aran Islander, the first real Modern in Irish; Seán Ó Ríordáin (1917-1977) from County Cork who shaped the Irish language to his metaphysic (an achievement that earned him much early criticism for his use, or alleged abuse, of the language); and Máire Mhac an tSaoi (1922 -), a Dubliner who spent much time in the Corca Dhuibhne Gaeltacht in County Kerry, who married a fine classical sensibility to modern themes.

Perhaps the renaissance of poetry in Irish, a renaissance that was subversive as it was affirmative, occurred at the end of the 1960s with the Innti poets out of University College, Cork. (*Innti* appeared first, as a broadsheet, in March 1970). These poets, most notably Michael Davitt, the editor of *Innti*, Nuala Ní Dhomhnaill, Liam Ó Muirthile and Gabriel Rosenstock, came under the influence of, among others, Seán Ó Ríordáin, then poet in residence, Seán Ó Tuama, poet and Professor of Irish, and Seán Ó Riada, the musician/composer, at the University. It was "the sixties," and the time was ripe for turning on to the Irish language. Large crowds turned up to their readings, and Irish language poetry was suddenly "in." Since then, the *Innti* magazine has become something of a flagship for poetry in Irish, an elder statesman rather than the cheeky pretender. But it has done its job. It brought Irish language poetry (and, more largely, poetry consciousness) to centre stage, and its poets were poets of real quality, many of them having consolidated their considerable reputations over the years.

The *Innti* poets were subversive in their approach to language; no dull revivalists, they shook up the language with verve and sass; their subject matter was equally unbridled. Indeed, Seán Ó Ríordáin would describe Gabriel Rosenstock's first collection, *Susanne sa Seomra Folctha* (1973), as Satanic.

The great Irish language novelist, Máirtin Ó Cadhain, saw in this poetic activity the swansong of the Irish language. Famously, he proclaimed: "Staid bhagarach, drochthuar é, an iomarca tóir a bheith ar fhilíocht a chumadh le hais an phróis . . . Sé an prós tathán coincréad, cloch saoirsinne an tsaoil, agus é chomh garbh, míthaitneamhach leis an saol féin . . . " ("It is a threatening and ominous portent when there is an excessive zeal to compose poetry rather than prose . . . Prose is the concrete base, the mason's cornerstone of life, and it is as rough and unpleasant as life itself . . . ") Whether this will come to pass is a much debated point. The death of the Irish language has been proclaimed before. Perhaps Nuala Ní Dhomhnaill best personifies the attitude of the Irish language poet at the end of the twentieth century – placing the Irish language, like the infant Moses, in a basket, a little boat of language, she sets it free to take its chances on the tide.

Ceist na Teangan

Cuirim mo dhóchas ar snámh
i mbáidín teangan
faoi mar a leagfá naíonán
i gcliabhán
a bheadh fite fuaite
de dhuilleoga feileastraim
is bitiúman agus pic
bheith cuimilte lena thóin

ansan é a leagadh síos
i measc na ngiolcach
is coigeal na mban sí
le taobh na habhann,
féachaint n'fheadaraís
cá dtabharfaidh an sruth é,
féachaint, dála Mhaoise,
an bhfóirfidh iníon Fháróinn?

The Language Issue

I place my hope on the water
in this little boat
of the language, the way a body might put
an infant

in a basket of intertwined
iris leaves,
its underside proofed
with bitumen and pitch,

then set the whole thing down amidst
the sedge
and bulrushes by the edge
of a river

only to have it borne hither and thither,
not knowing where it might end up;
in the lap, perhaps,
of some Pharaoh's daughter.

poem translated from Irish Gaelic by Paul Muldoon

—*Gabriel Fitzmaurice*

Eithne Strong
(1923 -)

Eithne Strong was born in 1923 in Glensharrold, County Limerick. In 1943 she married Rupert Strong, poet and psychoanalyst, who died in 1984. A teacher, broadcaster, poet and short-story writer in both Irish and English, her collections of poems include *Songs of the Living* (1961) and *Sarah in Passing* (1974), a novel *Degrees of Kindred* (1979), *Flesh . . . The Greatest Sin*, a long poem first published in 1980, and a collection of short stories, *Patterns* (1981). Her first collection of Irish poetry *Cirt Oibre* was published in 1974 and a second, *Fuil agus Fallaí* in 1983. *My Darling Neighbour* was published in 1985. *Aoife Faoi Ghlas*, a collection in Irish, and another volume in English were published in 1989.

Mar A Fuarthas Spreagadh (Response to Munch's *Scream*)

[As An Scread le hEdvard Munch]

Féach
mo thacaíocht mheánaicmeach
—ní háil liom ganntanas—
eagar is ord mo thí
—crácálaí is fuath liom—
éirim is slacht mo mhéin
—is gráin liom óinseach—

Ach
deich n-uaire in aghaidh an lae
ionsaím dún na céille; compord
an oird scriosaim as alt;
maise na seascaire, loitim í;
pléascaim an dlús teolaí:
is gealt os íseal mé.

Éist
is éigean dom réabadh san uaigneas,
dualgas an gheilt 'chur i gcion
thar ghnácht an ghnáis,
scéird-bhrú na mire 'chomhlíonadh
—cuibhreann na huaighe am thachtadh san só:
an scread rosc catha mo shaoirse.

Response to Munch's *Scream*

See
my middle-class bastions
—scarcity I detest;
the order and method of my house
—I abominate a scatterbrain;
decorum and reserve my manner
—one abhors gush.

But
ten times a day
I assail the walls of sanity
tear comfort raw
slash at padded ease
wreck the engulfing cloy.
Secretly I am a lunatic.

Hear
I must shatter the void
rend to maniac necessity
beyond the stale of habit
burst to crazy power:
comfort chokes in muffling tyranny
the scream is my survival.

—translated from Irish Gaelic by the author

Seán Ó Tuama
(1926 -)

Seán Ó Tuama was born in Cork in 1926. As Professor of Irish Language and Culture at University College Cork, he lectured extensively in American, English and French universities. Poet, playwright and editor, his anthology, *An Duanaire: 1600-1900 Poems of the Dispossessed* (1981) with Thomas Kinsella, introduced the poetry in Irish of that period to a new and wider audience.

Cá Siúlfam? (Where Shall We Walk?)

Cá siúlfam? Tá na cosáin reoite,
carnáin chalcaithe de shneachta cruaite
ar bhlaincéadaí an bhóthair mar a mbíodh ár siúl.
'S tá an ghaoth ag aimsiú ioscada na nglún
chomh géar chomh glic le fuip . . .
Ní shiúlfad leat. Tá an corp ina chloch.

Tiomáinfeam? Racham ar an aifreann déanach
ag éisteacht le Hosanna in Excelsis
á ghreadadh amach go buach caithréimeach,
is bainfeam sásamh as an at gan éifeacht
a thagann ar an gcroí . . . .
Chauffeur mé, lá seaca, ar dheabhóidí.

Ar deireadh: ní chorródsa amach inniu,
tá fuil i gcúl mo bhéil le mí ón sioc,
is ó inchinn go talamh síos
tá bánú déanta ar gach artaire
a dhéanann duine den daonaí . . . .
Fanfam féach an bhfillfidh teas arís.

Where Shall We Walk?

Where shall we walk? The paths are all iced over,
on the grassy blankets of the roads we've known
calcified mounds of slush and snow,
the wind stings the hollows of the knees
as slyly and as sharply as a whip . . .
I shall not walk with you. The flesh is stone.

We shall drive then, go to Mass,
listen to Hosanna in Excelsis
being ground out triumphally,
and feed upon the silly satisfaction
of music swelling up the heart . . .
On a frosty day I act as chauffeur to the mysteries.

No, just no: I will not move today
the chill has bloodied up my throat this long month past,
and every artery that makes a human burn
from brain down to the ground
has been whitened to debility . . .
We'll wait and see if heat returns.

— translated from Irish Gaelic by the author

Love Game

It was a quiet fame with no knives:
she lighted up the desert all about her
and you submitted;
on a night of frost her pipers blew
a hundred welcomes in a spacious airport,
and you swelled up in tune:
but afterwards there came the shrinking:
her butler dragged you through the narrow sewage pipes
and squeezed the vestiges of light from both your eyes.

— translated from Irish Gaelic by the author

Christy Ring*

He aimed at the impossible
each Sunday on the pitch;
sometimes he succeeded.

Down on one knee,
trapped in a corner of the field,
when his prechristian electronic eye
lit up in combat,
and the ball, a missile,
sped from him straight above the bar,
the air shook in awe.

When a driving lunge
brought him clear beyond
the ruck of men,
and the ball, propelled,
self-destructed in the net
to smithereens of light,
our cheering became a battle cry.

In one moment of raw frenzy
as his playing days ran out,
he summoned Cú Chulainn
to aid him on the pitch:
his trunk swelled up
in sight of thousands,
one eye bulged
and danced, demented,
through clash and crash
hue and cry
men were toppled
hot blood spurted
and as he rammed in
three lethal goals
all the gods of ancient Ireland
lent his hurley** a guiding hand.

Looking at his corpse laid out,
the day of his untimely death,
a woman said:
"It would be a sin to bury such a man."

I have not managed yet to bury Christy Ring.
Sometimes I imagine him
being venerated
in the care of the great god, Aengus,
on a slab at Newgrange
and at each winter solstice
for just one half an hour
a ray of sunshine
lighting up his countenance.

But no friend of his could think
of laying Christy Ring eternally to rest
locked in with ancient miracles—
for oh the miracles of the living flesh
we saw when his countenance lit up
Winter days and Summer days,
Sundays in and Sundays out,
on the playing pitch.

— translated from Irish Gaelic by the author

the Babe Ruth of hurling

**stick used in hurling*

Biddy Jenkinson
(1929 -)

Biddy Jenkinson, who writes only in Irish, is rarely translated as a gesture signifying that everything in Irish cannot be "harvested and stored" without loss in English. Her work has been published in *Innti, Poetry Ireland, Comhar, Feasta, Déidre* and *Riverine*. Her collections *Bàisteadh Gintlí* (1987), *Uiscí Beatha* (1988), and *Dán na hUidhre* (1991), all published by Coiscéim, seek to recreate a sense of the sacral world of nature and women's role in sustaining it. Her poetic manifesto appeared as a letter to the editor in the *Irish University Review* (Spring/Summer 1991).

Cruit Dhubhrois (The Harp Of Dubhros)

Bruith do laidhre im théada ceoil
ag corraíl fós, a chruitire,
clingeadh nóna ar crith go fóill
im chéis is an oíche ag ceiliúradh.

Oíche thláith, gan siolla aeir,
a ghabhann chuici sinechrith
mo shreangán nó go dtéann falsaer
grá mar rithí ceoil faoin mbith,

Go gcroitheann criogar a thiompán,
go gcnagann cosa briosca míl,
go sioscann fionnadh liath leamhain,
go bpleancann damhán téada a lín.

Is tá mo chroí mar fhuaimnitheoir
do chuisleoirí na cruinne cé
ón uair gur dhein mé fairsing ann
don raidhse tuilteach againn féin.

Nuair a leagann damhán géag
go bog ar théada rite a líne
léimeann mo théada féin chun ceoil
á ngléasadh féin dod láimhseáil chruinn.

The Harp Of Dubhros

Harper, hot your fingers still
stirring me on every string,
look, the night has climbed the hill
yet your noon-day strummings ring.

Balmy night bereft of air
slowly take the murmur-strain!
All that is, was ever there,
fugued to fullness and love's reign.

Until the cricket's drumming rasp,
and insect leg of silver gut,
grey moth-fur emits a gasp,
on music's web the spider-strut!

A sounding box within my chest
for busy buskers everywhere,
for every decibel compressed
recurring in the brightening air.

When the spider tests his weave
sweetly on each glistening line:
all my harp-strings leap and heave—
knowing that the tuning's fine.

— translated from Irish Gaelic by Gabriel Rosenstock

Silence

How I welcome you, little salmon
who leapt the womb, impatient to commence life.
I undertake to be a river to you
as you follow your course from the haven of my belly to far distant seas.

Let yourself go, and drink up your fill.
Suck sleep from me. By the terms of the breast-contract
I'll suck back from your puckered lips
love, with which I'll suckle another time, and for that I'm grateful.

How I welcome you, salmon of sleep
who made a tranquil pool in my life-stream.
In the rhythm of your heartbeat
I hear the music of the Heavens, and it guides my way.

— translated from Irish Gaelic by Pádraigín Riggs

Spray

If I were the spreading tide sheets I would overwhelm your insteps
I would fetch up round your ankles with the sunbleached wrath of storms
I would coax you to step closer with the swishback of the gravel
and swoosh back up behind your knees in curls.

If I were the tugging backwash I would tetter you and tease you
send waves of gooseflesh up your legs in squames
Thigh holes of my skin for you, my greenest silk to please you
High combers up your reefy ribs, your shoulders spumed in squalls

If I were green in essence I would melt your eyes and take them
I would hold your mind suspended like the water in a wave
Down, you'd flow; deep down to me, while over you most blithely
The harbour's breasts would jut with intimations of a war.

For the day is fine, the sky is bright and I am full and friendly
and I'd leave no sea shag crucified if I could plume its feathers
Swelling sea and shining sun and . . . . Oh my dear, be merry
The sea staff through the sea membranes is delicately stirring.

— translated from Irish Gaelic by Alex Osborne

Gréagóir Ó Dúill
(1946 -)

Pertaining to his poetry, Gréagóir Ó Dúill says: "As elsewhere, I insist that a Gaelic poet exists in a timeless continuum of violence and loss." Born in Dublin in 1946, he grew up in County Antrim. Educated in Saint Malachy's College, he was a prize scholar in Queen's University. He taught in Saint Malachy's for two years, then went to Dublin as an archivist. After a career in the cultural and central public service, he became a fulltime writer and spends half his time in the Donegal Gaeltacht area of Gort an Choirce. He holds an M.A. in History from University College, Dublin and a Ph.D. in English from Maynooth. His writings include six collections of poetry, an influential anthology of contemporary Ulster poetry in Gaelic, and a full-scale biography of nineteenth-century poet, translator and cultural administrator Sir Samuel Ferguson, as well as work in literary criticism, cultural history and sociolinguistics. He has been a writer in residence in the Verbal Arts Centre, Derry, a research officer with Poetry Ireland, and literary editor of *Comhar*. He is married to Belfastwoman Catherine Murray, a teacher, and has four adult children.

His books, all published by Coiscéim in Dublin, include *Innilt Bhóthair* (1981), *Cliseadh* (1982), *Dubhthrian* (1985), *Blaoscoileán* (1988), *Crannóg agus Carn* (1991), *Saothrú an Ghoirt* (1994).

Geimhreadh (Winter)

Faoi scáth na díge, fanann an sneachta go mailíseach,
Luíochán ciúin nach n-airím.
Imím go rúitín sa fhliuchlach bhán,
Mo mhéara coise mar leaca oighre ag slupadáil.
Cúlaím faoi shioc-shock.
Cuimhním ar lá ar bhris mo bhróg
Tré chabhail bhán chorp caora i ndíog dhorcha eile.
Ligh an samhnas mo fhiacla.

Tá mianach tréasach i ndíoga.
Is mithid fanacht ar an bhóithrín chúng,
Sin nó airdeall síoraí, cos ar an pháipéar scrúdaithe,
Súil le talamh, dall ar gach réalt
Nach mbíonn sioctha i linn oighre.

Winter

In the shelter of the ditch, the snow waits maliciously:
I fail to see the quiet ambush,
Drop ankle-deep in the white wet.
My toes are ice-floes floating
I'm freeze-framed, backing down.
I remember the day my shoe broke
Through the white corpse of a sheep in another ditch–
Nausea licked my teeth.
Ditches have a treacherous quality.
Better to stay on the narrow path,
That, or eternal vigilance, a foot on the examination paper,
Eye to the ground, blind to every star
Not frozen in a pool of ice.

— translated from Irish Gaelic by Aodán Mac Póilín

New Year

Our best plan now
(While the wind lashes the winter snow)
Is to sit tight
And batten down against the storm.

At the end of this month of cruel whiteness
And malicious ice, we will go out the door
And see the changes in the country's appearance
On thorn, tree, lake and river, mountain and corrie.

The country will not be the same at either end of winter
And there will be loss, cattle and sheep, old people
But we will be there, likewise changed
And the plough's snout will enter the enduring earth in the unfamiliar spring.

— translated from Irish Gaelic by Aodán Mac Póilín

Sonnet For A Six Month Old Cease Fire

I watch them walk the valley, two men after a fox.
They have guns and dogs and ideas.

I listen to a helicopter belly the air in flight to Tory
While boats lie beached, the sound is angry, someone is being evacuated.

I see him on the night road, when winter cuts,
His anorak hood up, light shooting in young eyes.

I lurch back from sudden noise in the hedge, white-faced,
I check the culvert under the road for fear it's blocked,
I bend under the car to free a trapped branch.

I see them in their kevlar waistcoats
All these anointed cardcarriers.
I hold my breath too long, my lungs almost explode.

Poison swims the Sea of Moyle from the canisters they dumped when I was young.

– translated from Irish Gaelic by the author

Note: *Violence remains inherent even in the pastoral scene. If Stokely Carmichael said "Violence is as American as apple pie," then an Irish version could be that "violence is as Ulster as the soda Fael." I grew up on the Antrim coast, facing Scotland, and the British surplus chemical weapons of World War II were dumped there, washing up as violence on our shores. (Kevlar is plastic body armour.)*

Dubhghall

I needed a safe place to land;
I'd had my fill of waves and steering oars,
Of sails filled by the come all ye whore of a wind in the Irish Sea.

I needed a safe place to land.
I pulled by hempen rope
My plough-share's snout, my sea-horse's neck.
I turned the longship into a camp, made fire
And raised the oars in earth as palisade until they bloomed.

Ireland

The oars stand still. Crinked hair at my feet.
There's a bonfire on the far hill, fire-brands coming,
The battle frenzy has faded
And the backwounds from the black knives have dried.

My people's practice is to launch the ship
Aflame, chief's body arrayed, to sea.
This ceremony is impossible for one man.
So they come to me. I start the lay of the pyre.

I wait, my ribs spread-eagling.

— translated from Irish Gaelic by the author / TRC

Pádraig Mac Fhearghusa
(1947 -)

Pádraig Mac Fhearghusa was born in County Kerry in 1947 from parents who came from the Sligo/Fermanagh area, whose heritage hails back to Scotland–as he says: "My own Scottish connections must be rather far fetched, but Fearghusa, as any good Gael would know, is Ferguson." As a poet and Irish language activist, his long poem, "Nótaí Treallchogaíochta ó 'Suburbia'" published in 1983, won the 1982 Open Poetry Award at Writer's Week, Listowel. His work has been published widely and anthologized in such collections as *An Crann Faoi Bhláth* (The Flowering Tree) and his books, *Faoi Léigear* and *Fá Shliabh Mis & Dánta Eile* (1993). He continues to live in his boyhood home of County Kerry.

Antinuclear Poem

On the step of the Church
the priest picked
the host out of the puke.
    Lord, hear us!

The light shrank
and Mullach a' Radhairc
spewed a spittle-mist
over the socket of the sun.
    Lord, graciously hear us!

As day brightens
on the slopes of Mount Elgon,
Africans raise their spit and breath
on outstretched palm.
    Lord, hear us!

Ireland

But here, throughout
the bowels of Oklahoma,
Leamhainéirí stroke their dwarfs
until they piss upon the sun.

Mixing spit and dust
will not put the pieces of an atom back,
and bombs cannot heal the blind man's eyes.

— translated from Irish Gaelic by the author / TRC

Near Fenit

A seaweed headland shears
The sky from the water;
An eye hangs in blue sky,
Wrack climbing the strand.

I can't live through
the poison of evening.
It drowns me.
Drains my fingernails of blood.

Let's make war on the darkness,
What's the point of the daily grind of yes and no's
Compared to the silence of crabs?

— translated from Irish Gaelic by the author / TRC

Cogar I Leith Chugam (Come Here, I Want To Tell You)

Cogar chugam, a Dhia,
Cén sórt áite é Neamh?
De réir mar a chloisim
Ní réiteodh an áit romhaith liom.

Bheadh sciatháin ar mo dhroim ann,
Is cláirseach im ghabháil,
Is mé i mo shuí ar scamall
Ar feadh na gcianta ag seinm stártha.

Sé a deir daoine eile
Nach eol dúinn roimhré
Cad a chífidh súil ann,
Nó cad a bhraithfidh croí.

Ach cogar chugam, a Dhia,
An mbeidh caife ar fáil ar maidin,
Nó piúnt leanna istoíche ann,
Is na haingil, bhfuilid baineann?

Come Here, I Want To Tell You!

Give us a hint, God,
What kind of place is Heaven?
According to what I hear,
That place isn't what I'd like.

I'd have wings on my back there,
An arm full of harp,
Sitting on a cloud I'd be,
Playing turns for eternities!

Other people say that
We don't know
What we'll find.
What our eyes will hear
Or what our heart will see.

Come on, God.
Will there be coffee in the morning?
A pint of beer before we go to bed?
And the angels, are they really girls?

— translated from Irish Gaelic by the author / TRC

Chemistry

I searched in the mind's trunk
That I might find relief,
Caressing woodworm eaten frames
Which were becoming fragments of forgetfulness,
Until I saw a withered photograph
Transformed beneath a hoarse covering of dust,

And years of mist blew back from
Your eye.
Through the smell of sausages
Beyond sultry windows
You are there,
Your mind glowing upon your cheek.
I sip the perfume in your ear, drink it
From your mouth—What's the use of screaming?
You have undergone a chemical transformation, and
We look for what's between us and can not find.

— translated from Irish Gaelic by the author / TRC

A Brother's Illness

I howl in horror
Through the woods of my skull
His eyes
Roll up into his head

When our father sighed,
I saw shadows of our death.
Terror took me.
But a whirlwind of shyness
Smothered me
In a gust of leaves.

In the morning,
The drugs we took
Put my brother to sleep.

I never sleep.
The sound of illness
Coming
Over the distant fields.

— translated from Irish Gaelic by the author / TRC

Micheal O'Siadhail
(1947 -)

Micheal O'Siadhail was born in Dublin in 1947 and has published nine collections of poetry including *Hail! Madam Jazz: New and Selected Poems* (Bloodaxe Books, 1992) and *A Fragile City* (Bloodaxe Books, 1995). Awarded an Irish American Cultural Institute prize for poetry in 1981, he has been a lecturer at Trinity College Dublin and a Professor at the Dublin Institute for Advanced Studies and is now a fulltime writer. A former member of the Arts Council of the Republic of Ireland, he is a member of Aosdána. He has read and broadcast his poetry widely in Ireland, Britain and North America. He lives in Dublin.

In A New York Shoe Shop

Canned blues rhythms hum the background.
Air-conditioned from the swelter, a choosy
clientele vets the canted wall-racks

Of new-look summer shoes. Unbargained for,
a handsome inky coloured man catching
the snappy syncopation, jazzes across the floor

to proof-dance a pair of cream loafers.
Beaming, he bobs and foot-taps; pleased
with his purchase, he jives a short magnificat.

A friend from Maryland had once described
seeing in his grandfather's cellar the rusted irons
that had fettered a chain-gang of black slaves.

Behind the polyrhythm, the scoops, the sliding
pitches and turns, I hear the long liquid line
of transcended affliction; women with gay

kerchiefs are prayer-hot in the praise-house
or whoop in Alabama's cotton fields. Life ad-libs
with a jug and washboard; sublimity forgives.

In submission to the pulse this customer lets go,
swings low to the bitter-sweet quadruple
time, unmuzzled, human and magnificent.

— translated from Irish Gaelic by the author

Visionary

What was it then, what commanded such ardour?
A scattering of lonely islands, a few gnarled
seaboard townlands, underworld of a language frail
as patches of snow hiding in the shadows of a garden.

But the dwindling were so living. In this wonderland
of might-have-been I fell for the rhythm, the undertone
of my father's speech, built a golden dream.
(As you dreamt that land was falling asunder.)

A world as it is or a world as we want it:
when to resist old fate's take-for-granted
or when to submit; had I known before I slid
into a snowy fantasy, a fairyland of squander . . .

Was it a lavishness, a hankering for self-sacrifice,
part arrogance, part the need of the twice
shy for a paradise of the ideal, pure and beyond,
where one man's will turns a hag into a princess.

Oh I was the fairy story's third son, the one
who, unlike his elder brothers would not shun
a hag by the roadside: surely I'd rub the ring,
summon a sword of light to slay the dragon.

Tell me now that land was a last outpost,
a straggling from another time no one's utmost
could save; the hungry beast of change roved
nearer, that vision was a ghost dance with the past.

Tell me now third brothers too have grown
older, have even learned to smile at highflown
dreams. Then tell me still somewhere in the thaw
a child is crying over a last island of snow.

— translated from Irish Gaelic by the author

Stranger

A youngster I came, pilgrim to the source;
fables of a native bliss stirred mottoes:
a land without a tongue, a land without a soul.
As the currachs drew alongside the steamer
men in dark blue shirts shouted exotic words.

In the kitchen a daughter returned on holiday
switches from her mother's tongue to chide
her London children. As I listen it seems
I am foreign to both, neither fish nor flesh.
Was I to be a stranger in this promised land?

I slip into a glove of language. But there's still
a vividness, an older mood, small courtesies
to fortune: the sea must have its own – to swim
is to challenge fate. Child of reason and will
I am at most a sojourner in that mind.

Talk then of the mainland as *the world outside,*
enter and become a citizen of this stony room:
handkerchief fields claimed from rocks, dung
dried for fuel, unmortared boulder walls,
calfskin shoes, stark artifices of survival.

A widower welcomes my visits, opens his sorrow
to the incomer. Gauchely, I mention his loneliness:
Hadn't he his turn? ask two neighbour women
swirling their petticoats. *What ails him?*
they banter, standing in the sunshaft of a doorway.

One evening on the flags dancing starts up;
no music, island women summering from Boston
lilt reels, long to be courted. But men
shy of plaid skirts or lipstick don't dare
(still too boyish, subtleties pass me by).

Nudges and smothered laughter among the men.
Over again the word *stranger.* I bridle,
yearn to be an insider, unconsciously begin
a changeling life; turning a live-in lover
I wear my second nature, a grafted skin.

– translated from Irish Gaelic by the author

Gabriel Rosenstock
(1949 –)

Gabriel Rosenstock was born in Kilfinane, County Limerick in 1949. He was converted from English to Irish at University College Cork, and became fully initiated in the Kerry Gaeltacht. He is former Chairman of Poetry Ireland/ Éigse Éireann, an honorary life member of the Irish Translators' Association and a member of the Irish Writers' Union. His published books include *Portrait of the Artist as an Abominable Snowman* (Forest Books); *Oráisti* (Cló Iar-Chonnachta); *Cold Moon* (Brandon, 1993). Among the authors he has translated into Irish are Alarcón, Heaney, Roggeman and Grass. Poet, playwright, children's author, broadcaster and journalist, his first collection *Susanne sa Seomra Folctha* (1973) was described by Séan Ó Ríordáin in the *Irish Times* as "Satanic." He is one of the most prolific of the poets in Ireland writing in any language.

Mustanbih

I am twenty years now barking
and the last bog has swallowed
my echo, rare echo.
I am more lonely than the cold dew
I drink to ease my throat.
In my shuddering heart I know
that my circling is without end,
but should I admit this?
I would do better to shut my mouth,
out-stare the stars,
lie back and die without a murmur.
I no longer know my Ireland.
They might as well toss her placenames
into the pot and boil them to mush,
distilling the poison of amnesia
from each famished syllable.

Pure gibberish now the blackbirds sing.
Even the simples forget their secrets.
Tadg the moonstruck has cleared off,
the rain will not clean my pelt,
the warm sun will not dry me,
the standing stone misdirects me and
the longnecked heron has no wisdom for me.
I have long forgotten
the signs to watch out for.
In Kerry I was a whining pup,
in Tipperary a speaking wolf,
in Kildare a hunting dog,
on the border a mild wolfhound.
In the County Clare, on a golfcourse,
a politician snarled at me −
a man who'd not know the sword of Oscar,
Hacker of Bodies,
from his own golf club.
In East Waterford there's a barbed-wire fence
thrown up by a Dutchman, a sign in English
saying KEEP OUT!
In the Shannon's neat tributaries 3,000 dead fish.
In Glenasmole it shook me to hear
St. Patrick mocking Oisín,
Oisín son of Fionn, who scorned the gift of Heaven
unless he'd his faithful hounds around him!
In Leitrim the lilt of a fiddle troubled my humours.
Blood of a badger, glistening on a road in moonlight.
In Aughrim a banshee
on the threshold of a heritage centre
stroking my coat kindly:
"Óch, what was it came over you, set you straying?"
I howled from a cliff in Connemara,
not even a seal to answer me.
A clam that a herring gull
dropped on my head
set me staggering for a week,
set me hunting for the bones of Cnú Dearóil,
the clever dwarf beloved of Fionn,
no more than four fists high!
Now he is dust, invisible on the wind,

and so is the neat bride they found for him,
Blánaid, gone from the memory of the tribe.
How strange this tongue of hounds
the hounds themselves don't understand!
They do . . . but they feign deafness.
All I can do is walk backwards now
clean clear out of myself
to where Cnú
with a heart as big as himself
is sending the worlds to sleep
with his wind-deft fingers.

— translated from Irish Gaelic by Theo Dorgan

Sometimes I'm A Phoney Man

I

Sometimes I'm a phoney man,
I frighten myself —
My lies crucify me.

Strip me of my clothes
Tear them asunder
Burn my entrails
Until I hear my own
Birth-cry.
I would walk the world then, a flame,
I would talk in tongues of fire,
I would dance at fairs
I would frighten children
What wouldn't I do!
I would leap in the air like the northern lights
Like stars running through the Milky Way.
Sometimes I'm a phoney man,
I frighten myself —
My lies crucify me.

II

Let the raven come
Let him pick my eyes out
I would laugh a black scorched laugh at a wedding feast

I would jump out of my skin at a baptism
I would eat the green grass:
I would drink hare's piss!
I am a phoney man
Between heaven and earth
Blind to destiny
Ignorant of pedigree
From the furnace of my soul
Sparks escape
Through my eyes.
Sometimes I'm a phoney man,
I frighten myself –
My lies crucify me.

III

This skull doesn't concern me
Any more –
Leave my hat on, however,
I would be confirmed
I would take the rings from the Bishop's fingers
I would buy some loaves of bread
And two cured fish
And would await the miracle
Until perished with hunger and thirst.
Sometimes I'm a phoney man,
I frighten myself –
My lies crucify me.

IV

Who tarred and feathered
My tongue?
Hold fast!
The wind will speak through me
Ceaselessly
From every quarter
In the forgotten tales
Of travellers
Fugitives' stories, stories of a roofless people.
Sometimes I'm a phoney man,
I frighten myself –
My lies crucify me.

Ireland

V

Take me to the river
The Boyne
The Nile
Immerse me in the Ganges
Or in the River Jordan:
I travelled through fire
Through desert
And through ice
Headless, faithful
By God
I demand to be taken to the brink.

— translated from Irish Gaelic by Gabriel Fitzmaurice

An Mhaenad (The Maenad)

Tá crónán beach dostoptha ina broinn
Nach múchfar ach i dtonn bháite
Go coim

Seasann an mhaenad sa sáile
Rud doráite
Ina súile ar déanamh na halmóinne

Gortóidh sobal goirt a pit ata
Ar ball agus gáirfidh sí
Cúbfaidh tonnta óna fraoch

Titfidh líomóidí is oráistí ina mbáisteach
Léimfidh éisc ildathacha
Agus beifear ar fad ar aon dord

Níos déanaí
Nochtfaidh réaltaí as an gciúnas
Faoi mar nár tharla faic
Faoi mar a bheadh an chéad chruthú ann
Fáiscfidh sí smugairle róin lena gabhal

The Maenad

She harbours in her womb the droning of maddened bees
Only a drowning wave waist-high will still that tumult

The Maenad stands erect in the salt-sea wave
The ineffable one
With the almond-chiselled eyes

Salt-sea spray will sting her swollen vulva
And she will laugh as waves recede before her rage

A rain of oranges and lemons will thunder down
Exotic fish will leap from the ocean
And all will echo and re-echo the one sound

Later
Stars will come forth out of the silent dark
As if nothing at all happened
As if the first creation began all over again
And she will clasp jellyfish between fierce thighs

— translated from Irish Gaelic by Seán Mac Mathghamhna

Letter To My Husband Slaving On The Great Wall

Greetings Chieftain of my heart and Lord
    of my soul!
It's now seven weary months since I laid eyes
    on your body and your face.
And since every star was quenched in the sky:
The moon has run off to hide;
The wind from the North brings terrible news –
That rice is scarce and millet
    scarcer still,
That mud and freezing ice cover you,
That the sky is black with vultures
And barbaric arrows fall on you
With the Great Wall crawling like a dragon
    over mountain and desert.

More men were lately recruited from
    this district. I won't mention
    their names. Scholars and poets.
Their scrolls were burnt. They were chained
    together and taken away
Without a word, dumbstruck,
    to the far North.
Two months tramping in bare feet and for what?
A wall between us and the frozen North!

Is it true what they say about the Xiung-nu?
That they eat their own offspring
When times are bad,
That red fur grows on the palms
    of their hands.
Bad luck to them!
Oh, if only the moon would shine tonight
And you, light of my heart,
were looking at it like me . . .
Do they really think the wall will last forever?
Against the wind, against rain,
Against frost, against the Barbarians?

In every direction the land is ruled by terror.
The other day a foal was born
With two heads!

The wind breeds treason in the pines.
A catfish leaped out of the Yellow River,
Stood on the bank and spoke to us
    in a foreign tongue:
"The night shines up North with bones
Like the Tail of the White Mare."

Since you left a hard wall has grown round
    my heart.
Come and knock it down.
But please, come soon!

            — translated from Irish Gaelic by Seán Mac Mathghamhna
                          version by TRC

Ravi Shankar

Glaonn	You
Tú	Call
Anuas	Down
Ó	From
Na spéartha	The sky
Chugainn	To us
Ealaí	Swans
Is druideanna	And starlings
Tá	The world
An domhan	Is
Ina	An ocean
Aigéan	Fluttering
Cluichearnachta	There is
Níl	No
Mórthír	Land . . .
Le fáil . . .	Breathing ceases.
Stopann	
Anáil.	

– translated from Irish Gaelic by Gabriel Fitzmaurice

Colette Gallacher
Colette Ní Ghallchóir
(1950 –)

Colette Gallacher was, as she says, "born in a glen in the Bluestacks and brought up in a house full of song and stories." She moved to the "Bloody Foreland" area of Donegal when she was ten years old – which she describes as a "traumatic event." She attended boarding school on a scholarship before going on to get her training and degree in primary school education – the field in which she now teaches. Her work has been published in most of the major literary journals in Ireland. In 1996 a selection of her poems was published by Cló Iar-Chonnachta in Galway in a book of five Irish poets. Aside from her teaching work in the schools, she is involved in projects and programs helping children to learn to write. She currently lives in Letterkenny, in County Donegal.

An Grá ina thost (Love Is Silent)

Ar an tráthnóna fómhair seo
Faoi scáth Chnoc Fola
Scairtim thar an chaorán chugat
Ach ní chloiseann tú mo ghlór.

Tráth dá raibh
Ba leor ár dtost
Lenár ngrá dá chéile
A chur in iúl.

Anois agus blátha an Earraigh
Ag brú aníos orainn
Tuigeann muid beirt
Borradh agus bás.

Love Is Silent

On this autumn evening
Beneath the shadow of Knockfola,
I cry out to you
Across the bogs
But you do not hear my voice.

Once
Our silence was enough
For it to be called love.

Now
The spring flowers
Are pushing up
We both understand
Blossoming and withering.

— translated from Irish Gaelic by the author

That Place You Are So Alone

Lying here in the hill field, I know
you are the mountain I cannot reach.
Long ago, in the marshes
I didn't care much for life or death.
The moment I saw you,
I knew, I would jump ditches, plough bogs
and steal you
from that place you are so alone.

— translated from Irish Gaelic by Barbara Parkinson / TRC

Requiem

Bás uaigneach
na n-uaisle, i Meirceá
Tórramh mór na mbodaigh.

Ach caoinfear anocht thú
ó bhruach Loch Finne
Go barr Chnoc Leitreach.

Requiem

You died
Your lonely death
Endured the funeral
Of the wealthy
In America.

We will cry for you tonight
From the banks of Loch Finn
To the top of Knockletra.

– translated from Irish Gaelic by the author

Michael Davitt
(1950 -)

Michael Davitt was born in Cork city in 1950. He graduated from University College Cork with a degree in Celtic Studies in 1971. Poet, broadcaster and editor of *Innti*, which is, more than any, the magazine of contemporary poetry in the Irish language.

We Will Stray

for Gabriel

> *Death, I still think, is answer*
> *Life is question –*
> *We will stray another while*
> *And see the land.*
>
> *– Seán Ó Ríordáin*

we will stray
south-west by south
from the north-west
we will expect the heat of voice
we will seek Almighty God
and in a rite
of candles and skin
in Cashel
we will singe our barren bards
in a bonfire
and scatter their ashes
on the mildew of tradition
we will stray
we will make mistake
upon mistake
in our mountain wandering

or steeped
in a marsh
between
Altan Mór
and Altan Beag
at the railway station
of Caiseal na gCorr
we will bid farewell
to the historic train
that goes astray
we will stray
phoning
from poll to poll
in the windowed squares
of Dublin two
until we are burnt
in the bloody whisperings
for the great voice
we will force a circuit
of the muddy empire
on chaffed knees
calling loudly on
the masters
Ó Bruadair
Eoghan Rua
Aodhagán
we will banish
the hereditary depression
and we will stray
the voice
is heralding a new age
the age of the small man
the age of the inner life
the age of the English
the age of the Irish
the age of new potatoes
we will anaesthetize
the heart of the bomb
our head in the eye
of the hurricane

we will sing birth-songs
growing songs
we will condemn only
the Angel of Pride
we will humanize the Church
we will end
conceit
we will stray
and at the end
of the day
we will live in heat
sending evenings
of clay pipes astray
changing
we will change
we will go proud
we will go low
we will go

– translated from Irish Gaelic by Gabriel Fitzmaurice

In Memory of Elizabeth Kearney

Once it was cards on the table,
Rosary and mugs of tea in candlelight
Beside a blazing fire;
Outside, a donkey in the night,
Dogs denied their diet
And an old woman destroying me with Irish.

Once, there was the after-Mass chatting,
And she would trim the sails
Of strangers with one caustic look of her eye
Putting the College Trippers
Firmly in their places
With 'pestles' and 'hencrabs' and 'haycocks'!

Once, at mackerel and potatoes
During the news at noon-time
She'd ask for a translation
Because her English was lacking

Ireland

And I'd say: "Yera they're killing each other
In the North of Ireland."

Once, she was like a statue
At the top-stairs window
Wandering west from the quayside
Home in a dream to her island
And if I suddenly came up behind her
She'd say: "Oh, you thief, may you long be homeless!"

– translated from Irish Gaelic by Michael Hartnett

An Sceimhlitheoir (The Terrorist)

Tá na coiscéimeanna tar éis filleadh arís.
B'fhada a gcosa gan lúth gan
fuaim.

Seo trasna mo bhrollaigh iad
is ní féidir liom
corraí;

stadann tamall is amharcann siar
thar a ngualainn is deargann
toitín.

Táimid i gcúlsráid dhorcha gan lampa
is cloisim an té ar leis
iad

is nuair a dhírím air féachaint cé atá ann
níl éinne
ann

ach a choiscéimeanna
ar comhchéim le mo
chroí.

The Terrorist

The footsteps have returned again.
The feet for so long still
and silent.

Here they go across my breast
and I cannot
resist;

they stop for a while, glance
over the shoulder, light
a cigarette.

We are in an unlit backstreet
and I can hear who
they belong to

and when I focus to make him out
I see there is
no one

but his footsteps
keeping step with my
heart.

— translated from Irish Gaelic by the author / Philip Casey

For Bobby Sands On The Eve Of His Death

We wait,
like people
staring up at a man
who stands, tensed
on a fourth-floor window ledge
staring down at us.

But is your sacrifice suicide?
Neither surrender, nor escape;
today you don't even have the choice
of jumping or not jumping.

Ireland

Uncertain of our role
in this madness
we dispute the rights and wrongs
over the background boozer-roar.
We wait for the latest news,
the latest videoed opinions.

We wait,
ducks in our cushy down
staring at hens in the mud
and the strutting cock
threatening his own brood
and his neighbour's
with a pompous crow:
"a crime is a crime is a crime."

You fell today,
into the sleep of death.
We hear on the radio
the grieving voice of your people
sorrow surmounting hatred:
our prayer for you
is that it prevail.

— translated from Irish Gaelic by the author / MO'L

Hiraeth

do Dheirdre

an tost seo tar éis amhráin
agus an lá ag folcadh san abhainn
idir solas agus clapsholas

an scréach ná cloiseann éinne
agus titeann an oíche gleann
ar ghleann ag tafann sa bhfuacht

Hireath

for Deirdre

this silence after song
as day bathes in the river
between light and twilight

the scream that no one hears
and night falls valley
by valley barking in the cold

— translated from Irish Gaelic by the author

Chugat (To You)

ná fan rófhada liom
mura dtagaim sa samhradh bán
uaireanta mealla an fharraige mé

ar an mbóthar fada chugat
níl inti ach mo dheora féin

slánaigh do chroí
ná habair gur thréigeas thú
abair gur bádh mé

To You

don't wait too long for me
if I don't arrive in white summer
sometimes I'm tempted by the sea

on the long road to you
it is no more than my own tears

keep your heart safe
don't say I left you
say I drowned

— translated from Irish Gaelic by the author / Philip Casey

Nuala Ní Dhomhnaill
(1952 -)

One of Ireland's most widely read and celebrated younger generation poets, Nuala Ní Dhomhnaill was born in Lancashire in 1952 and grew up in the Kerry Gaeltacht and in Nenagh, County Tipperary. She studied at University College, Cork. She spent seven years wandering in Turkey and Holland and now lives in Dublin with her Turkish husband and four children. She has published three collections of poems in Irish, *An Dealg Droighin* (1981), *Féar Suaithinseach* (1984), and *Feis* (1991). The Gallery Press has also published *The Astrakhan Cloak* (1992) and *Pharaoh's Daughter* (1990)–both of which were collaboratively published in the U.S. in following years by Wake Forest University Press in bilingual editions with translations by many of Ireland's best-known poets.

Blodewedd

Oiread is barra do mhéire a bhualadh orm
is bláthaím,
cumraíocht ceimice mo cholainne
claochlaíonn.
Is móinéar féir mé ag cathráil
faoin ngréin
aibíonn faoi thadhall do láimhe
is osclaíonn

mo luibheanna uile, meallta
ag an dteas
an sú talún is an falcaire fiain
craorag is obann, cúthail
i measc na ngas.
Ní cás duit
binsín luachra a bhaint díom.

Táim ag feitheamh feadh an gheimhridh
le do ghlao.
D'fheos is fuaireas bás
thar n-ais sa chré.
Cailleadh mo mhian collaí
ach faoi do bhos
bíogaim, faoi mar a bheadh as marbhshuan,
is tagaim as.

Soilsíonn do ghrian im spéir
is éiríonn gaoth
a chorraíonn mar aingeal Dé
na huiscí faoi,
gach orlach díom ar tinneall
roimh do phearsain,
cáithníní ar mo chroiceann,
gach ribe ina cholgsheasamh
nuair a ghaibheann tú tharam.

Suím ar feadh stáir i leithreas
na mban.
Éiríonn gal cumhra ó gach orlach
de mo chneas
i bhfianaise, más gá é a thabhairt
le fios,
fiú barraí do mhéar a leagadh orm
is bláthaím.

Blodewedd

At the least touch of your fingertips
I break into blossom,
my whole chemical composition
transformed.
I sprawl like a grassy meadow
fragrant in the sun;
at the brush of your palm, all my herbs
and spices spill open

frond by frond, lured to unfold
and exhale in the heat;
wild strawberries rife, and pimpernels

flagrant and scarlet, blushing
down their stems.
To mow that rushy bottom;
no problem.

All winter I waited silently
for your appeal.
I withered within, dead to all,
curled away, and deaf as clay,
all my life forces ebbing slowly
till now I come to, at your touch,
revived as from a deathly swoon.

Your sun lightens my sky
and a wind lifts, like God's angel,
to move the waters,
every inch of me quivers
before your presence,
goose-pimples I get as you glide
over me, and every hair
stands on end.

Hours later I linger
in the ladies' toilet,
a sweet scent wafting
from all my pores,
proof positive, as if a sign
were needed, that at the least
touch of your fingertips
I break into blossom.

— translated from Irish Gaelic by John Montague

Poetry

Almost spent
the small bird landed
on my window-sill,
don't know where from,
don't know where gone,

a scantling,
he nested – circumspect – in my arms,
got back his strength, began to sing.

I lost myself,
lost day and night,
followed the music
east of the moon
and west of the sun
and oh red-ripe the garden-o . . .

when I awoke
he was gone,

I open my window,
I place on the sill
the bowl of water,
the reddened grain.

— translated from Irish Gaelic by Tom Mac Intyre

Jerusalem

Thinking of you
milk fills my breasts.
I'm Jerusalem, the holy city,
the milk-and-honey flow,
carbuncle and sapphire
ground me, rubies
my gable and my roof-tree,
the gates are of crystal . . .

I won't tell you,
you'd get a swelled head.
Nor would I satisfy you
to think I have it *that* bad.
Rest assured, for my condition
there's no cure known.
I declare myself helpless.
Say: I'm a woman,
milk fills my breasts.

— translated from Irish Gaelic by Tom Mac Intyre

The Black Train (An Traein Dubh)

As surely as the Headless Horseman
came to Ichabod Crane,
into the station every night
comes the black train.
Waiting on the platform
are the passengers themselves,
easily distinguished though they wear
no yellow stars on their sleeves.

Some are young, in the prime
of life, still on the up and up,
some so well past their prime
their backs are bent like hoops.
Many of them, you'd hardly think
were marked for death,
what with smiles all round,
the jaunty cap, the fag in the mouth.

But one by one
they all will mount
the gangway of the Windigo
that stands there, adamant,
blowing steam
from its great nostril-valves
before slouching away
to the strains of no whistles nor fifes.

As far as the rest of us are concerned,
we wash our hands
of them. We give them a wide berth.
We bury our heads in the sand.
We grab another espresso
and, with renewed zest,
go about our business
as if they didn't exist.

We're so taken by the fun and games
of power and money – such is the allure
of the glistering world
and our wish for the life of Reilly –
we forget

we're all in the same holding-camp; we forget
there's no way out
but through the gateless gate

where the guards
are waiting in uniform
to herd
us down the platform
to the left and into the cattle-wagons
and on to Dachau or Belsen.
There's no one for whom it's not a foregone
conclusion.

— translated from Irish Gaelic by Paul Muldoon

Immram (The Voyage)

1. Cathair Dé Bhí (The City of God)

An té a bhreac i scrioptúr ar bith
nach amhlaidh atáimid tar éis teacht go dtí
rudaí somhínithe; ar chlé scamaill dhúdhorcha
agus duifean agus spéirling, blosc stoic agus glór gártha
a thugann ar lucht a éisteachta luí síos is impí
is triall ar thoscairí a sheachadadh ag iarraidh anacal anama.
An té a bhreac an méid sin
do bhreac sé an diabhal d'éitheach! Le dhá ghlúin nó trí
táimid gafa trí róipíní — dhá chogadh dhomhanda,
spalladh triomaigh is gortaí, sé mhilliún Giúdach
ídithe ina n-íobairt dhóite, gan trácht ar cad
a dhein a dtaoisigh féin le muintir Chambodia . . .
is gan sinn tagaithe céim níos cóngaraí do Shliabh Shíón,
nó Cathair Dé Bhí, a Iarúsailim neamhaí.

Uaireanta chím uaim í, ag íor na spéire
mar oileán, áit nach raibh éinne roimhe riamh.
Uaireanta eile taibhsítear dom í i lár an ghaineamhlaigh,
suite ar bharr stocán cloiche, in áit éigin
mar Dakota, nó Nevada nó Wyoming.

from: **The Voyage**

1. The City of God

Whoever wrote in scripture, of whatever kind
or kidney, that it's not as if we might quite suddenly find
all made abundantly clear – to the left, dark clouds
and thunder-claps and trumpet-blasts and the voices of crowds
that have those who hear them get on their knees
to pray that peace emissaries
be dispatched – whoever made such a revelation
was full of it: over a mere couple or three generations
we've been subjected to two
World Wars, droughts, famines, at least six million Jews'
burnt offerings, not to speak of the impieties
visited upon the people of Cambodia . . .
and we've not come one step closer, all the same,
to Mount Zion, nor the City of God, that heavenly Jerusalem.

Sometimes I glimpse it, though, that heavenly city,
however evanescently, there, at the very horizon,
like an island where no one has ever set
foot: sometimes it appears to me in the middle of the desert;
on top of a sandstone chimney-pipe or column
somewhere in South Dakota or Nevada or Wyoming.

– translated from Irish Gaelic by Paul Muldoon

Gabriel Fitzmaurice
(1952 –)

Gabriel Fitzmaurice was born in 1952 in Moyvane, County Kerry where he now lives and teaches in the local National School. He has published eleven books to date including poetry in English and Irish, children's verse, an anthology of poetry in Irish with verse translations, *An Crann Faoi Bhláth/ The Flowering Tree* (Wolfhound Press, 1991) and collections of ballads and folksongs. His latest book of poetry is *The Father's Part* (Story Line Press, Oregon, 1992).

Gaeilge★

for Micheál Ó Conghaile

I was wild and wonderful
With many dialects –
Erratic, individual
As the genius that expressed

Itself through me;
On my terms suitors wooed –
I revealed to those who pleased me
My hidden voice and mood.

I was Queen of dialect
And language through me sang
Like poetry, the thrill
Of words upon my tongue.

I gave myself to language –
We agreed like rhyme,
Different yet harmonious.
Widowed now by time,

Ireland

Dependent on the grammar
Prescribed for me – this crutch;
Doctored by officials
Who care about as much

For wilderness and wonder
As a Civil Servant's Form,
Oh for the tongue of passion!
To be swept again by storm!

– translated from Irish Gaelic by the author

★Gaeilge – the Irish language.

Hence The Songs

i.m. Billy Cunningham, singer

How soon great deeds are abstract . . .

Hence the songs –
The mighty deeds the tribe sings in the bar:
Gaisce★ diminished by the video.

Men I never knew still star
In North Kerry Finals,
Their deeds not history but myth
Alive upon a singer's breath;

Again local men are martyred
In a lonely glen;

Now love is lost,
A Rose is won –

Things insufficient till they're sung . . .

– translated from Irish Gaelic by the author

★Gaisce – (Irish) valour, great exploits, boasting.

Survivor

Captain, I remember you
Praying every day
At the statue of Saint Anthony
For the men you shot. They

Haunted you in your old age
To your asylum – prayer:
This faith that once divided you,
That fought a Civil War

To forge order from division,
Sustained you, though the state
That both sides fought for
Neither could create;

But, for all that, a Republic
Where you played the Captain's part
Biting every bullet,
Knowing in your heart

That, though the war is over
And we vote in liberty,
There's a *Britain* in all of us
From which we're never free.

– translated from Irish Gaelic by the author

Áine Ní Ghlinn
(1955 –)

Born in 1955 in County Tipperary, Áine Ní Ghlinn is a poet and journalist who works with Raidió na Gaeltachta and RTÉ. Her work has been included in several anthologies and school textbooks and has been broadcast on various radio and television programs. She is the author of three collections of poetry: *An Chéim Bhriste* (Coiscéim, 1984), *Gairdín Pharthais* (Coiscéim, 1988), and *Deora Nár Caoineadh* (1996). She has also written two books for teenagers: *Mná As An nGnáth* (An Gúm, 1990) and *Déithe Is Daoine* (An Gúm, 1995). Awards for her work include an Arts Council Bursary in 1992, Duais Bhord na Gaeilge, Listowel Writers' Week Award in 1987, and the Oireachtas Award in 1985 and 1987. She currently lives in Dublin.

Cuair (Curves)

Ó ghoid máinlia
a banúlacht uaithi
bíonn sí de shíor
ag stánadh
ar éirí na gréine
ar chomhchruinneas na gcnoc.

Ar pháipéar déanann
stuanna ciorcail
ceann i ndiaidh a chéile.
Ó fagadh coilm sceana
mar a mbíodh a brollach
tá sí ciaptha ag cuair.

Curves

Since a surgeon
stole her femininity
she is constantly
staring
at the rising sun
at the roundness of the hills.

On a piece of paper she draws
arcs of circles
circle after circle.
Since a scar replaced
her breast
she is haunted by curves.

— translated from Irish Gaelic by Pádraig Ó Snodaigh

The Grass House

We built a grass house – you and I –
at the foot of the meadow. You were 30.
I was no higher than the walls.

You knocked on our stone door. And came in.
"I'll be Daddy, you be Mam," you said softly.
"and I'll be coming home from my day's work."
We drank some tea out of toy cups.

"Come on, my love. It's time for bed. Strip off."
I stripped. You ripped out a pillow from the kitchen
wall. Your 30 years smothering me.

You cleaned me with your handkerchief.
You kissed my blood to heal the wound and we
went home – you and I – to the house of
my mother, your daughter.

Now, whatever look I throw over my shoulder I
can still see the gaping
wound you left in the kitchen wall.

— translated from Irish Gaelic by the author and Pádraig Ó Snodaigh / TRC

Release

She would not go to the funeral
but went to the wake
Laid her hand on his head
Smiled and
traced the line of his nose
down over lips closed forever
on his slimy tongue
his blubbering spit
his foul-smelling breath
Down, over his rosaried hands
and under the white sheet of death
she saw the small organ
that would never again play
in her small dark cave

She offered condolences
to his widow and
his children
and ran
out the door
down the road
towards the wood
She found
the cold bed
where he first
raped her
and screamed
the scream of horror
that had been stuck in her throat
for more than twenty years.

– translated from Irish Gaelic by the author and Pádraig Ó Snodaigh / TRC

Cathal Ó Searcaigh
(1956 –)

Cathal Ó Searcaigh, poet and playwright, lives on a small hill farm at the foot of his beloved Mount Errigal in the Donegal Gaeltacht. Cathal has, over the past decade, emerged as one of Ireland's most distinguished modern day poets. He is now widely regarded as one of the greatest Irish language poets of the century; a fitting heir to that great triumvirate of Máire Mhac an tSaoi, Seán Ó Ríordáin and Máirtín Ó Direáin. "His confident internationalism," according to Theo Dorgan, writing in *Irish Poetry Since Kavanagh* (Four Courts Press, 1996), "has already begun to channel new modes, new possibilities, into the writing of Irish language poetry in our time." One of the few Gaelic poets writing full-time, he was writer-in-residence in Queens University, Belfast and the University of Ulster, Coleraine 1992-1995. He has also completed a six-month residency in University College, Galway. His work is an integral part of all courses in modern Irish poetry at universities in Ireland and at many American universities. Recently Cathal Ó Searcaigh was elected a member of Aosdána, the ultimate accolade of achievement for creative artists in Ireland. (Aosdána is an elite group of writers, painters and composers who have made a significant contribution to the arts. Only the top echelon of creative artists are elected to the eminent ranks of Aosdána. It includes among its living legends Seamus Heaney, Brian Friel, John McGahern, Jennifer Johnson, Máire Mhac An tSaoi.) Ó Searcaigh is fast becoming a poet of international renown. He is frequently invited to give readings at arts festivals and literary celebrations all over the world. In the past two years he has read his work in Belgium, Italy, France, Spain, Germany, Wales, Scotland, England and Canada. He has been an Irish representative at the prestigious L'Imaginaire Irlandaise Festival in France and at the renowned Frankfurt Book Fair in Germany. A French edition of his poems, titled *Le Chemin Du Retour* (Exiles Return) has been issued by the publishing house La Barbacane in Paris. A Catalan edition was published by Columna in Barcelona. Selections of his work have already been published in German and Italian. His bilingual collection *Homecoming/An Bealach 'Na Bhaile* (Cló Iar-Chonnachta, 1993), now in its third printing, received wide international acclaim on its appearance. Colm Tóibín reviewed it as "one of the international books of the year" in the *Times Literary Supplement.* He has been the recipient of numerous prizes for his poetry: the Seán Ó Ríordáin Prize in 1993; Duais Bhord na Gaeilge, 1995; a number of major Arts Council bursaries in Literature. Both the BBC and RTÉ have made television documentaries on Cathal and his works entitled *File An Phobail* and *An Bealach 'Na Bhaile,* respectively. His collection *Na Buachaillí Bana* was recently published by Cló Iar-Chonnachta, followed by *Out in the Open* in 1997.

I gCeann Mo Thrí Bliana A Bhí Mé (When I Was Three)

do Anraí Mac Giolla Chomhaill

"Sin clábar! Clábar cáidheach,
a chuilcigh," a dúirt m'athair go bagrach
agus mé ag slupairt go súgach
i ndíobhóg os cionn an bhóthair.
"Amach leat as do chuid clábair
sula ndéanfar tú a chonáil!"

Ach choinnigh mé ag spágáil agus ag splaiseáil
agus ag scairtigh le lúcháir:
"Clábar! Clábar! Seo mo chuid clábair!"
Cé nár chiallaigh an focal faic i mo mheabhair
go dtí gur mhothaigh mé i mo bhuataisí glugar
agus trí gach uile líbín de mo cheirteacha
creathanna fuachta na tuisceana.

A chlábar na cinniúna, bháigh tú mo chnámha.

When I Was Three

For Anraí Mac Giolla Chomhaill

"That's muck! Filthy muck, you little scamp,"
my father was so severe in speech
while I was messing happily
in my mud-trench by the road.
"Out with you from that muck
before you freeze to death!"

But I continued shuffling, having fun,
all the time screaming with delight:
"Muck! Muck! It's my own muck!"
But the word was nothing in my innocence
until I felt the squelch of wellies
and, through the dripping wet of clothes,
the shivering knowledge of water.

Ah! Muck of destiny, you drenched my bones!

– translated from Irish Gaelic by Thomas Mc Carthy

A Portrait Of The Blacksmith As A Young Artist

for Máire Nic Suibhne

I'm sick and tired of Dún Laoghaire,
Of my bedsit in Cross's Avenue,
A pokey place that cripples my wordsmith's craft
And leaves me nightly in the dumps
Scrounging kindred among the drunks
Instead of hammering poems for my people
On the anvil of my mind.
Almighty God! It's gone too far,
This damned silence.
If I were back in Caiseal na gCorr
I'd not be awkward, half-alive.

No way! But in the smithy of my tongue
I'd be hale and hearty
Working at my craft daily
Inciting the bellows of my mind
Stirring thoughts to flame
Hammering loudly
The mettlesome speech of my people.

– translated from Irish Gaelic by Gabriel Fitzmaurice

Shelter

"It will storm," you said, "an awful storm."
Restless, you pace the floor, up
and down plaintively, your eyes suppliant.
Outside the night blows and drifts
about the house, clattering at the windows,
shouting and threatening through the keyhole.
"It would breach a place to come inside,"
you say, jamming the door with an armchair.
Volleys of rain knock on the window.
Suddenly, as if in fright, the kitchen blind
rolls up. Quaking, you spring to my breast
for shelter.
Hugging you, my fingers catch
your skin, squeezing, squeezing.
Heat on heat, your lips part to kiss me
as the storm gusts through me.
I flash and a fireball hits your skin.

− translated from Irish Gaelic by Gabriel Fitzmaurice

Silence

For Micheál Ó Máirtín

These bogs all round me, north and south
from the *Seascann Mór* on out to *Altán,*
may they effect my poem
as they do the bog-bean −
mature it with silence.

− translated from Irish Gaelic by Gabriel Fitzmaurice

Beyond

In your sleep you raise
Neither refuge nor sanctuary

All night I haunt
The hidden world behind your eyes

That is truer blue
Than the Virgin Mary's blouse.

On the hidden side of words
Lies a world of echoed melody.

− translated from Irish Gaelic by Joan McBreen

A Braddy Cow

For Liam Ó Muirthile

He got fed-up, I'd swear,
of the loneliness that constantly seeps down,
through the rolling hills, through the valleys
sluggish as a hearse;
of the lazy hamlets of the foothills
empty of youth as of earth;
of the old warriors, of the sodbusters
who turned to red-sod the peaty soil
and who deafened him pink, year-in, year-out,
bragging of the old sods of the past;

of the small, white bungalows ugly
as dandruff in the sedgy headlands of the Glen;
of the young trapped in the cage of their fate
like wild animals who have lost their cunning;
of the three sorrows of storytelling in the misery
of the unemployed, of low spirits,
of the backwardness, of the narrowmindedness of both sides of the Glen,
of the fine birds below in Ruairí's
who stirred the man in him
but who couldn't care less about his lusting;

of tribal boundaries, of ancient household ditches,
of pissing his frustration at race and religion
that walled him in.
He got fed up of being fettered in the Glen
and, bucking like a braddy cow one spring morning,
he cleared the walls and hightailed away.

– translated from Irish Gaelic by Gabriel Fitzmaurice

To Jack Kerouac

For Séamus de Bláca

> *"The only people for me are the mad ones,*
> *the ones who are mad to live, mad to talk,*
> *mad to be saved, desirous of everything at*
> *the same time, the ones who never yawn or*
> *say a commonplace thing but burn, burn like*
> *fabulous yellow roman candles"*

from: *On the Road*

Thumbing through your work tonight the aroma of memories came from
every page.
My youth rewoke and I felt rising in me the dreamy beat that imitated
you at the start of the '70s.
1973. I was hooked on you. Day after day I got shots of inspiration from
your life which lit my mind and stretched my imagination.
I didn't see Mín 'a Leá or Fána Bhuí then, but the plains of Nebraska and
the grassy lands of Iowa
And when the blues came it wasn't the Bealtaine road that beckoned but
a way stretching across America.
"Hey man you gotta stay high," I'd say to my friends as we freaked
through California's Cill Ulta into Frisco's Falcarragh.

Your book lies shut on my breast, your heart beating under the skin cover
in the muscle of every word.
Oh man I feel them again, those highs on youth's Himalayas from coast
to coast we roamed together, free, wild, reckless:
A hitchhiking odyssey from New York to Frisco and down to Mexico
City.
A mad beat to our lives. Crazed. Hurtling down highways in speeding
cars, skidding over the verge of sanity on the wings of Benzedrine.
We crossed frontiers and we scaled dreams.
Celebrations at every turn of life's highway, binges and brotherhood
from Brooklyn to Berkeley; booze, bop and Buddhism; Asian verse;
telegrams from a Sierra eternity; marijuana and mysticism in
Mexico; frenzied visions in Bixby Canyon.

Orpheus emerged from every orifice.

O I remember it all Jack, the talk and the quest.
You were the wild-eyed poet walking free, searching for harmony,
    searching for Heaven.
And although it is said there's no shortcut to the Gods you opened one
    up now and then, harnessing your mind's Niagara with dope and
    divinity.
And in those rapturous moments you generated the
    light that you saw eternity by
And that guided you, I hope, the day of your death, home to Whitman,
    Proust and Rimbaud.

My road is before me "a road that ah zigzags all over creation. Yeah man!
    Ain't nowhere else it can go. Right!"
And someday, on the road of failing sight and knotted limbs
Or a less distant day, perhaps
Death will face me at Fate's Crossroads
And then, goddammit Jack, we'll both be hiking across eternity.

*   — translated from Irish Gaelic by Sarah Berkeley*

Piccadilly: Nightfall

For Angela Carter

I am waiting for somebody
in the dusk.
Here in the centre of Piccadilly, around
the menacing mouth of the Underground
a cold nippy wind
bites into me savagely;
hunger gnaws at my guts,
my limbs are gone jittery
and you
you with your mouthful of kisses
where are you, now the hour having struck?
If I looked for kindliness,
if I collapsed in a heap
here, right here where I'm standing
would some big-hearted stranger
step forward benignly
from these sullen Londoners,

these hurrying, self-conceited Londoners
who slip by me, curtly
as if I were a cess-pit
befouling their way?
And I recall immediately
Joe Beag in Prochlais
giving his timely advice before
I left my home and my country:
"If you ever need a helping hand, lad,
you will always find the most reliable one
secured to the end of your arm."
Thank God for the saving grace of irony.
Without its blessings
where would I get an uplift
in this hour of anxiety.
I am waiting for somebody
in the dusk,
listening to fifties rock'n'roll
Buddy Holly and Chuck Berry
thumping from a street vendor's foodstall.
An angelic face out of a Botticelli
now passes by;
there are swallows in flight
in the flip-flap of her shoes
but like the ace of hearts in a pack of cards
she is shuffled out of sight
by fate's sleight of hand trick.
A hunchback busker
plays on the sheltery side of the corner
in Lower Regent Street;
the jazz sobs of his saxophone
like a pet dog whimpering
in a deserted bedsit.
Above us
the technicolor heaven of advertising
and the seven gifts of knowledge
pour down in tongues of light
from the Holy Spirit of Consumerism.
"You wanta make it dontcha"
says a skimpily clad tart,

the cling-clang of a cash register
in her pseudo-American drawl.
In this age of deceit
the whores parade by, cocksure,
like Christ's temptations in the desert,
their hearts on their sleeves.
And my mind chills
for no kind friend comes
to kindle the damp tinder of my intellect
and I reflect a little frivolously
which would be better, a change of climate,
a swig of the punch of Truth
or a wee Aspro of inspiration
to straighten out my disorders.
I am waiting for somebody
in the dusk,
yearning in my imagination
for the call of the hills and the bogs
from Mín 'a Leá and from Mín na Craoibhe
from Prochlais and from Dúnán.
I am alone and alone has no friend
but memory, but memory is a snap-shot
that wept upon, goes out of focus,
blurs.
Oh Good God
is there any escape route
other than the suicidal one
taken by Celan and Berryman
but deep in my heart
I know full well
that suicide is no escape door
merely the image
of a door painted on the walls of Despair.
But despite all that
it's difficult to overcome this ominous gloom
in myself, I
who a year ago was as lively
as the spring mist
dancing the High Caul Cap
on the top of Errigal.

Ireland

But now
the groan of a ship's siren
is closer to this gasping in my throat
and no matter how hard I try
I'm left floundering
in the exhaust fumes of the city.
I'm waiting for somebody
in the dusk.
Almighty God
I understand finally
the homesickness and heartbreak of the exile
having myself gone astray
on this mind-disordering spot in Piccadilly
amongst people deprived of their patrimony
and here I am
thinking amidst my profanities
that this city will always be for me
like the potter's field
bought with Judas' blood money
as a graveyard for the abandoned.
I am waiting for somebody
in the dusk
waiting and waiting
like that phone ringing
in the empty booth on the corner;
like the spider
crouched there in his web on the wall;
like that pointer dog
craning his neck;

like the poet with his words.

— translated from Irish Gaelic by Gréagóir Ó Dúill

SCOTTISH GAELIC

Scottish Gaelic

By any logical assessment, the language we know as Scottish Gaelic should be extinct by now. It has lived with centuries of government hostility and neglect, ranging from the Statutes of Iona, enacted in 1609, with a view to breaking the clan system, and bringing the Gaelic chiefs under control, to the 1872 Education (Scotland) Act, drafted as if Gaelic did not exist. The fight back to acknowledgement that the language is a valuable thread in the tapestry of Scotland's culture has been a long one.

But even the radical improvements of the last couple of decades leave Gaelic in the most vulnerable position imaginable. Parents can now opt to have their children educated through the medium of Gaelic, throughout their pre-school and primary education. Provision of television programming has been enhanced to the extent that Gaels enjoy a daily news bulletin in their own language – all of five minutes – and several hours per week of mixed programming, which includes a highly popular soap opera.

Yet neither education system nor media is structured in a way which ensures that Gaels, young or old, can inhabit an environment where they are totally immersed in their own culture. Outside those specialised classrooms, and the few hours of Gaelic broadcasting, English pervades. Even in the most Gaelic-intensive home, with the language spoken across the generations, television and radio speak English for the overwhelming portion of the time. Likewise, the printed media: apart from one quarterly magazine and the very occasional newspaper column, everything we read is likely to be in English. Yet Gaelic survives, and if not thriving, it certainly seems to be riding a long and buoyant wave of confidence.

And Gaelic literature has seen a remarkable flowering in this century. Readers of Gaelic in the nineteenth century, or earlier, would have been hard put to find anything in print that wasn't a poem or a sermon – especially a sermon. In the twentieth century, the library of an average literate Gael is likely to contain a range of short story collections, novels, plays, autobiographies and historical monographs, as well as a substantial list of contemporary poets.

Chief among the latter stands Sorley MacLean, acknowledged by Seamus Heaney, among others, as a writer of world stature. MacLean, a graduate in English Literature at Edinburgh University, acknowledges influences ranging from "Eliot, Pound and Auden, MacNeice and Herbert Read" to the French Symbolists of the nineteenth century, but pays particular tribute to anonymous (largely female) composers of the classical repertoire of traditional Gaelic song.

MacLean speaks of "those Gaelic songs of the two and a half centuries between 1550 and 1800 – the songs in which ineffable melodies rise like exhalations from the rhythms and resonances of the words, the songs that alone make the thought that the Gaelic language is going to die so intolerable to anyone who knows Gaelic, and has in the least degree the sensibility that responds to the marriage, or rather the simultaneous creation, of words and music." In the same essay, MacLean expresses his conviction that "Scottish Gaelic song is the chief artistic glory of the Scots, and of all people of Celtic speech, and one of the greatest artistic glories of Europe."

That's a discovery he could only have made through being born into a family steeped in the Gaelic oral tradition. At school, his reading would have been confined to the two anthologies edited for use in schools by Prof. W.J. Watson – *Rosg Gàidhlig* (Gaelic Prose), first published in 1915, and *Bàrdachd Ghàidhlig* (Gaelic Poetry) which appeared in 1918. Both were still in use, and were still the only real books in Gaelic we had access to, when I attended Portree High School, in the late 1950s, more than three decades after Sorley MacLean. I'd lay a bet on some very dog-eared copies still being in use into the next millennium, in a school or two.

Any serious consideration of Scottish Gaelic poetry in the twentieth century has to begin with Sorley MacLean. Some of those who preceded him brought modern consciousness and an instinct for innovation to their work, but none, before or since, has achieved the extraordinary fusion between a deep continuum of tradition and the widest imaginable range of contemporary influences.

Marrying those elements to the theme of love, experienced and lost, MacLean created a poetry of wonderful sonority and almost unbearable intensity. Expressing his despair at the thought of writing in a dying language, he has done much to show that the language has the vitality to see it safely into the next century, at least.

Following MacLean is Derick Thomson, Professor of Celtic at Glasgow University until his retirement in 1991. He is the son of a schoolmaster, James Thomson, who was also a poet. Though he has himself identified earlier Gaelic exponents of *vers libre,* he has to be acknowledged as the first Gaelic poet to use the modern form with consistent success, becoming, because of that, a significant influence on younger poets. Yet, an awareness of the old Gaelic forms and values permeates the poetry, as does an acute sense of the local, and the colloquial.

Iain Crichton Smith comes from Bayble, the same village as Thomson. A former English teacher, he writes poetry, prose and drama, in both Gaelic and English. Among the influences he acknowledges, Auden and Lowell are ranged alongside Carlos Williams and the Japanese Haiku masters, but Smith's is a restless, open and ever questing mind. Among many memorable poems on such themes as love, age and language, "Tha thu air aigeann m'inntinn" (You are at the bottom of my mind) always comes to mind first.

These three (along with George Campbell Hay and Donald MacAulay), the oldest of whom was born in 1911, the youngest in 1930, may be regarded as the founding fathers of the Twentieth Century Gaelic Renaissance. Each, in his own way, broke with tradition, in so doing reinforcing the tradition. At the same time, traditional poetry, composed to be sung, continued to be made. And a succession of younger poets have taken up the baton. And, in those newer writers, we continue to find the balance struck between new forms and old assonances, between public concern and personal reflection. Love and politics remain central themes, with aspects of place and nature providing a pervasive filter through which they are worked.

The place is usually home – from which we are usually exiled, by economics, and we are usually, though not always, dissenters. Of those anthologised here, two are learners of Gaelic. William Neill is old enough to be placed with the senior list, but is a relative newcomer to Gaelic. Like George Campbell Hay, he also writes in Scots and English. For Fearghas MacFhionnlaigh, it was a way of making contact with "the tap-root of Scottish Identity." There are a number of other non-native speaking poets. Most prominent of those, and regrettably absent, because she has no new work to offer, is Meg Bateman, whose rare lyrical gift is married to a marvellous metrical confidence.

Crucial absentees among the native Gaelic writers are the sisters Catriona and Morag NicGumaraid (no relation to Mairi – they're from Skye, she from Lewis), John Murray, well known as a fine short story writer and dramatist in Gaelic, whose few published verses reveal a poet of considerable power and distinction.

It should, however, be noted that, while there will be many native Gaelic writers, there are other bardic penmen and women assured of acceptance as bone fide poets, whose words have been heard by millions, yet have been marginalized as mere "songwriters." For example, Calum MacDonald, percussionist and lyricist with the Scottish rock group Runrig, is also part of a central thread in the Gaelic literary tradition, that which Sorley MacLean alluded to in his essay "Old Songs and New Poetry." As a maker of songs, MacDonald, and his kin working in the oldest literary tradition in this country, is as concerned as the rest of us to make that tradition new.

– Aonghas MacNeacail

Sorley MacLean
Somhairle MacGill-Eain
(1911 - 1996)

Sorley MacLean was born in 1911 on the island of Raasay off Scotland's west coast. He was raised in a Gaelic-speaking family and was introduced for the first time to English at age six. He received his formal education degree in English at the University of Edinburgh. In the 1960s he was instrumental in the movement toward the preservation of the teaching of Gaelic in the schools.

Revered as one of Scotland's leading literary luminaries of the twentieth century, Sorley MacLean's work has been a touchstone for writers half his age. Often referred to as "the Yeats of Scotland," his poems such as "The Great Famine" and "The Cave of Gold" are masterpieces of Scottish Gaelic literature. Of his many books, the most recent is a series of collected poems, *O Choille gu Bearradh/From Wood To Ridge* (Carcanet, 1989). A volume in honor of his 80th birthday (*Somhairle: Dàin is Deilbh*) was published in 1991 by Acair and edited by Angus Peter Campbell. Having lived in the community of Braes on the Isle of Skye in his later years, he died in the fall of 1996. This volume is dedicated to him as one of the pillars of the Celtic language renaissance as well as one of its greatest poets.

Celtic Twilight (*from:* **Realism In Celtic Poetry**)

It is a very different type of romanticism that has been predicated of the Gael and his poetry. The special brand of romanticism attributed to the Gael and his poetry is a romanticism of the escapist, other-worldly type, a cloudy mysticism, the type suggested by the famous phrase, 'Celtic Twilight'. This Celtic Twilight never bore any earthly relation to anything in Gaelic life or literature. It was merely one of the latest births of the English literary bourgeoisie, and its births are to Gaelic eyes exceedingly strange, whether they be Mr John Duncan's St Bride or the late Mrs Kennedy-Fraser's 'Mairead òg with her sea-blue eyes of witchery.'

. . . I suppose that many with Celtic pretensions will be shocked at a declaration that Gaelic poetry has not less but more than common realism. They invoke the names of 'Ossian' MacPherson, 'Fiona MacLeod', Kenneth MacLeod and Marjorie Kennedy-Fraser, and hosts of lesser Twilightists, but they will have no competent native critic on their side. Of course, with the kind of people who call Mrs Kennedy-Fraser's travesties of Gaelic songs 'faithful reproductions of the spirit of the original', I have no dispute. They are harmless as long as ignorance and crassness are considered failings in criticism of poetry. They have had their hour in the drawing-rooms of Edinburgh and London; they have soothed the ears of old ladies of the Anglo-Saxon bourgeoisie: they have spoken after dinner, hiding with a halo the bracken that grew with the Clearances; they have cherished the Iubhrach Bhallach and forgotten the 'Annie Jane' that went down in the Kyle of Vatersay, and some of them have had their earthly reward.

Reothairt (Spring Tide)

Uair is uair agus mi briste
thig mo smuain ort is tu òg,
is lìonaidh an cuan do-thuigsinn
le làn-mara 's mìle seòl.

Falaichear cladach na trioblaid
le bhodhannan is tiùrr a' bhròin
is buailidh an tonn gun bhristeadh
mu m'chasan le suathadh sròil.

Ciamar nach do mhair an reothairt
bu bhuidhe dhomh na do na h-eòin,
agus a chaill mi a cobhair
's i tràghadh boinn' air bhoinne bròin?

Spring Tide

Again and again when I am broken
my thought comes on you when you were young,
and the incomprehensible ocean fills
with floodtide and a thousand sails.

The shore of trouble is hidden
with its reefs and the wrack of grief,
and the unbreaking wave strikes
about my feet with a silken rubbing.

How did the springtide not last,
the springtide more golden to me than to the birds,
and how did I lose its succour,
ebbing drop by drop of grief?

— translated from Scottish Gaelic by the author

A Church Militant

There is a church militant in his head
shouting about the condition of man
and about the state of every creature
that is suffering the pain of the flesh
and the soreness of the spirit,
which we call the heart.

It is girning all the time
when it is not shouting
about the innocent girl in cancer
and about the whore in her disease,
about the martyr on a rack
and his repute in the lying mouth.

Its cry is on the top of a mountain
and smothered in the quagmire
in the mouth that gets no hearing,
about the good man and the hero nameless
and about the martyr of whom there is no tale.

Its eye is without sleep or peace
on the innocent oppressed poor creature
and on the insane murderer
who did not ask to be born,
on the child's belly
almost splitting with famine;
on the loathsome cholera
and on the horrific cancer,
on the intolerable pain of one creature.
On the gas chambers,
on every Belsen that was,
on the atom and neutron bomb
and on the utter destruction that has no words.

— translated from Scottish Gaelic by the author

A Poem Made When The Gaelic Society Of Inverness Was A Hundred Years Old

Ghosts on a ridge tonight,
on a fleeting peak in the mist
that surges thickly and spreads thinly,
when one bare summit comes in sight
and when another goes away from the eye
and when a rock face is darkened in deep shade.

Smoke of the generations climbing
over peaks of memory of varying value,
the great men and the small
appearing and being lost in the hardship
that squinting fortune gives, or the choice
made by vision and devotion.

His own ghosts to every man
and its choice of image to every aspiration;
to each man his choice of ridge
that his eye reaches with the division
made by acute perceptions, or the struggle
that is between Scotland and himself.

Walking the streets of Inverness
from the ridge of the untractable century,
wise men and scholars that stayed
against the onset made against all
who preferred their inheritance to the gold,
and who did not ask for the new choice.

The venomous fog is on the street,
on the peaks and on the towers,
the smoke of the rout from Culloden
and from other routs before it
and from routs after it
twisting perception and hope.

A mist gilded with gold,
the worst mist that ever came,
the cavalry and guns of the sheep
and their wild and surly bleating on the mountain,
and the little band striving
when giving in would be good sense.

In the flabby mist of a tale
there is no certainty in a cold vision
and there is not much to tell
that cannot be perverted in the telling.
In the un-Gaelic town of Inverness
a small group once did a great thing.

Twenty-four there were,
and two out of three are lost in the mist
and no tale of them on one ridge,
their shadow on not one rock face,
but only four or five;
the rest on ridges in deep shadow.

Men on ridges tonight
and not one as high as he ought to be—
wise men and scholars of the Gaels
whose loved heredity was a blazing fire,
some in the swift gleam
and some lost in the mist.

Ridges rising in the eyes of some
and lost utterly in the ignorance of others,
twenty of that group without fame
without which no banner would stand,
twenty of that band nameless,
with no fame in the dim mist of death.

— translated from Scottish Gaelic by the author

A' Ghort Mhòr (The Great Famine)

I

Neòil na gorta le samh sgreataidh
Ann an deàrrsadh na gréine,
A' seargadh feòil ai cnàmhan,
A' dèanadh culaidh-ghràin de bhòidhche.
Cìochan a bha daingeann corrach
'Nan ròpan an crochadh ri cléibh,
Sléisdean is calpannan a bha cuimir
'Nam biorain chrìona connaidh,
'S a' bhrù a bha cho slìom seang
'Na bolla tioram teann oillteil.

II

'S ioma gort is tart mhòr
A bh' air an t-saoghal o thùs,
Gun telebhis gan craoladh
Gu na bailtean reamhar saoibhir,
Gun ghuth réidio gan innse
Do chluasan coibhneil no coma,
Agus do chluasan teth le nàire,
'S do chluasan nan naomh 's nan aingidh,
'S do chluasan a bha 'g éisdeachd
Ri acras an cloinne fhéin.

III

'N e 'm peacadh a rinn an sgrios seo,
An sgrios fada fichead uair as motha
Na teine 's prunnasdan nam frasan
A dhòirt air Bailtean na Machrach?
Bheil nàdur coma co-dhiù
'S an Taghadh fuar-chridheach borb?

IV

Còrr is fichead muillion,
Barrachd, barrachd ioma h-uair
Na bhàsaich ann an Gort na h-Eireann,
Còrr is fichead muillion.
Có a thomhaiseas an cràdh,
An ciùrradh a shracas an cridhe
Ged nach robh ann ach a h-aon,
Aon leanabh air nach fhacas
Blàth iongantach na h-òige,
Am blàth a dh'fhaodadh mairsinn
Ioma bliadhna gun sheargadh,
Ròsan a' fosgladh gu làn àilleachd.

V

Cridheachan màthar is athar
Agus peathar is bràthar
Riabte leis na tàirnean meirgeach,
Le spealgan iarainn nan sligean
A thig gun sian ás an adhar
A dh'innse mu chor an t-saoghail.

Scotland

VI

Có ás a thug sibh a' choiseachd
'Nur triùir chompanach an-iochdmhor,
A' ghort 's an laige 's an calar?
Có ás a thàinig sibh le 'r sgreamh,
Có ás a thàinig sibh idir?
'N ann ás an aineolas rag,
No ás an leisg gun shuim,
Ás a' pheacadh bheag,
No ás a' pheacadh mhòr,
No ás an fhéinealachd choma,
No ás an aingidheachd fhéin
No ás a' ghamhlas as miosa,
Is mac an duine cho còir,
Cho iochdmhor coibhneil laghach,
Cho cùramach mu chor a chloinne?

VII

Tha 'n Afraic fada thall
Ach tha 'n telebhis faisg
Air rumannan comhfhurtail
'S air bùird beairteach le biadh
Is deoch is airgead deàrrsach
'S gach sochair eile th' aig an stamag
'S aig an t-sùil 's aig a' bhlas
Agus aig miannan na colainn.

VIII

Ciamar a roinnear am biadh?
Ciamar a dh'uisgeachar an fhàsach?
Bheil bàs na gorta 's a' chalair
Do-sheachanta mar a bha
Fad gach ginealach a thàinig,
Fad gach ginealach a thig?

IX

Am faigh gach fear is bean is nighean
Is mac is leanaban a mhillear

Agus a mharbhar le gort is calar
Pàrras shìorruidh an spioraid
Fad àlan buan na biothbhuantachd?
Bu mhath am prionnsapal 's an riadh
A bhiodh 'nan éirig air na thachair,
An éirig a dh'fheumadh na mìltean
'S na ciadan muillion de chreutairean
An dèidh anacothrom na beatha.

The Great Famine

I

The clouds of famine with loathsome stink
in the glitter of the sunlight,
withering flesh on bones,
making beauty a disgusting thing.
Breasts that were firm, upstanding
ropes hanging to rib cages,
thighs and calves that were shapely
brittle sticks of firewood,
and the belly that was sleek and slender
a dry tight hideous buoy.

II

Many a famine and great thirst
were in the world from the start
without television broadcasting them
to the fat wealthy towns,
with no radio voice telling of them
to kindly or uncaring ears,
and to ears hot with shame,
to the ears of saints and of the wicked,
and to the ears that were listening
to the hunger of their own children.

III

Was it sin that made this destruction,
a destruction far more than twenty times greater
than the fire and brimstone of the showers

that poured on the Cities of the Plain?
Does Nature not care at all
and is Predestination cold-hearted and cruel?

IV

More than twenty million,
more, more many a time
than died in the Famine of Ireland,
more than twenty million.
Who will measure the pain,
the torture that tears the heart
though there was only one,
one child on whom there was not seen
the wonderful bloom of youth,
the bloom that might last
many a year without fading,
roses opening to full beauty.

V

Hearts of mother and father
and of sister and brother
torn with rusty nails,
with iron splinters from shells
that come without whizz from the sky
to tell of the world's plight.

VI

From where have you walked,
you three merciless companions,
famine, weakness and cholera?
From where have you come with your loathsomeness,
from where have you come at all?
Is it from stubborn ignorance
or from the uncaring laziness,
from the small sin,
or from the great sin,
or from the indifferent selfishness
or from wickedness itself
or from the worst malice,
though mankind is so generous,
so merciful, kind and pleasant,
so careful of the state of his children.

VII

Africa is far away
but television is near
comfortable rooms
and near tables rich with food
and drink and gleaming silver
and every other privilege of the stomach,
of the eye and the taste
and the desires of the body.

VIII

How will food be shared?
How will the desert be watered?
Is death from famine and cholera
unavoidable as it was
throughout every generation that has come,
throughout every generation that will come?

IX

Will every man and woman and daughter
and son and infant that will be spoilt
and killed with famine and cholera,
will all of them get the eternal Paradise of the spirit
throughout the lasting generations of infinity?
How good would the principal and interest be
as ransoms needed by the thousands
and hundreds of millions of creatures
after the great distress of life.

— translated from Scottish Gaelic by the author

Derick Thomson
Ruaraidh MacThómais
(1921 –)

Derick Thomson was born 1921 in Stornoway, Isle of Lewis, Scotland, son of James Thomson (schoolmaster and poet) and Christina Smith, and was educated at the Nicolson Institute, Universities of Aberdeen, Cambridge and Bangor (North Wales). He has taught Celtic at Universities of Edinburgh, Aberdeen and Glasgow, and was Professor of Celtic Languages at Glasgow from 1963 to 1991. He has published widely in Gaelic and English, and is the author of *The Gaelic Sources of MacPherson's Ossian* (1952), *Branwen Uerch Lyr* (1961), *An Introduction to Gaelic Poetry* (1974, 1989), *The Companion to Gaelic Scotland* (1983, 1994), *European Poetry in Gaelic* (1991), *The MacDiarmid Ms Anthology* (1992), *Alasdair MacMhaighstir Alasdair: Selected Poems* (1996). He has been the long-standing editor of the Gaelic quarterly *Gairm* since 1952. His many volumes of poetry run from *An Dealbh Briste/ The Broken Picture* (1951) to *Meall Garbh/The Rugged Mountain* (1996), with his collected poems, *Creachadh na Clàrsaich/Plundering the Harp* (1982), still available. He is married to former Mod Gold Medallist Carol Galbraith. They have a family of six, including six grandchildren, and live in Glasgow, which is the largest Gaelic "colony" in Scotland.

Aig Tursachan Chalanais (At Callanish Stones)

Cha robh toiseach no deireadh air a' chearcall,
cha robh ìochdar no uachdar aig ar smuain,
bha an cruinne-cè balbh a' feitheamh,
gun muir a' slìobadh ri tràigh,
gun feur a' gluasad ri gaoith,
cha robh là ann no oidhche –
is gu sìorraidh cha chaill mi cuimhne
air do chuailean bàn 's do bheul meachair,
no air an aon-dùrachd a shnaoidh sinn
ri chèile an cearcall na tìme,
far nach suath foill ann an tràigh dòchais.

At Callanish Stones

The circle had neither end nor beginning,
our thought had neither start nor finish,
the still universe was waiting,
sea not stroking the land,
grass not moving in wind,
there was no day, no night –
and I shall never forget
your fair hair and tender lips,
or the shared desire that wove us
together in time's circle
where treachery will not touch hope's shore.

– translated from Scottish Gaelic by the author

Thursday Morning, In A Glasgow Post Office

From the streets
and from the back-streets of the city
they converged
on the Post Office,
the lame and the halt:
a man dragging his crooked legs along,
a young man with black scars on his face,
another whose eyes bulged from his head,
a youngish woman
haggard with drink,
an old man in his slippers,
stubbly beard and long hair,
wearing thin trousers,
each one looking to the head of the queue,
holding his slip of paper,
going to the spring in the desert
where the feast was,
blind and following the light,
deaf and eager for music.
I looked to see if Christ
was behind the counter,
but the halt were there too.
Standing in the queue there
thinking I was whole.

– translated from Scottish Gaelic by the author

The Herring Girls

Their laughter like a sprinkling of salt
showered from their lips,
brine and pickle on their tongues,
and the stubby short fingers that could handle fish,
or lift a child gently, neatly,
safely, wholesomely,
unerringly,
and the eyes that were as deep as a calm.

The topsy-turvy of history had made them
slaves to short-arsed curers,
here and there in the Lowlands, in England.
Salt the reward they won
from those thousands of barrels,
the sea-wind sharp on their skins,
and the burden of poverty in their kists,
and were it not for their laughter
you might think the harp-string was broken.

But there was a sprinkling of pride on their hearts,
keeping them sound,
and their tongues' gutting-knife
would tear a strip from the Lowlanders' mockery –
and there was work awaiting them
when they got home,
though they had no wealth:
on a wild winter's night,
if that were their lot,
they would make men.

– translated from Scottish Gaelic by the author

Budapest

Dùn chlosaichean ri oir nan stràid,
torrghan nan tanc, làmhach nan gunna mòr,
snaidheadh nam peileirean air balla mìn
a' sgrìobhadh eachdraidh shoilleir mar air clàr
no leac a dheasaich clachair –
tha aodann snaidht' a' chlachair nis fon chruaidh.

Ballachan Bhudapest – bithidh 'n dealbh seo deargt'
air retina na saorsa iomadh linn,
ged 's goirid cuimhn' na colainn air a cràidh,
ged sgaoileas ceò brat-falaich thar nan lot,
ged chòmhdaicheas an duilleach iad ri tìm,
ged reodhas sneachda geal le 'thùirling mhìn
faileadh na daonnachd air a' chabhsair lom.

Budapest

A heap of corpses at the roadway's edge,
rumble of tanks, the volley of huge guns,
carving of bullets on a smooth wall
writing history plain as on a plaque
or tablet sculptured by a mason –
now the carved face of the mason lies under the chisel.

The walls of Budapest – this image will be seared
on freedom's retina for many an age,
though short the body's memory of pain,
though smoke extends a pall over the wounds,
though leaves will cover them in course of time,
though white snow, smoothly gliding down, will freeze
the human stench on the deserted road.

– translated from Scottish Gaelic by the author

Strathnaver

In that blue-black sky,
as high above us as eternity,
a star was winking at us,
answering the leaping flames of fire
in the rafters of my father's house,
that year we thatched the house with snowflakes.

And that too was the year
they hauled the old woman out on to the dung-heap,
to demonstrate how knowledgeable they were in Scripture,
for the birds of the air had nests
(and the sheep had folds)
though she had no place in which to lay down her head.

Scotland

O Strathnaver and Strath of Kildonan,
it is little wonder that the heather should bloom on your slopes,
hiding the wounds that Patrick Sellar, and such as he, made,
just as time and time again I have seen a pious woman
who has suffered the sorrow of this world,
with the peace of God shining from her eyes.

— translated from Scottish Gaelic by the author

Uilleam Neill
William Neill
(1922 -)

William Neill, or Uilleam Neill as he is known as a poet of Gaelic verse, was born in 1922 in Ayrshire. He was educated at Ayr Academy and Edinburgh University. Coming to Gaelic later in life, he is also fluent in Scots and English, and writes and translates in all three languages. As poet and translator, he is a SAC Book Award winner and the author of many volumes, including: *Cnù à Mogaill*, *Wild Places*, *Buile Shuibhne*, *Making Tracks*, and *Selected Poems 1969-1992*. Of his work Tom Scott says: "He is in the front rank of Scottish poets of this century." And Kathleen Raine has added: "He has the fluency and ready inventiveness of the born Makar." A true pillar among the older generation of writers and translators in Gaelic, he makes his home in Kirkcudbrightshire, Scotland.

What Compelled You To Write In Gaelic?

I would say that was my right,
probably Walter Mor's to blame,
dressed up in the Gaelic fashion;
though not mean about the breeches
he went bare-kneed with saffron hippings
shouting 'Up with the Gaelic'
before An Comunn was with us at all,
and posh English coming into fashion
in the big smoky city of Edinburgh
a place that William (Dunbar) much liked
and he saying that one lowland arse
would make a better noise, indeed.

Grumbling down in Galloway,
the habit of yon gallows breed,
muttering and deedling (like a piper)
with my traitor tongue, doubtless,
that has taken a Highland twist.

Scotland

Travelling in Kennedy's country
from 'Carrick to the Cruives o Cree'
if I find no other speakers (of Gaelic)
o horo won't I be joyful
speaking to each tree that's there.

Would it not have been better to spend my powers
writing faultless London English,
so I could get a little poetry book
with clean hard covers on it,
than that I should bring the Carrick clay
to Edinburgh Cross, my dear.

I would not say I came from people
as lordly as the Kennedies,
but farmhands in Culzean,
Morrison, Kellie, Neill and Orr
crying aloud in my veins,
hungry highland ghosts they were,
before braid Scots came in among us
every man and woman had Gaelic –
a pity that it was denied
to Robert (Burns) in that same country.

O horo am I not joyful
to be a relic of the Southern Gaels;
warm Gaelic of Walter Kennedy
between Rathlin and the Isle of Man
between (St. John's Town of) Dalry and Kintyre,
and Ailsa Craig like the jewel
on the boss of the shield of the land of Kennedy
of Bruce, of Angus (of Islay) and of the MacDowalls,
the land of the Bluchbard and Cian,
Rabbie and the Highland Captain,
and if some should complain
that I write too much in Gaelic,
it was Kennedy that pointed the way;
with some eloquence (Gaelic exclamation),
as Gaelic poets use (Gaelic exclamation),
is set my capricious (literary) taste.

Too late now to be twisting
a rough tongue to the accents of London,
but blabbering with my Carrick lips
Gaelic and villain I must bide,
impudent in saffron back and side.

— translated from Scottish Gaelic by the author

Stuth Toirmisgte (Contraband)

Ma bhios mi nam sheasamh
an seo air Oirthir Ghallobha
is urainn dhomhsa fhaicinn Eilean Mhanainn
gorm glan air fàire às an tàinig
an stuth toirmisgte mar bhranndaidh,
sìoda, clàireat, saorsa, Ghàidhlig.

Contraband

If I stand here
on the coast of Galloway
I can see the Isle of Man
clear blue on the horizon,
from whence came
contraband such as brandy,
silk, claret, freedom, Gaelic.

— translated from Scottish Gaelic by the author

Nightmare

When the high tower-blocks fell in the Cities of the Plain
after the withering that came on the people
with disease, poverty, spiritual sickness,
the remainder scattered from each shabby ruin.
There was every chance for the great ones
who grew so rich in Unjust-Mammon-City
to take their gamekeepers
to the empty and extended new grouse-moors.
Now and again a wretch would be found
on the point of starving with hunger, crawling

like a rabbit through bracken,
and who would blame his friend
for putting an end to that kind of misery
with a good-natured shot entirely without malice.

or else . . .

The Great Ones grew fat and sleepy
with luxury, gluttony and sloth,
the captain of the guard drunk every night
believing the wild tribes to be at peace.
The whisperers arose in the mean streets,
lifting every tool that was close to hand,
petrol-bomb, bayonet, knife and scythe.
Bloody bubbles in their jacuzzis
and a heat in the saunas that they had not sought.
The slaves raised up the guillotine
in the Stock Market building.
Heads were seen rolling
under the blind eyes of computers,
and their foolish squeaking was silenced.

I heard an echo, waking in a start of fear:

'The cruelty of men is not imprisoned
within the rusty fences of Belsen.'

— translated from Scottish Gaelic by the author

Graves Of Gold

There are no fish in the Loch of Swans

There are no twigs in the hazel-wood
and no grass on the grassless moors

In the City
men are counting money
that will bury them one day
in graves of gold

— translated from Scottish Gaelic by the author
version by TRC

Clàrsair (Harper)

Ri pongan finealta fonnmhor nan cruit gleusda
is bodhar na suinn an-duigh san t-seòmar àrd;
is feàrr leo geòcaireachd seach amhran bhàrd.
Do chraobh bhrèagh nan teud cha toir iad èisdeachd.

Is liath mo cheann is chan iarrainn a-nis ach ceòl,
coma leam gach call eile ma mhaireas sin;
'nam aonar a' cluinntinn fuaim na clàrsaich binn
san talla a bhoillsgeas le airgead is òr.

Harper

To the delicate harmony of the tuned lyre
the heroes are deaf today in the high room;
they prefer gluttony to the songs of poets.
To the beautiful tree of harps they give no ear.

My head is white and I seek nothing now but music,
I care nothing for the loss of all else if that will endure;
alone and listening to the sweet harp's sound
in the hall that shines with silver and gold.

– translated from Scottish Gaelic by the author

That's Gone And This Has Come

The Gaelic refrain is the same as the title.

I speak just the fine English now,
my own ways left behind;
the good schoolmaster taught me how;
they purified my mind
from the errors of my kind.
Dh'fhalbh sin is thàinig seo.

High in the service of the south
grand words will gain a place;
the subtleties within my mouth
will soon disguise my race,
the poets' ancient grace.

Scotland

Dh'fhalbh sin is thàinig seo.

When there's one speech upon the tongue
they can't tell Fionn from Fred.
Though words remembered, sweetly sung
may echo in the head,
we'll smile and call them dead.
Dh'fhalbh sin is thàinig seo.

— translated from Scottish Gaelic by the author

Iain Crichton Smith
Iain Mac a' Ghobhainn
(1928 –)

Iain Crichton Smith is one of Scotland's most prolific, honored and enduring writers. As an award-winning poet, novelist, short story writer, playwright, critic, translator and film writer in both English and Gaelic, he is the recipient of ten Scottish Arts Council Awards, the PEN Poetry Award, the Scotsman Short Story Prize, the Saltire Award, the Forward Award, the Commonwealth Poetry Prize, as well as awards and prizes for his work in theatre and television. His work has been documented by others in essays, books and biographies. He is the author of thirty volumes of poetry in Gaelic and English, including such titles as *Bìobuill is Sanasan-Reice* (1965), *An t-Eilean is an Canan* (1987), *The Long River* (1955), *Thistles and Roses,* and most recently *Ends and Beginnings* (1994) and *Collected Poems* (1992). A major contributor and mentor to younger writers and to the resurgence of Scottish literature and Gaelic literature in particular, Iain Crichton Smith makes his home in Argyll.

The Clearances

The thistles climb the thatch. Forever
this sharp scale in our poems,
as also the waste music of the sea.

The stars shine over Sutherland
in a cold ceilidh of their own,
as, in the morning, the silver cane

cropped among corn. We will remember this.
Though hate is evil we cannot
but hope your courtier's heels in hell

are burning: that to hear
the thatch sizzling in tanged smoke
your hot ears slowly learn.

— translated from Scottish Gaelic by the author

A' Dol Dhachaidh (Going Home)

Am màireach théid mi dhachaidh do m'eilean
a' fiachainn ri saoghal a chur an dìochuimhn'.
Togaidh mi dòrn de fhearann 'nam làmhan
no suidhidh mi air tulach inntinn
a' coimhead "a' bhuachaill aig an spréidh."

Dìridh (tha mi smaointinn) smeòrach.
Eiridh camhanaich no dhà.
Bidh bàt' 'na laighe ann an deàrrsadh
na gréin iarail: 's bùrn a' ruith
troimh shaoghal shamhlaidhean mo thùir.

Ach bidh mi smaointinn (dh'aindeoin sin)
air an teine mhór th'air cùl ar smuain,
Nagasàki 's Hiroshìma,
is cluinnidh mi ann an rùm leam fhìn
taibhs' no dhà a' sìor-ghluasad,

taibhs' gach mearachd, taibhs' gach cionta,
taibhs' gach uair a ghabh mi seachad
air fear leòint' air rathad clachach,
taibhs' an neonitheachd a' sgrùdadh
mo sheòmar balbh le aodann céin,

gu'm bi an t-eilean mar an àirc
'g éirigh 's a' laighe air cuan mór
's gun fhios an till an calman tuilleadh
's daoine a' bruidhinn 's a' bruidhinn ri chéile
's bogha-froise maitheanais 'nan deuran.

Going Home

Tomorrow I shall go home to my island
trying to put a world into forgetfulness.
I will lift a fistful of its earth in my hands
or I will sit on a hillock of the mind
watching 'the shepherd at his sheep.'

There will arise (I presume) a thrush.
A dawn or two will break.
There will be a boat lying in the glitter
of the western sun: and water running
through the world of similes of my intelligence.

But I will be thinking (in spite of that)
of the great fire at the back of our thoughts,
Nagasaki and Hiroshima,
and I will hear in a room by myself
a ghost or two ceaselessly moving,

the ghost of each error, the ghost of each guilt,
the ghost of each time I walked past
a wounded man on a stony road,
the ghost of nothingness scrutinising
my dumb room with distant face,

till the island becomes an ark
rising and falling on a great sea
and I not knowing whether the dove will return
and men talking and talking to each other
and the rainbow of forgiveness in their tears.

– translated from Scottish Gaelic by the author

Two Songs For A New Ceilidh

When she took the great sea on her
Lewis went away and did not return.
It was not necessary for me to sail
away off to far Australia.

Our Hiroshima is round about me
and Pasternak's book in my hand –
I'll not drink a draught from the spring
of the healthy deer of May

but from water full of eels
electric and shivering on my flesh,
like Venus bursting through the brain
and dark green of the clouds.

But it was the fine bareness of Lewis
that made the work of my head
like a loom full of music
of the miracles and nobility of our time.

•

'Go to London,' they said to me.
'In the great city you will make songs
from the sore hard light of your breast.'
And I strove with myself for many years

thinking of those streets,
men with sharp power in their gaze,
and illuminated glittering taxis
lighting the windows of my mind.

But tonight sitting by the fire
and the hills between me and the sky
listening to the empty silence
and seeing the deer come to my call

I am thinking of another man
who spoke the words that are true:
'Look directly down through wood and wood.
Look in your own heart and write.'

— translated from Scottish Gaelic by the author

Dearcagan (Berries)

Chruinnich sinn dearcagan air feasgar foghair
o chraobhan a bha fàs ris an rathad.
Bha an fheadhainn abaich air cul dheanntagan.
"Dé 's aobhar do seo?" ars thusa.
Bha an latha cho ciùin 's cho bòidheach.
Bha na dearcagan mar chlagan dubha
as nach robh fuaim ag éirigh.
Sheall mi ri mo làmhan: bha iad dearg gu léir
mar gum biodh fuil orra, fuil shoilleir dhearg.
Bha am feasgar cho ciùin 's gun cluinninn do smaointean
's tu a' coiseachd gu faicilleach a-measg dheanntagan
le do bhrògan dearga, le do chasan àrd is geal.

Berries

(for my wife)

We gathered berries on an autumn day
from trees that grew beside the road.
The ripe ones were behind thorns.
"What is the reason for this?" you said.
The day was so calm and beautiful.
The berries were like black bells
from which no sound came.
I looked at my hands: they were entirely red

as if there was blood on them, bright red blood.
The evening was so calm that I could hear your thoughts
as you walked carefully among thorns
with your red boots, with your tall white legs.

— translated from Scottish Gaelic by the author

Young Girl

Young girl that walks
with straight back along the street,
there are baskets of flowers in my breast,
my table is furnished with your laughter.

A woman will say to me, 'There is pride in her walk,'
but I will answer properly,
'Is there pride in the sun in the sky?
Is there jealousy between stone and gold?'

And when a storm goes past
in its own world of wind and rain
will you say 'Pride and arrogance!' to it
that turns forests upside down?

Will you disparage the diamond for its glitter
or the sea for its calm radiance?
There is a white vessel among the ships,
among the black hats there is a crown.

from: **Selection** (To Derick Thomson)

The cuckoo is in the mouth of the hawk.
The chicken is in the mouth of the raven.
The sore wind is in a hurry.

I will not wear my silken coat,
my summer coat, in the bad weather,
and my jester's coat now in pieces.

This century is throwing enough water at us
like that upright coloured bus
that makes hollows in the roadway.

I will not jump from it, it is too fast,
it is pulling the earth topsy turvy,
it is putting welcome and horror on me,

and my hair streaming to that wind
and my white face becoming a diamond
against elegies and hymns

against the *Iolaire* and Holm,
that song among the psalms,
against the blackness and the blue

and we now about our time,
and white fine lights around us,
and Stornoway as small as a pin

and the riddle of the world about us
with no cows seen in the meadow

but a gold hawk in that tall sky
like God looking in a mirror.

— translated from Scottish Gaelic by the author

The Letter

Here is my letter to you out of the mirror,
God who created us.

Why did you put the rabbits in the bellies of the foxes?
Why did you put man in the middle of the days?
Why did you raise us with frail bones?

Why did you give us hearts
that will feel hubbub and injustice,
why aren't they like watches
small, round, and golden?

Why did you leave the eagle alone
in a nest of clouds
hanging from ropes
transfixed by nails?

Why did you not make angels or beasts of us
with cold wings, with barbarous heads?
Why did you raise the sea in front of us
with wide absurd face?

In the mirror
there is a boxer's face,
in the mirror
there is a rusty helmet.

In the mirror there is your book with a steel fastening,
with an edge red as a rose.

In the mirror there is one rose,
our hope growing
red, shaking in the winds,
in a circle of dew.

— translated from Scottish Gaelic by the author

from: **Oban**

2

Shall I raise a town of paper?
With coloured lions on the wall?
With great fierce tigers,
and the wheel of music spinning?

Shall I raise a sky of paper?
Clouds of paper, white lights?
Shall I make myself into paper,
with my verses being cut on paper?

3

Tonight the sea is like an advertisement,
book after book shining.
My shadow is running down to the sea.
My skin is red and green.

Who wrote me? Who is making a poetry
of advertisements from my bones?
I will raise my blue fist to them:
'A stout Highlander with his language.'

— translated from Scottish Gaelic by the author

Aonghas MacNeacail
(1942 -)

Aonghas MacNeacail was born in 1942 in Uig on the Isle of Skye. As one of the most widely known 60s generation Gaelic writers in Scotland, he is a poet, journalist, researcher, broadcaster, scriptwriter and filmmaker. He has published collections of poems in both Gaelic and English, including, most recently, *Rock and Water* by Polygon. His poems have appeared in most Scottish literary journals and in many international magazines from Australia to America, Switzerland, Italy, Belgium, Croatia, Finland, Israel, and Spain as well as in various Irish, Welsh, and English publications. He has lectured and performed his own work in North America, Japan, Poland, Germany, Belgium, Croatia, Israel and Ireland. In commemoration of the centenary (1991) of Caithness novelist Neil Gunn, he edited *A Writers' Ceilidh,* an anthology of contemporary Highland writers.

A recipient of several fellowships and teaching and lecturing residencies in various universities across Scotland, he has also collaborated with a wide range of artists and musicians on albums with such musician/recording artists as the Capella Nova choir as well as contemporary operatic productions with such composers as Alasdair Nicolson. His writing for theatre includes short pieces for 7.84's *Long Story Short* and Eden Court's *The Hielanman's Umbrella,* and his first full-length theatre piece, *Atoms of Delight.* Television and film script credits include documentaries such as *Ceòl Mòr* (The Big Music) and *Craobh an Eòlais* (A Tree of Knowledge) as well as scripts for the Gaelic serial drama *Machair* as aired on Scottish television. His radio writing includes *Sound The Pibroch, Sgathach* and *Driven West* – a telling of a Highland family's involvement with the American saga of the Cherokee "Trail of Tears."

His most recent collection of Gaelic poetry is *Oideachadh Ceart* (A Proper Schooling; Polygon, 1997). His short film *An Iobairt* (The Sacrifice) directed by his wife, the actress Gerda Stevenson, was commissioned by BBC Scotland. He currently makes his home just outside of Edinburgh, traveling back and forth to the Isle of Skye and his teaching position at the Gaelic College.

the gàidhlig beò (gaelic is alive)

mar chuimhneachan air caitlín maude

cuireamaid an dàrna taobh
obair an là an-diugh
dèan dannsa ri
port-a-beul na gaoithe

"tha gàidhlig beò"
a dh'aindeoin gach saighead
's i streap nan sìthean
fiùran daraich fo h-achlais
a sùilean dùbhlanach
a' sìneadh gu fàire fad' as
's i sireadh na fàire fad' as
lasair-bhuan leugach 'na broilleach

'n aire nach gabh i sùrdag ro bhras

ach dèan dannsa dèan dannsa
's e obair a th'ann a bhith dannsa

gaelic is alive

in memoriam caitlín maude

let's put aside
today's work
and dance to
the wind's port–a–beul

"gaelic is alive"
despite all arrows
she climbs the hillside
sapling of oak in her arms
her defiant eyes
reaching the far-off horizon
she aims for the far-off horizon
a bright lasting star in her breast

defend her from too bold a leap

but be dancing be dancing
it is work to be dancing

– translated from Scottish Gaelic by the author

249

flags

when you smell the motion of bluebells
when you hear a hoofmark honeycomb
after long summer grasses are scythed
and a fist of angry bees guards their labours
you know that industry is various, you know
you're not standing in the immediate
vicinity of the sheen of granite flags
(here flags are green, are stalk and leaf
have heads of gold, pale gold susceptible
to winds, machines and seasons)
while you're not here, you know the
level granite flags you walk were
cut from hillsides such as these,
the gaping hole in great ben X is
all the streets you walk, the bridges
underpasses, viaducts, the shortcuts
shady places, towerblocks, the flyovers,
the shoals of rushed and isolate
humanity that's sitting with the radio
on, listening to conversations between
(fluid eloquence) the voices of sharp
talkshow hosts and tinny callers speaking
down the line from elsewhere, down
the distant instant meet the people
be familiar on the airwaves, never
really meeting, phone-in line,
beyond the glass are factories
which manufacture memories
and echoes, silage, rust, you
cannot ask the pavingstones to be
a mountain once again, and time
will only hold the past you've
etched in flame upon your
mapping point or else this
could be any where, or when,
(the purse of history snapped
shut) a pattern discontinued,
there's a language here that sings

with fragrant accents of grasses,
heathers, brackens, that's shaped
by the distance or nearness of
oceans, how steep are the
hillsides, where rocks overhang –
where birches grow tall
spring is blue underfoot, slow
vowels are honeyed with laughter
every field gracenoted by bees

– translated from Scottish Gaelic by the author

in the season when crocuses

in the season when crocuses
raise peaceful spears of colour
and the doves still
peck at old bread
and always the anguished faces
dumb, in the ravenous windows of televisions
indifferent to the eyes watching them
through those voracious windows
and the eyes are ground smooth
being so used to the pitiful scenes
and the stock-market reports
and the hit-parades
and the burdensome days of princes
and footballs in orbit,
the doves are so glutted they cannot move
with the kindness of old women
and see the crocus opening
a cup of hope,
but wait till it fills – is it
wine, is it blood

– translated from Scottish Gaelic by the author

an aimhreit (the contention)

tha caolas eadarainn a-nochd
mis' air m'eilean, thus' air d'eilean-sa.
aon fhacal bhuat, a luaidh, is buailidh
mi le ràimh mar sgiathan sgairbh na tuinn.
bidh eòlas eadarainn a-nochd

the contention

there's a kyle between us tonight
i on my island, you on yours.
one word from you, love, and i'll beat
with oars like scart's wings the waves.
there'll be accord between us tonight.

— translated from Scottish Gaelic by the author

gleann fadamach (glen remote)

plèan a' dol tarsainn
cho àrd 's nach cluinnear i
long a' dol sìos an cuan
ach fada mach air fàire

cuid dhen t-saoghal
a' siubhal 's a' siubhal

sa bhaile seo,
chan eileas a' siubhal ach an aon uair
's na clachan a rinn ballaichean
a' dol 'nan càirn

glen remote

plane crossing
so high it can't be heard
ship going down the ocean
far out on the horizon

a part of the world
travelling travelling

in this village
people only travel once
and the stones that made walls
become cairns

— translated from Scottish Gaelic by the author

dèanamh ime (making butter)

chan eil a shamhla ann —
tionnadadh 's a' tionndadh a ghilead òrach
am broinn dorcha na h–eanchainn
ag éisdeachd ri suirghe is
dealachadh is pòsadh
nan lid luasganach leaghtach
ag éisdeachd airson nam boinne
blàthaich a' sileadh air falbh o
ghramalas òrbhuidhe dàin

making butter

there's nothing like it —
turning and turning the golden whiteness
inside the darkness of the brain
listening to the wooings and
partings and weddings
of soluble tossed–about syllables
listening for the drops
of buttermilk trickling away from
the golden-yellow firmness of a poem

— translated from Scottish Gaelic by the author

man has been

man has been
making
an orderly garden
ever
    since —

Scotland

now
what remains
of the wilderness

— translated from Scottish Gaelic by the author

shamanic song

o
staying here
travelling while
staying here
o

— translated from Scottish Gaelic by the author

Myles Campbell
Maoilios M. Caimbeul
(1944 –)

Maoilios M. Caimbeul/Myles Campbell was born in Staffin, Isle of Skye in 1944. He graduated from Edinburgh University in 1976 and after qualifying as a Gaelic teacher, he taught in the Isle of Mull for a number of years. He now lives in Skye and teaches and writes. A winner of Scottish Arts Council Bursaries, his collections of poetry are *Eileanan* (Glasgow University Celtic Department, 1980), *Bailtean* (Gairm, 1987), *A' Càradh an Rathaid / Ag Coíriú an Róid* (Coiscéim, 1988) and *A' Gabhail Ris* (Gairm, 1994). *Bailtean* has facing translations in English. Selections of his verse also appear in various anthologies such as *An Aghaidh na Sìorraidheachd* (Polygon, 1991) and *Scotland o Gael an Lawlander* (Gairm, 1996), which is a collection unified under the symbol of the village – whether it is the village of love, of old age, or of desolation. This book is unusual in that it has facing translations in Scots rather than in English. (It being almost the done thing nowadays for Gaelic poetry collections to have facing translations in English.) Campbell has also published several novels and adventure stories for children, including *Clann a' Phroifeasair* (Gairm, 1988) and *A Ulbha gu Geelong* (Acair, 1992).

To Any Lewisman

Now that we have NATO,
buy a gun!
If one day you are in the moor
and you see the sky flaming
with an unnatural light,
do not look to Stornoway
but fall on your stomach in the peat-bog,
covering your eyes and skin.
Wait until the heatwave is past
and the wind decreases.
Do not look at the fireball.

Run home.
Fetch the gun from the closet
and start with the youngest child.
If a neighbour should come half-roasted
wanting a loan, be kind.
Then kill your wife,
the cattle, the dog, the cat and anything
that you love.
But save a bullet for yourself.
You wouldn't want to see
the world as it dies
and turns to stone.

Note – *Of the Iolaire disaster Norman MacDonald says, "The tragedy of the sinking of the Iolaire in the Hebrides on New Year's morning 1919 ranks with the great disasters of the world in its appalling inclusiveness. Within minutes, one hundred and eighty-one men from a small island community were wiped out on the shores they called home. They had survived the World War and were coming home at last."*

– translated from Scottish Gaelic by the author / TRC

I Remember Death

I remember death.
My father would put on his black coat
and polish his shoes
and come home with
the earth on his soles.

And again at a funeral
the people standing around
with question in their eyes,
bowing their heads.
There was always a prayer
for death not to touch
my father and mother,
and there is still.

What can I say
but that the home is empty
and the grave full
and the wind blows
over the foot of the croft,
like a mystery
or the only One who knows.

– translated from Scottish Gaelic by the author / TRC

An Clamhan (The Buzzard)

Muile nam monaidheam farsaing
agus nam bailtean gun daoine;
an clamhan air chaithris 'na rìoghachd
ag èisdeachd ri beul-aithris na gaoithe.

The Buzzard

Mull of the spacious moors
and the deserted towns;
the buzzard wakes.
Listening to the oral tradition of the wind.

— translated from Scottish Gaelic by the author / TRC

Sea Emperor

The emperor is nude
in the new world;
beside the sea
he listens for the beat of the waves,
placing shells to his ear
for the least thrum from Fujiyama,
rising pap-like from a body
lost in the mist of myth.

The heat of the sun,
on my bald pate
and the bronze gods gone.
Why don't you believe
I'm a god
and Amaterasu's land holy
with the miracles of Mitsubishi?

— translated from Scottish Gaelic by the author

Cànan (Language)

Siùrsach is òigh
's tu agam an seo
ga do dhealbh
ga mo dhealbh.
Pògan naomh agus aingidh
thugad is bhuat
anns an dorcha,
anns an t-solas,
thu a' cruthachadh
mar as miann leat
fada o m' mhiann.
'S cò aig' tha fhios
dè thig asad –
an e ùrnaigh, dàn,
no òrdugh bàis
ann am Belsen.

Language

Whore, virgin
with me here
making you
making me.
Holy, wicked
kisses
given and received
in the dark
in the light
you create
as you wish
far from my desire.
And who knows
what you'll produce –
prayer, poem,
or a death warrant
in Belsen.

– translated from Scottish Gaelic by the author

Fearghas MacFhionnlaigh
(1948 –)

"I was born in 1948 in the Vale of Leven at the southern end of Loch Lomond. We emigrated to Canada when I was three. I enjoyed my boyhood in rural Ontario, initially at a place called The Willows, and then at Forest Stream Park (one winter recess my lips stuck to the outside brick-wall of the school – Cherrywood Public). I remember the birds – chickadees, bluejays, cardinals, the Baltimore oriole, the cedar waxwing, the indigo bunting. Scottish species are just wee brown things in comparison. The space of Canada, like Scotland, still inhabits my head. A mental space of uncharted distances. An elemental space of wood and snow and creek and sky. We returned to the 'Vale' in 1958. In my early teens political awareness dawned on me with the self-evident fact that Scotland should be an independent republic. This remains as obvious to me yet as the sky is blue. Gaelic wasn't taught (or mentioned) at school, and apart from some token Burns, neither was Lallans. It struck me as odd and then increasingly outrageous that we were being schooled almost entirely in the language and literature of another country. I saw how language to an alarming extent predetermines and sets the parameters of thought. I saw the totalitarianism of English, whatever its speakers' nationality. Had not Scotland two languages of its own? I would declare a republic of the mind. I chose radical 'opaque' Gaelic rather than the more pellucid Lallans, which blends into and out of English. Some do find the energy to use both. I observed that the surrounding placenames were Gaelic. I discovered that the people who gave their name to Scotland were Gaelic-speaking. Teutonic tongues were doing quite well, thank you very much. Nowadays I am as much motivated by the belief that all languages are the resource of all men. If Celtic speech dies from the face of the Earth, we all stand to lose. Human thought will have that bit less room for maneuver. In 1967 I went to Art College in Dundee. Since 1974 I have taught art in Inverness. Currently I am also teaching a bit of Gaelic-medium art, though as the government is declining to support Gaelic-medium initiatives in high schools, the future for this is uncertain. I am married (to Mary) with two children (Cara, 12, and Ciaran, 14 – both Gaelic-speaking). My first book published was a children's novel – *Cò Ghoid am Bogha-Froise? / Who Stole the Rainbow?* (Celtic Department, Glasgow University, 1978). Two other long poem-sequences have been A' *Mheanbhchuileag* / *The Midge* (Gairm, 1980), and *Iolair, Brù-Dhearg, Giuthas* / *Eagle, Robin, Pine* (Glasgow University, 1991). The bilingual group-anthology *An Aghaidh na Sìorraidheachd* / *In the Face of Eternity* (Polygon, 1991) has some shorter poems. I have received a Scottish Arts Council bursary. I have also taken part in two SAC-sponsored poetry-reading tours of Ireland. *Bogha-Frois san Oidhche/Rainbow in the Night* will be my next book, which is forthcoming from Handsel Press, Musselburgh."

from: **Eagle, Robin, Pine**

for Catherine Nugent

1
From beyond the sunrise I have come,
from beyond the mountains of the mind,
from horizon to horizon my eyes scan, my wings span.

I am transcendent Truth which strikes from on high
and bites to the bone. I am ungraspable.
I am Eagle.

2
From within the garden I have come,
from within the arboretum of the heart,
from hedgerow to hedgerow I flit, I sit.

I am immanent Truth. Though I am homely
you yet delight in me. I am indomitable.
I am Robin.

3
From beneath the fibrous forest floor,
from beneath the radix of the brain,
from generation to generation the sap flows, and grows.

We are incarnate Truth. We are the transient form
the content takes. We are uncountable.
We are Pine-needles.

4
The Pine-tree represents Time.
The needles are numberless watch-hands
or silently cascading grains of sand.

The Robin represents Now:
intimate but elusive. No needle escapes
the compass of his concentrating eye.

The Eagle represents Eternity.
It is he who shakes the Tree.
He is the beginning and the end of the Circle.

5
The Eagle senses the Robin
The Robin senses the Fir-tree/Coffin.
The Fir-tree pines.

The Eagle burgeons from an upper bough.
The Pine-tree trembles to each earth-bound tip.
The Robin attends the tear-shed green.

6
Above the grief –
Belief.
This is the spiralling Circle of the Eagle.

Within the pain –
Human chain.
This is the inner Circle of the Robin.

Beneath the loss –
Forgotten dross.
This is the age-old Circle of the Pine.

7
Darkness. Doing 65 on the highway to Dumbarton.
Beethoven's 7th fills the car. The 2nd Movement.
The air pulsates with slow insistent eagle-wings of sound.

10
Thank God for Beethoven on the road to Dumbarton.
The wings broad.
The talon sharp and precise.

35
The night is black. My car is white.
Beethoven's scalpel opens a parturient red mouth in my breast.
Gives sudden Caesarean birth to my grief.

I hear the infant howling, howling, howling.
Howling for the Mother
who is dead.

55
The pistol-shot of a frost-bitten pine
splitting in the snow-stunned forest.
But who will hear my breaking heart?

57
My car is white. My breast is red.
A window opens. I am by your bed.
A door. I flutter in the Face of God.

— translated from Scottish Gaelic by the author

Angus Peter Campbell
(1954 –)

Angus Peter Campbell is a native Gaelic speaker originally from the islands off the west coast of Scotland, where he lives today in Sleat on the Isle of Skye. As a Scottish Gaelic language poet he is the author of two books of poetry: *The Greatest Gift* (1992) and *One Road* (1994), both from Fountain Publishing. He is also the editor of *Somhairle: Dàin is Deilbh* (A Celebration on the 80th Birthday of Sorley MacLean) published by Acair in 1991. His poems, such as "Suisinish" and "The Dump, Outside Portree" are indicative of his allegiance to place and the powers that have invaded the life, culture and landscape of his western Highlands homeland.

from: Suisinish

The morning light is a mirror.
My speculations are mythological.
Across the sound,
a film-crew is putting away their gear.
My history has been digitalised.
The Clearances, like electricity and the angels,
have been reduced to the film essentials:
it is all stones and flames and emptiness.

They have not recorded anything.
The wind that I suspected
has risen again and is keening,
like a dying child,
across the firth:
it has your name on it,
and mine,
lighting and extinguishing a million Suisinish fires.

– translated from Scottish Gaelic by the author
version by TRC

The Dump, Outside Portree

Seagulls,
scavenging,
above broken washing-machines and smashed mirrors.

A child's pram,
askew,
a torn rubber tyre.

A doll without a head,
a spade without a shaft,
a car without doors.

Filament-nets protect debris from the circling crows
who have their eyes on a fish-bone beside the headless doll.

Is this my country?
A dump of nets and headless doors.
A mirror of jaded light, the rusted wars –

– translated from Scottish Gaelic by the author
version by TRC

Landseer

The older I get
the more I want my terrible country
to resemble a Landseer landscape:
all dewy-eyed Highland cattle and moody Ossianic lochs,
as if the people all lived in misty reverie.

And no wonder I want this,
for I have seen the best blood of my generation
poured out in the bars of Glasgow,
one dissolute generation removed from actual starvation.
Goddammit, I want them to be blissful in a painting,
as if clearance and despoliation and the loss of their language
had never taken place,
as if all these horrors were in another painting,
Guernica, say, or my wife's painting of savage Dundee.

But, alas,
Strathnaver is Guernica
and each empty glen the real version of cardboard city
praying for a Gaelic Picasso to tear the fundaments apart
with the fierce anger of God.

— translated from Scottish Gaelic by the author

Consumerism

It's not that my grandfather wasn't a consumer.

Without a telly,
or even a wireless, or the Internet,
he toyed with old addictions:
his clay pipe, lobster-fishing, and going to the Mod.

Or, a generation further back,
my great-grandfather
(just before he was cleared to Canada),
kelp-gathering, soldiering, and dying at Culloden.

Window shopping,
the hunter-gatherers were dazzled by wooden spears
as my own children are dazzled by Barbie's latest gear.

— translated from Scottish Gaelic by the author

The Highlands

Acre after bloody acre of it lies empty,
as if the millions weren't dying in Bombay.

As you drive north,
the desolation, of course, becomes ever more beautiful,
as if you were impregnating Snow White
and suddenly discovered that she was still miraculously alive.

On bright summer days,
it hoards so much beauty
that it seems to have no other purpose,
much like the glass buildings of Manhattan.

Scotland

It offers so many wonderful mirages.
When you see Suilven in August
it is as if MacCaig were alive again,
dram in hand on Rose Street, the Festival in full swing.

But the braes of Glenelg,
the steeples of Kintail,
the great piobroch of the Cuillin
are like shrouds covering the dead,
blankets of splendour flung over so much horror,
for the world is not empty without reason.

For men have evicted men,
and men have raped women,
and men have murdered children
to leave such a grave silence,
like a kirkyard on an eternal Sabbath.

– translated from Scottish Gaelic by the author

Siùsaidh NicNèill
(1955 –)

After Secondary (High) School, Siùsaidh NicNèill went on to study drama at Queen Margaret College in Edinburgh. It was at this time she first started to write poetry and short stories. From there she went on to work in various roles in television in both London and Glasgow until 1982 when she returned to the Isle of Lewis in the Outer Hebrides. After a number of years freelancing in television, radio and newspapers, she was given a full-time job as a producer on the Isle of Skye with ABU-Tele, a Gaelic language production company. During this time her poems started to appear fairly regularly in anthologies and in 1996 her first collection, called *All My Braided Colours*, was published by Scottish Cultural Press as part of the *Scottish Contemporary Poets* series. She writes in both English and Gaelic and currently is living and writing in her little house by the shores of Lewis. Together with activist Iain Sinclair she has been working with the Wounded Knee Survivors Association in Pine Ridge, South Dakota to have a Ghost Dance Shirt repatriated from Glasgow Museum to its rightful resting place in the United States.

Dannsair Taibhse (Ghost Dancer)

Ca' bheil thu, mo laoch?
A bheil d'anam lom
rach air seachran gu fuarachadh,
spealachadh am measg taighean àrd,
a'ranail airson na gleanntan àrd
den Cnocan Dubha coisrigte.

Cùm do làmh dhearg a leigeil fuil
gu h-àrd,
ag aslaich An Athair Speur.
Tha do bhroilleach athailteach
la Dannsa fo Greinne
nighe gu uallach ann an soilleir taibhsearachd.

Scotland

Agus far an suidhicheadh
iteag bho sgiath seabhaic
air an aite cridheil, uaine
bidh oraid seachad
bidh do spioraid sgeadaich,
thig thu dhachaidh
agus cha chaill sinn càil
ach an eòlas aoibhneach
gur bha thu a'fuireach nam measg
airson ceud bliadhna.

Dannsair taibhse!

Ghost Dancer

Where are you, warrior?
Does your naked soul
Still wander coldly,
Shivering between high tenements,
Crying for the high canyons
Of the sacred Black Hills?

Hold your bleeding red hand
Upwards, supplicating Father Sky.
Your Sun Dance scarred chest
Proudly bathed in the ghostly light
And when a feather from the hawk's wing
Settles on that green place I love
Talk will be done,
Spirit will be clothed,
You will come home
And we will have lost nothing
But the joy of knowing
You lived among us
For a hundred years.

Ghost dancer!

— translated from Scottish Gaelic by the author

Wanagi Waci Kin (Lakota version)

Mita Akicita kin toki ilala huwo.
Ninagi kin nahanhci hacola sniyel omayani huwo.

Tiwankatuya kin agna ncancan huwo.
Paha Sapa kin iguga
wankatuy i
kin oweyeceya huwo.

Ninape kin w eyeals e laguate,
na wakan tanka hoy yakiye.
Maku kin osnaze niyuke,
Wayaci kihe un,
na cetan hupahauhwanji wahwayela hinhpay iyecel,
kin hehan wooglake kin hena inajin kte,
eyes, wonhahun waste kihe waniyetu opawinge unkiciyaun.

Rody Gorman
(1960 –)

Rody Gorman was born in Dublin in 1960, but migrated to Scotland early on to become fluent in Scottish Gaelic. A student of the Gaelic poet Meg Bateman, and one of the Gaelic Resurgency's younger voices, his book of Scottish Gaelic poems *Fax and other poems* was published by Polygon in Edinburgh in 1996. He is currently awaiting the publication of his first book written in Irish Gaelic (*Bealach Garbh*). He is a former Director of Sabhal Mòr Ostaig, the Gaelic College, on the Isle of Skye and now lives on Isle Ornsay on Skye.

Oraid (Lecture)

Chaidh mi a dh'èisdeachd ri òraid
Ann an Tall' a' Bhaile nochd
Air dol air ais an dualchais againn

'S fhad 's a bha fear na h-òraid a' cur dheth
'S ann a dh'èirich gaoth làidir
'S bhris an uinneag mhòr,
A bha mar thaic ris, air feadh an làir
Na sgionabhagan

'S dh'èirich a h-uile mac màthar
'S thòisich iad air na basan a bhualadh.

Lecture

I went to a lecture
In the village hall tonight
About the decay of our culture

And while the lecturer was spouting off
A strong wind rose up
And the big window,

Which was supporting him,
Broke in smithereens all over the floor

And everybody stood up
And started applauding.

— translated from Scottish Gaelic by the author

Glainead (Purity)

Chaidh do ghlainead a chur nam chuimhne
Nuair a sheall mi mach air an uinneig reòthta sa mhadainn
'S an aon lèine gheal a th' agam a' tiormachadh ann an shin
Na sneachda air feadh Aird Shlèite.

Purity

I was reminded of you
When I looked out the frozen window this morning
With my one white shirt drying out there on the line
Like snow covering the Aird of Sleat.

— translated from Scottish Gaelic by the author

Gaelic

Someone's wife died in the village
With loads of Gaelic
Unbeknownst to herself:

It was no great surprise
The day of her funeral
That there wasn't a sound on our lips
But the apposite silence
Suiting her speech forever.

— translated from Scottish Gaelic by the author / TRC

Two Loves

My two loves
Are sometimes two beautiful swans
Swimming in Loch an Tuim

And other times
Two work horses
Tearing me apart.

— translated from Scottish Gaelic by the author

Separation

We split up
After sitting in the pub all night

And afterwards
I walked home on my own

And there I was,
Walking on my own, full of thoughts,

That weighed on my heart
(And also my bladder)

After I took a piss
I felt better.
Aye, just fine.

— translated from Scottish Gaelic by the author / TRC

Beside The North Sea

I walked beside the road
Beside the North Sea
In the dark

I have forgotten you
Like the receding tide
Or a haar on the water
Like senility

Broken and clarity born like memory
Like light
From an oilrig on a distant shore.

— translated from Scottish Gaelic by the author / TRC

Anne Frater
(1967 –)

Anne Frater, born in 1967 on the Isle of Lewis and raised in the community of Bayble before leaving to go to Glasgow and Glasgow University in 1985, is one of the more prominent Gaelic poets of the younger generation. Graduating with a degree in Celtic and French in 1990, she went on to train as a secondary school teacher of Gaelic and French at Jordanhill College in Glasgow 1990-1991. She took her Ph.D. in Celtic (Scottish Gaelic Women's Poetry up to 1750) from Glasgow University in 1995, and is currently working in television as a researcher, subtitler and location dialogue supervisor. Her work has been published in many Scottish literary journals such as *Gairm*, *Verse*, *Chapman*, and in anthologies: *An Aghaidh na Siorraidheachd* (Polygon, 1991), *An Anthology of Scottish Women Poets* (Edinburgh University Press, 1991), *Siud an t-Eilean* (Acair, 1993) and *Dream State* (Polygon, 1994). The first collection of her own work, *Fon t-Slige / Under the Shell* was published in 1995 by Gairm. She lives in Glasgow.

Aghaidh Choimheach (Mask)

A' coimhead dhan sgàthan
chan aithnich mi mi-fhìn:
aghaidh choimheach a' sealltainn a-mach
le gàire air an t-saoghal;
tè nach aithnich mi a' gluasad
's a' còmhradh ri daoine,
a' dannsa 's a' seinn gun chùram;
tè a fhuair seachad ort,
tè a tha slàn.

Ach ma thogas tu an aghaidh choimheach
tha tèile ri 'faicinn,
tè le sùilean falamh
a tha 'lorg a' ghaoil a lion iad;
tè a tha 'càradh a slige
mus tig tuilleadh pian;
tè a tha a' feuchainn ri a h-aghaidh choimheach
a dhèanamh fìor.

Mask

Looking in the mirror
I do not recognize myself:
a false face reflected
laughing at the world;
one I do not know
moving and conversing,
singing and dancing without care;
she is over you,
she is whole.

But if you lift the mask
you will see the other one,
one whose empty eyes are searching
for the love that filled them;
one who is mending her shell
in case more pain comes;
one who is trying to make the false face
real.

— translated from Scottish Gaelic by the author

Glasgow

They scrubbed your face well:
the dirt of centuries scraped
and swept away
with sandy soap;
and your dark head is now
red and fair and lovely.

Mould still grows
on your walls,
but who cares . . . ?
As long as nobody looks inside you
they will not see the cancer
that is festering;
they will not see the wretchedness
behind the gleaming windows,
hiding in your deceiving eyes.

And when your beauty dazzles us
and your merit entices us
never mind about the holes
in the soles of your shoes.

— translated from Scottish Gaelic by the author

She Was Beaten Again Last Night

She was beaten again last night.
Two black eyes and a broken arm
as payment for her love.
But it wasn't him who did it!
It was the drink that made him
raise his fist
and leave its mark
on her face.
And it was her fault –
his food had grown cold
as she waited for his return
from the pub.

She shouldn't have let the fire
go out.

The police came
again,
and she told them everything;
the tears of years pouring out of her,
her life unravelling at her feet
leaving her naked
on their notebooks.
She saw the bruises on her mind
and promised that she would break
away from his brutality
and that she would have a new life,
free
clean
and whole.

But all the same
when he came with a blanket
and the warm words of regret,
with excuses and lies,
she believed him
and went home with him
as always
one more time.

– translated from Scottish Gaelic by the author

The Cry Of The Bear

He broke your chains
but he did not cut your claws,
and, his heart in his mouth,
he left you in the woods,
in the darkness.

The eagle circled above your head
and the lion was waiting.

You put your claws to use,
and you ripped the red star
out of your forehead.
Amazed, you saw the blood
pouring out,
until it made you blind.

The eagle circled overhead
and the lion came closer . . .
his tongue hanging out.

And then the pain.
You had not imagined that the ripping
of the star that pinched you
would leave you so wounded,
so bloody,
so pained;
and you did not understand
that it would heal.
A red mist filled your mind
and you started with your claws
to rip your fur,
tearing your own flesh;
and your terrible cries
shook the forest.

The eagle stopped circling
and the lion had fear in his eyes.

— translated from Scottish Gaelic by the author

(Kernow)
CORNWALL

CORNISH

Cornish

Outcroppings of granite punctuate the Cornish landscape. Immense volcanic forces are bound up in dense, taut crags able to face any storm. And yet, geologists tell us, these ragged piles are woven from an unimaginably fine fabric, jewel-like beneath the microscope. What if the forces within such a weave of gems were released? This same question faces poets writing in the Cornish language. Emerging from the parent Brittonic some fifteen hundred years ago, Cornish clung tenaciously to its territory as invader after invader swept in. It only ceased to be a community vernacular towards the end of the eighteenth century, leaving an attenuated oral tradition and a manuscript legacy. In that span of time it had produced verse drama, lyric, prose narrative, religious polemic, grammar and rhetoric.

Scholars began to merge the oral and manuscript traditions in the second half of the nineteenth century. The fusing engendered a renewal of poetic activity. In this phase, lasting into the 1970s, Cornish was a classical language, learnt from texts and confined to elevated domains such as ritual and literature. Henry Jenner made the Age of Saints, the Arthurian matter and pre-industrial life the central themes of his work. R. Morton Nance added folklore and a commitment to Celtic kinship. These two men set the tone of Cornish poetry for generations, distancing it from the contemporary Cornwall of declining industries and schismatic Methodism. Too much of the poetry was trite and slipshod, and far too much still is so. But three people heralded change. In the 1940s, Peggy Pollard composed witty and erudite verse dramas parodying forms and conventions of the classical period, but dealing with existential themes of belief, integrity and feminism. A.S.D. Smith wrought anew in Cornish the great story of Tristan and Isolde. Edwin Chirgwin was writing meditatively on personal themes, introducing an almost colloquial tone. In the next decade, two men began poetic careers still innovating and astonishing. Personal themes of love and loss enabled Richard Gendall to experiment with free verse. With his broad vision of the nation's place in humanity and nature, he was able to create songs now irrevocably part of the popular repertoire. An existential crisis about the nature of the Cornish language compelled him to repudiate the entire body of his work during the 1980s. Since then, he has begun to write again, in a new diction and with a quiet, stoical tone. Tony Snell began to experiment with the tight discipline and demanding techniques of early Celtic poetry. He fell silent during the 1960s, subsequently returning with the additional craft of song. In the next decade, he created an integral vision of the personal, the national and the universal. Silent again during the 1980s, he has now turned to terse narrative poems with a taut dramatic structure. Where Gendall provided the *naïve Dichtung* of Schiller's formulation, Snell provided the *sentimentalische*. It is as if Villon and Boileau were contemporaries. The two men provided a starting point for what followed: During the 1960s, Nicholas Williams wrote lyric and verse drama with strong patriotic and religious themes. Discouraged by the language's continued demographic failure, he drifted away. However, Cornish began to function as a vernacular once more from the mid-1970s. Common daily experience of the language deepened all the perceptions as the language entered a phase similar to that of Hebrew a hundred years earlier. Graham Sandercock made himself the master of *chanson,* causing people to recognize with sudden delight the corners and passageways of their own lives. Brian Webb's tragic life bore a rich crop of lyric and song, with a deep anger adding colour and pungency. Tim Saunders, taking Gendall and Snell as his starting point, explored a wide range of themes in every possible mood. Pol Hodge attacked the present crisis of Cornish society with rough-edged vocal vigour. Katrina Waters cut finely-proportioned corners of steadily increasing scale, a feminist sensibility informing her vision.

Attempting further freedom from invaders, Cornish is now running free, unrestrainable by any of the competing schools of thought. Differences of orthography encourage wild accusations of political and religious deviation, but much energy is released to vivify the renewed vernacular. Colloquialisms add depth and colour to the delicate language of poetry. As the last exponents of the decayed school of Jenner and Nance reach the end of their careers, Cornish poetry loses the last remains of self-consciousness, and attacks its proper tasks with renewed vigour.

− Tim Saunders

Richard Gendall
(1924 –)

"My father, starting as a blacksmith's apprentice in Penzance, became ordained, and Rector of the Turks and Caicos islands, where I was born on 12th April 1924. The family resettled in St Blazey in 1926; I grew up there, at St Winnow, than at St Stephen, Lanson. I was sent to St John's Leatherhead, leaving in 1942, then spent six months studying harmony under Gerald Knight. In the autumn I entered Leeds University; in March 1943 joined the Navy, serving on the destroyer *HMS Offa*, then with a commission on major landing craft. I re-entered Leeds in 1946, studied Modern Languages, Music and History, and qualified as a teacher. Teaching first in Barbados, with incurably itchy feet I moved to Lanson College (twice), Middlesex, the London Nautical School, New Zealand (three times), Bramley, Romsey, Penryn, Helston (twice), in Cornwall living at St Stephens, Egloskerry, Redruth, Gwinear by turns. My mother taught me my first Cornish when I was four. As early as I can recall, I was deeply affected by music, boats, wildlife, home, the latter developing into a passionate awareness of Cornish identity. I was writing songs and tunes from the age of nine. In 1970 Brenda Wootton took an interest in singing my Cornish songs, which triggered intense activity resulting in some 400 songs and as many unused melodies, and two folk operas. I was the first Chief Moderator of the Cornish language for the CSE. I founded Teere ha Tavaz, a language and heritage research group, in 1986, and the Cornish Language Council in 1987. I retired in 1981 to devote myself to my boat, trees, and music. Most of my time is now spent researching and writing about modern Cornish, and tending my self-planted woodland which is managed as a wildlife reserve."

Vor Wella Dena Oyow (How To Suck Eggs)

Whathe mouy edn Sows seeandgack!
Dew! Thur peleah iggans toaze?
Ree gwase en'gye ha gadgack
En powe go hunnen tha voaze
Dressans neb subban wheelas
Than goth angye, dreth treegas
Mesk teeze judgez behatna,
Andelha omweele broaza?

Ree leadan Powe an Sausen,
Ha kellez whathe en Worthen,
Resta credgy dreze neb poll
Hunz ubma ha broaza fooell
Itna tha hunnen gwellas,
Gorthez gen leeas meeras?

Kee trea, Sows bean, tothda,
Haake esta treegas ubma,
Ha desky theth henvabmow
VOR WELLA DENA OYOW!

How To Suck Eggs

Yet another conceited Englishman!
God! Where do they come from?
Too insignificant and sickly
In their own country to be
That they should seek some sop
To their pride, through dwelling
Among people adjudged lesser.
Thus make themselves greater?

Too wide England,
And yet lost in Ireland,
Didst thou think that there is some pool
Down here, a greater fool
In it thyself to see,
Swollen by many a gaze?

Go home, little Englishman, quickly,
Persona ingrata art thou living here,
And teach thy grandmothers
HOW TO SUCK EGGS!

— translated from Cornish by the author

The Snow

When I set foot upon the grey rock,
or else on the grassy meadow, or on the road,
or on the beach that is washed by the sea,
I know that I stand
where before have stood many others,
and will do so again.
The tinner, he too,
digging through the ground,
though he is the first
cannot be sure to be the last
where he draws his breath.

But the snow,
fallen from the sky,
white, clean, bright,
and when I note its fresh cleanness,
transforming the bleak hillside
where I walk,
it is certain that I am the first,
that I shall also be the last,
for soon each flake will be lost,
melted away, turned to water,
and with it every trace that has been made
by me upon its matchless face.

— translated from Cornish by the author

United We Will Be

When will end all the anger?
When will the sky clear?
When will the promised day come
that there will be an end of pain?

Long is the road,
great is the anger around us!

Come, brothers,
Come, you sisters too,
Why will we not unite?
A wonderful thing that would be!

Cornwall

Two thousand years it is, and more,
since we came over the sea . . .
Are we divided by that sea?
For the land will there now be anger?

While there is still strife with us,
and we have so much anger,
they steal our land . . .

Neighbours, let us come together
from across mountains, across seas!
In glory, in strength
united we will be!

— translated from Cornish by the author
version by TRC

Comet

I stood beneath the clear sky of the night
set all about with bright stars.
breathing the breath of the leaves
hanging ever so quiet on the scented trees.

There was one star among them
surpassing, and with ease, the beauty of
        the others,
that was white, was green, golden indeed,
"Look, here am I!" seeming to say.

I could not turn my gaze away,
cleaved ever to her unable to move,
but soon I saw her
slant towards me like a burning eye.

And I ran forward,
my hands outstretched before,
and caught her then,
and clutched her in my arms,
and pressed her against my breast,
but oh! she burned, she burned,
she burned cruelly without mercy,
and burned out my heart.

— translated from Cornish by the author

Gwennol (Swallow)

A wennol, A wennol, deez lavar an gweer,
mar bell peleah ve che dreth termen gwave heer?
Me geath tewa sooth pols bean, ma guthman,
Leb ma a whirny da stella an previan.

A wennol, A wennol, ma ubma tha nyth,
en skeber aworra en trester ew gwrez.
Per thaa me a ore, rag me an gwraze enna,
ha me an owna car drova en kensa.

A wennol, A wennol, tha che me veth scose,
en kidniath mor menta buz gurtas en close.
Na algam gweel hedna, na, leez me a verow,
buz me vedn doaz trea en gwainten, me an thethow.

Edn voze ma a adgan en sooth war an oon,
ha nam bes omwetha rag cara hye downe,
buz pecarra gwennol na vedn gortas pelha,
dreth oll an beaze hye a vedn moaz tha wandra.

Swallow

O swallow, O swallow, come tell the truth,
so far where hast thou been through the long winter time?
I went to the south for a while, my friend,
where insects ever hum.

O swallow, O swallow, here is thy nest,
in the barn up on the beam where it is made.
I know very well, for I made it there,
and I will repair it as it was before.

O swallow, O swallow, I will shield thee,
in the autumn if thou wilt but remain near.
I could not do that, no, lest I die,
but I will return in the spring, I promise it.

A maid I know in the south on the down,
and I cannot but love her deeply,
but like the swallow she will not stay longer,
across all the world she will go to wander.

– translated from Cornish by the author

Richard Jenkin
(1925 –)

Born in 1925 in Derbyshire, "son of a Mousehole man in exile," Richard Jenkin was educated at William Hulme's Grammar School in Manchester, attended Exeter College, Oxford (1943-1944) and joined the army in 1944 (1944-1948), attended Manchester University from 1948-1951 where he attained a Bachelor of Science degree in Honors Chemistry before going on to attend University College of the South West, Exeter for an education degree in 1952. During his teaching career to follow, he lived and taught in Wales, Devon and Cornwall, to which he returned in 1959 and where he still lives. In 1947 he entered the Cornish Gorsedd. Since that time he has served as Grand Bard of the Gorsedd; President of the Federation of Old Cornwall Societies; International President of the Celtic Congress; Chairman and Founding Member of Mebyon Kernow; co-editor of *New Cornwall*; co-author of *Cornwall, The Hidden Land*; and editor of *Delyow Derow* – a position he still holds. He has written poetry in English since 1942 and in Cornish since 1957. His work has been published extensively in such literary journals as *The Cornish Review, The Cornish Magazine, The Poetry Review, Old Cornwall, New Cornwall, The Meneage Book, Book of Mawgan, Kernow ha'n Mor, Delyow Derow,* and *The Celtic Pen.* He is married to Ann Trevenen and has four children.

An Gour Tullys (The Deceived Husband)

An gour yu tullys yu ges pupprys
Mes den a'n gor he whath y berthy
Yu neptra aral. Y'n dorgrys
A'y vewnans brewys ef a wra fethy
Meth ha coll ha cam ha drok,
Mes nefra ny yaghha an wan.
Y fyth bys vyken bewnans cok,
Colon yeyn, an dre hep tan.

The Deceived Husband

The deceived husband is always mocked
But the man who knows and keeps quiet
Is different. In the earthquake
Of his life he overcomes
The shame and loss he suffers,
And a wound that will never heal.
His life is empty,
His heart cold.
He goes home to a hearth where
there is no fire.

— translated from Cornish by the author
version by TRC

Brythennek (For Brian Webb)

Brian, brythennek, barvek, bras,
Campyer cref Kernewek mas,
Gwyader gwyas gwres a gan,
A vu haval dh'y 'Avon Splan.'

Yn dughan down dagrow a dyf,
Ow-lenwel lyn lagasow yn lyf
Erna res goverow warnans
Rak coll car kerys yn mysk cans.

For Brian Webb

Brian, freckled, bearded, big,
Strong champion of good Cornish,
Weaver of a web made of song
Which was like his 'Avon Splan.'

In deep sorrow tears grow,
Filling a lake of eyes in flood
Until streams run down
From the face of our friendship, like blood.

'Avon Splan' means "bright river" in Cornish

— translated from Cornish by the author
version by TRC

Garfield Richardson
(1925 –)

Garfield Richardson was born in England in 1925 of Cornish descent. He has lived in Cornwall, Wales and England during the course of his life and is now based in Wales. He writes in Cornish and English and has won literary competitions in one or other language in each of the first five triennial Esethvosow Kernow and places in the annual Gorseth literary competitions. His work has been published in both Cornish and English, including poetry and short stories. His poems in Cornish have only been seen in the Cornish publication *Delyow Derow*. He currently lives in Llandysul, Wales, which is also the home of Welsh poet Menna Elfyn.

An Dynas (The Hill-fort)

An dynas coth a sef 'vel dans
Dhe var an vre a-ugh an nans,,
Ha du erbyn an ebron las
Whath ef a wyth war wun ha pras.
Yndan an don 'ma bedhow down. –
Enevow gyllys yn Annown
Ha corfow cref yu lemmyn pry,
Ankevys yns hag oll 'ga bry.
Mes whath an gwynsow glyp a wheth
A wor an wesyon y'ga deth.
Ha'ga gos a wra resek ruth
Y'gan corfow yn gwythy cuth.

The Hill-fort

The old fortress stands like a tooth
On top of the hill above the valley,
And black against the blue sky
Still it watches over moor and field.
Under the turf there are deep graves. –

Souls gone to Annown
And strong bodies are now clay,
They are forgotten.
But still the damp winds blow
That knew the lads in their day
And their blood runs red in our bodies.
In secret veins.

— translated from Cornish by the author

Yet I Have Hope

What are they doing to my Cornwall now?

They're building bungalows with roofs of tile,
With picture-windows letting in the view
And all-electric central heating, too.
Yet I have hope that slate and stone outlast
The creeping concrete walls, pre-cast.

What are they doing to my Cornwall now?

They're tearing down the hedges of the fields,
Stone by stone, to get the tractors in
And send birds soaring by their strident din
While ploughing all the farmstead to one field,
To gain a few percentage more in yield.
Yet I have hope that wild flowers still will shoot
When gorse and heather flood back here to root.

What are they doing to my Cornwall now?

They're making sail-lofts into piskey shops
And cafes out of cellars by the quay
Where tourists stuff themselves and watch the sea,
And pump the sewage a mile into the bay
To float back on the beach where children play.
Yet I have hope that Winter storms will sweep
The whole damned lot away into the deep.

What are they doing to my Cornwall now?

They're putting our old language in new dress,
Devising scientific spelling rules
That hide familiar forms from simple fools –
A Celtic Esperanto of the mind
That leaves the land of Cornwall far behind. –
Yet I have hope this latest kiss of death
Won't choke our Cornish tongue and stop its breath.

What are they doing to my Cornwall now?

There's two-way traffic over Tamar bridge, –
The English in, the Cornish out, it seems,
And nothing stops the ever-flowing streams.
No work, no house for native Cornishman
For he can't pay as much as English can.
Yet I have hope that he will fight to stay
And keep his Cornwall safe another day.

Yet I have hope, but no guarantee
That what I hope will ever be.

– translated from Cornish by the author

There Is A Shower Threatening

"There is an ugly shower
Threatening, on my faith."
So once spoke Ham
When he saw the wall of water
That drowned all the world.
When gentle rain was turned
To steel arrows, and all life on earth
Struck swiftly to the ground –
Man, woman, animals and plants –
Brought, from water, into a boat by Noah
To begin again.

Is there threatening now
An ugly shower upon us which will be
More terrible than that, in time
To come, leaving nothing alive?

A rain of fire from heaven we will see,
    – A thousand times worse than lightning –
Ugly death with cruel pain.
    We will be wounded with light,
Its flash burning every eye.
    In a fraction of a second our clothes will be
Ignited by the heat of Suns.
    A tempest will blow away towns,
Bearing dust with hidden sting
    Which will fall in rain and stab the earth
When atomic fire replaces death with birth.

– translated from Cornish by the author / TRC

An Als (The Cliff)

A-ugh an lyf an als a sef.
Y clewaf an lef – y'n gwelaf –
Gwylan an gwyns, yu gwyls ha gwyn
'Vel gwlan py ewon glan, ylyn.
Arta y cry kepar ha cath,
Ow-scryja, hag ow-nyja whath
Adr dhe'n als, lamleder dhu
Ha serth. A, uthek yu hy vu.
Adro dh'y thros an mor a don;
Kepar ha taran yu y son.
Nefra ny heth; byth ow-conys
Rag dyswul selven an norvys.
War-van y wheth awellow cref,
Anal an mor, ow-ton y lef
Dhe'm dywscovarn mar vodharys
Hag orth-ow-thenna peryllys
Dhe vyn an als, yn-cren ena,
Ha res yu dhym, ow-crowedha
Synsy ton an als rag bos sur
A sawder dyworth tonnow mur.

The Cliff

Above the flood the cliff stands.
I hear the voice – I see it –
A gull of the gale, wild and white
As wool or clean bright foam.
Again it cries like a cat,
Shrieking, and flying still
Around the cliff's steep black precipice.
Below, the sea beats
Like thunder and the sound
That never stops.
Upwards blow strong breezes, and
The breath of the sea, carrying its voice
To my ears deafened
And drawing me endangered
To the lip of the cliff. Trembling there,
And lying down I must grasp
The turf of the cliff-top
The only safety from wind and waves.

– translated from Cornish by the author / TRC

Pawl Dunbar
(1947 –)

Pawl Dunbar was born in May 1947 in Hooe, a Cornish enclave "just the wrong side of the border but in sight of Mount Edgecumbe." His father was of Scots descent, his mother Cornish/Irish. After training as a boatbuilder, he lived on a fishing boat and then a yacht. After largely rebuilding the yacht and sewing his own traditional canvas sails by hand, he sailed for 12 years in Cornish waters and became a marine surveyor, which he recently gave up before "inane yachtsmen and even more inane insurance companies drove me mad." After becoming a fluent Cornish speaker he became involved in Cornish politics, joining Mebyon Kernow ("Sons of Cornwall," the Cornish autonomist party) in 1985, "qualifying me for automatic classification as a subversive in MI5 files." In 1988 he sold the yacht, bought land near Liskeard and a year later founded the political and cultural magazine *Kernow* which he still edits and "which is known to create regular surges of paranoia in Unionist circles." In 1990 with actor Will Coleman he founded the organisation Cornwall Against the Poll Tax, which gave a chance to ". . . rant Cornish separatist sedition at bigger crowds than English politicians had ever addressed in Cornwall . . ." (The highlight of CAPT's career was when an effigy of the then British Prime Minister Margaret Thatcher was burnt in the centre of Truro city following the St Piran's Day march. Pawl was later invited in for questioning by the police on suspicion of having set fire to the effigy and inciting a riot, but was released for lack of evidence.)

Pawl currently lives in a primitive cottage in a vineyard on the edge of Liskeard, Cornwall, "the venue of wild parties of international reputation." In 1996 he was selected as the Mebyon Kernow Prospective Parliamentary Candidate for South East Cornwall. Currently writing a who-dunnit in Cornish and a regular participant in debates on Cornish issues in the press, he is the author of articles in both Cornish and English on a wide range of topics which have appeared over the years in *Kernow* and various newspapers. A collection of Pawl's poems was printed by Gwask Bramm an Gath in 1996 under the title *The Revolutionary Rhymes and Provoking Poems of Machiavelli Tregaegle and Friends.*

Yth esa Plommwas . . . (There Was A Young Plumber . . .)

Yth esa plommwas a'n kynsa degre,
Ow plommya y vowes war an vre,
Yn medh hi: "Hedh, sos!
'ma nebonan ow tos!"
Yn medh ev, hwath ow plommya, "Ya, my!"

There Was a Young Plumber . . .

There was a young plumber called Lee
Who was plumbing his gal by the sea,
She said "Stop your plumbing!
I hear someone coming!"
Said the plumber, still plumbing, "It's me!"

– translated from Cornish by the author

Skeusow An Enev (Shadows Of The Soul)

Skeusow an enev
Skeusow an nos
Bos heb eneb
Bos heb tros.

Tewlder efan
Hwans a wolow
Tewlder bran
Enevow, olyow.

Gorhen, gorgoth –
Tra kudhys.
Mynnes, bodh –
Tra sedhis.

A-dhistowgh flamm –
Skeusow a lamm.

Shadows Of The Soul

Shadows of the soul
Shadows of the night
Someone without a face
Someone without a sound.

Wide darkness
A want of light
Crow darkness
Souls, spoors.

Very ancient, very old —
A hidden thing.
Wanting, desire —
A submerged thing.

Suddenly a flame —
Shadows jump.

— translated from Cornish by the author

An Skeus (The Shadow)

Dres pellder an oesow
Eskern ow hendasow
A syns dhymm hwath.
Brys ha korf i a vrath
Enev ha kolonn, anlev, stag,
Goes a sev ha dhymmo tag:
Skeus du, furv an tir.

The Shadow

Across the distance of the ages
My ancestors' bones
Grip me still.
Mind and body they bite
Soul and heart, voiceless, fixed,
Blood rises in me and I choke:
A black shadow, the shape of the land.

— translated from Cornish by the author

Old Woman

With her back bent,
She walks the road.
Against the wind.
Her coat is the cold of winter
Wrapping her bones and
Her hips of steel.

Her grey hair,
Her two slow legs,
Her white face,
Her thin blood,
Old age laughs at her
Holding on to that stick
For dear life.

The wind blows harder.
Rain starts to fall.
Somewhere
A door opens and shuts in silence.

— translated from Cornish by the author
version by TRC

Graham Sandercock
(1950 –)

Graham Sandercock was born in March of 1950 of a St Austell (mid Cornwall) family. He graduated with a degree in geography from the University of Liverpool, England, where contact with fellow Celts, especially from Ireland and Wales, led to a renewed interest in the Cornish language which he had learned of as a child from grandparents. On return to Cornwall, he began to teach and write in the language and became a leading figure in the revival of Cornish after 1970. He founded the all-Cornish magazine *An Gannas* (The Messenger) in 1976 which has appeared monthly under his editorship ever since. He has been active in the Cornish cultural and political scene and has risen to be chairman of both Kesva an Taves Kernewek (The Cornish Language Board) and Kowethas an Yeth Kernewek (The Cornish Language Fellowship) the oldest and largest language organisation with open membership in Cornwall. He is well-known as a singer in the Cornish language and has written the Cornish words and music to a large number of songs. A successful first album, *Poll Pri* (Clay Pit), was produced in 1992 and a new collection is currently being recorded as a follow-up CD. All his poems have been written to music, many of them following a story-telling ballad tradition. His book of Cornish verse and songs was published in 1994, titled *Geryow* (Words).

Quiberon

An explosion was heard in the middle of the sea,
black oil smoke pierced a clean sky,
a call for help made through the airwaves,
one man died in a ball of fire.
Alan Etienne was the name of the man,
and his age no more than twenty-eight years,
the sea was his fate like many Bretons before,
killed without warning in pursuit of his job.
The engine room of the Quiberon was the place,
the seventeenth of July was the time,

Cornwall

Alan Etienne choked in a cave of smoke
and a young soul did go from the world.

> Never mind what is done,
> events happen,
> death perhaps
> accidents of course;
> and it's not necessary to hurry –
> it will never be of any use –
> let's pause a minute,
> always let's be careful.

All the passengers were herded out,
climbing the stairs from the decks below,
tears of smoke were seen on many a cheek
although the sun was high and the weather fine.
The ferry Quiberon was quiet in its path,
asleep, rocking there a long time;
we knew nothing of the misery of Alan Etienne
or if the stories were false or true.
The television circus came to play its part,
as all the emergency services arrived,
the ferry was crippled, that was clear enough
and I knew well that the night would be long.

> Never mind what is done,
> events happen,
> death perhaps
> accidents of course;
> and it's not necessary to hurry –
> it will never be of any use –
> let's pause a minute,
> always let's be careful.

One eye closed against the brightness of the sun
tired I lay down on the deck
and all the people chattering and coming and going
I watched them for I don't know how many hours.
The ferry was towed safely to the port
and the argument began about all the case;
but me, I remember only one thing –

the death of Alan Etienne in a hateful explosion.
I don't take any notice of the daily paper;
I don't believe big headlines;
you shouldn't guess a truth which isn't true;
a man died and with the sea so blue.

(a true story; the writer was on board the ship at the time of the fire)

— translated from Cornish by the author

Surf

Before the sea was polluted,
and with the weather fine,
and the strong currents pulling against me;
eyes tired and bleary,
throughout the summer,
the surf was so high and so white.

Those summers were longer,
so it seems to me,
and Cornwall's beaches, tidy, parched and bleached;
the hope we had was truer,
and the desire keen,
a life spent under a splendid sky.

Love in the dunes
under the stars
all the elements
were so clear.

When we were healthy and young,
long ago,
without any worries at all in the world;
carefree in our days of escape,
real children,
following a just craving all the time.

Bold was the body and the spirit,
drinking too much,
girls and lightheaded friends;

on our favorite north coast,
we enjoyed ourselves
through long days and summer nights.

And now, how beautiful the sand is
in the early morning,
without the footsteps of anybody, in the breeze;
many a smile, many a choice,
there was of course,
before it was washed clean by a sweep of the sea.

O Friends, where are you now?
spread so thin,
with your traces on so many beaches;
separated, our world in pieces,
across many lands,
and our time together, gone.

Today, fear beats in my fiery heart.
On the crest of a wave that runs from the world;
and on the back of a thundering white horse
I will ride
always
with one more chance to be free.

— translated from Cornish by the author
version by TRC

View From The Street

There's an old man in the shade of a
dark, grey building,
a ragged straw hat on his head;
a wooden stick in his hand,
and a small dog lying at his feet
as the water runs from a circular fountain;
a man who knows everyone
and every secret like the back of his hand.

There are two secretaries in a cafe
drinking strong coffee.

It is the middle of the morning.
An old yellow lorry passes by,
followed by a black
cloud of dirty smoke,
disturbing the town;
on this same lorry, a name written from
another place;
on wide tracks under a cover of dust
to another land it goes, heavily burdened.

There are two young soldiers conversing
quietly, under the moon.
People rush by.
They will go to war before long,
to the frozen mountains
and the night will be long;
every family's prayer
following them, like clouds, over each field.

The concierge stands at her door. Wide-eyed and
throwing mean looks at me.
She has seen me come this way before;
she doesn't know who I am or what new
business I bring.
But I am forgiven.
And I will return to my covert lover;
where I will suffer a tongue-lashing like a purge
for being gone.
In a time of precious freedom, perhaps,
she will love me.
And in the distance, the barking of an old man's dog.

— translated from Cornish by the author
version by TRC

Tim Saunders
(1952 –)

One of the most widely-read poets in the Cornish language of the younger generation of writers, Tim Saunders was born in 1952 in Hexham, Northumberland. He attended primary schools in England and Cornwall (1957-1962), King's College, Taunton (1962-1969), Christ Church, Oxford (1970-1971), University College of Wales (1971-1979) and University of Middlesex (1994-1996). As a student of Celtic languages, he is fluent in Welsh, Cornish, Irish, French, Breton and German. He has held a variety of jobs including that of a language instructor at the University College, Cardiff in Welsh and Cornish; Welsh Folk Museum, St. Fagans, Wales; BBC Wales, Cardiff; Workers' Educational Association, Barry, Wales; and as a freelance translator and researcher. Some of his book titles include: *Selected Poems; Teithiau / Voyages* (1977); *Geriadur Arnevez Kernaouek-brezhonek / Modern Cornish-Breton Dictionary* (1990); *Y Saer Swyn* – childrens stories (1994). Other contributions of his work have appeared in a large number of literary journals in the United Kingdom, Cornwall, Wales, Ireland and the United States, including: *Barn, Kernow, New Welsh Review, Planet, Taliesin,* and *World Literature Today*. He currently lives in Cardiff, Wales.

The Cornish Society, University College, Cardiff, St. Piran's Day, 1985

Here I am come to the college one evening, despite sorrow of heart and despite the weather, standing on St. Piran's day at the end of a long and hard year, before lively students who are watching and listening.

I shall speak of that ancient Irishman who crossed on a stone altar to our very shores long ago to escape a hateful enemy, of his pure vigorous faith and of his drinking exploits, of his exploit in drawing tin from the stone in a bonfire on the sand.

"Come and give us a speech," said the secretary to me, "not more than half an hour, please, and then we must rest, a little bit of patriotism, a little nostalgia, a little laughter, and then all and one, boy, will hurry to the pub."

I explain how there crossed to this city by the Severn Channel, to earn a hard living, those who were not happy students, to turn the wheels, dry the mines, steer the ships, to send fuel across the sea to give warmth to the world.

I speak of that hidden world at the dark bottom of the mines, a world of stone that has no horizon, where the air and the light die, of the courage of the old tinners I speak sincerely, praise those who did not give a straw for precious life in danger.

I remind of that battle on the green fields of Ireland, when an army followed the Black and White Flag across the river, but my voice almost breaks when my memory flies back thirty-six hours to an army proudly marching to the top of a certain deep valley.

Warriors of the dark fields of the coal, courageous warriors who had stood for an entire year against the rich and powerful, in a great march back to work without fear, without shame, without regret, but oh! in the face of their fate a heart of rock would melt!

Once great crowds used to cut the black wealth from the depth, and where the mine is the gentle breeze will blow, but yesterday there were red flags, and the echo of *L'Internationale* (take care, you mighty ones, take care and be terrified!).

In front of me in the pub many pints will be put – how generous are these young people, how thick the fog in my head! – the voices rise singing of *Camborne Hill*, rise far above the pools of black tears in my heart.

– translated from Cornish by the author

The Great Hunger

When a miasma of corruption blew the length and breadth of the land of Britain and Ireland, a smell of deserted ruins in the damp valley-bottoms, the sigh of a cool-dropped Spring when the roots were melting in the earth, the seeds of death awoke amongst the soil and the gravel.

A heavy fist on the green island will squeeze from its earth blood and sweat, will squeeze out half its people, will squeeze from its bones the marrow, will squeeze from its fields wealth, will squeeze from its flesh naked want, will squeeze from its peace ill-will, will squeeze from its quietness peace.

A clerk's pen will record the breaths of a lifetime, coin by coin; in the columns of the account books, it is gold that will grant life to people: when the parchment is dry, naked will be the white bones: at the bottom of every page the grant will come to an end.

The iron fist of Roman belief on a heart will squeeze will-power to dust, will squeeze every energy from the muscles, will squeeze every light from the stars, will squeeze strength from a sword arm, will squeeze every warmth of sun from the day, will squeeze a living stream from the veins, will squeeze every root from the clay.

What is earth, that it swallows completely hour, working day, year of life, consumes flesh and life without any finish ever to its desire? And what, pray, is land that it gives of its unceasing generosity to the hands that never touch it? Why does the ne'er-do-well receive every benefit?

It is the tight fist of hunger on the entrails that will squeeze with the blind grievous strength of a grave, squeeze the colour from the skin, squeeze love from lad and maid, squeeze pity from the soul, squeeze from the Earth the hope of Heaven, squeeze air from the throat, squeeze every thought from the head.

Heavy the mist on the acres, light the seeds of magic without feathers or hum, sleep on every tilth and green field, deep a dream of easy fair weather: gold the ears on every harvest, silver the dew on every field, iron the heart of the son of Trevelyan, empty every chest that has formerly been full.

White and ripe the field of harvest, white the bones in the earth of a field of battle, grey the air of the edges of the sky, grey the young hair on a thousand heads: it is wealth that will suck from the barn every nourishment for the great common people, it is thin soup and potato mash for the one who wields the spade.

When a sharp burning scalds from the long leaves through all the roots from one to another, and leaves foul muddy ash, a dark mess cold like night, it is famine that will burn now through town and valley, field and hill, devour townland and barony through every single horizon where it tramples.

On the fertile pasture of Skibbereen when the copious white dew lies down, the bolt and the key will give to the house of silence the dignity of a grave: by the cells of the Cistercian monks neighbours will sink out of sight where the grass will give voice to the song of the memories of the silent host in the gravel.

No ship will stride the salt amphitheatre when an army arrives at Wadebridge, quarrymen rank upon ordered rank on the march against sour hunger: nourishment will win the day, when avarice cleaves to food; no boat will leave the harbour before they all receive a loaf.

It is false witnesses who will tell us that no meaning at all will cleave to a word, that no rain will fall from a cloud, that no foot walked where there is a print: a martyr bears witness through living deed, a fresh work, surely on behalf of truth (to us it is scholars who told).

Ancient clerics spoke of the colours (let us learn quickly) of martyrdom, the red of a slaying, the white of exile for a holy motive: what colour for an absence, the slow martyrdom of an ebb, blind the windows of the cottage, the rustle, you and me?

It is a healthy wind that will chase away the fog of oblivion from the names condemned without proof, rescue from the shadow of Hades the grey martyrdom of the hunger: on fire for tomorrow we shall turn disaster to advantage, open the treasure chests, give to hope the breadth of the sea.

– translated from Cornish by the author

Ow Thaz (My Father)

Ha'y dhorn ganz raj ow' tava'nn prenn
y'nadhe'nn wydhenn war alteur staj
yn-pareuz dhÿ drummaj na'dhoe dhÿ-benn.

My Father

With his hand touching the wood carefully,
he hewed the tree on the altar of a slipway
ready for a voyage that would not come to an end.

– translated from Cornish by the author

Ty Ha' My (Great Heart, Beat By Beat / You And I)

Dowlagaz down ann nos ma y'sudh,
feuntÿni tywl, feuntÿni kudh;
frozow kelyz hudh c'hwanz hag own,
dowlagaz leun, dowlagaz down:
    hynzi ewn, hynzi kamm,
    kolonn veur lamm ha'lamm.

Ann bysyez kryv ha'nn dalghenn tomm,
gwres jolyv gwoez ha'nn tava tromm;

ann balv worth palv ha'nn bys worth bys,
erwi gwresenn yn-dan ann krys:
    hynzi ewn, hynzi kamm,
    kolonn veur lamm ha'lamm.

Trëyz ow' rima, troez vyw ganz troez
war hen fordh las bÿz kreis ann koez;
gwodhnow war welz ha' kneuz was dhoar,
ponya yn-ghwylz, pawes yn-kloar:
    hynzi ewn, hynzi kamm,
    kolonn veur lamm ha' lamm.

Feuntÿni kloar y'nn goezwig dhown,
peub froz ow' lemmyl yn hy lown;
anadhlow arav dywedh dydh
donz lent ann deil y'nn awel rydh:
    hynzi ewn, hynzi kamm,
    kolonn veur lamm ha'lamm.

Great Heart, Beat By Beat / You And I (Song)

Two dark eyes into which the night sinks, dark springs, secret springs; hidden springs of merriment, desire and fear, two full eyes, two deep eyes.
    straight paths, crooked paths, great heart beat by beat.

The strong fingers and the warm grasp, the lively warmth of blood and the sudden touching; the palm to palm and the finger to finger, acres of fertile soil beneath the shirt:
    straight paths, crooked paths, great heart beat by beat.

Feet rhyming, living foot with foot on an ancient green lane right into the middle of the wood; soles on grass and flesh on earth, running wildly, resting coolly:
    straight paths, crooked paths, great heart beat by beat.

Cool springs in the deep forest, every stream leaping in its own spot; slow-moving breaths of an afternoon, the slow-witted dance of the leaves in the free breeze.
    straight paths, crooked paths, great heart beat by beat.

— translated from Cornish by the author

In The Country Of The Blue Rock

The town lies on the hill amongst the thick clouds; the voice of the winds, by my faith! is like the anger of a lion: but still I love the place, and its people so kind and bold who have no fear of the keen winds in the country of the blue rock.

In the fields on the bare slopes we once played noisily, singing under the lead sky, or laughing all in the rain: and every boy who has no fear of the keen winds in the country of the blue rock will soon be a man with a big and warm heart.

In strike or in grievous accident, in illness or in hunger, for the sake of the truth like black on white we all stood without fear strongly together against them, full of deep determination, since we had no fear of the keen winds in the country of the blue rock.

Like a ripe harvest of corn we were all scattered very far through many countries at the limits of the world to get away from cruel need: by wandering through all the breadth and length of the world we shall not hope to find better than those who have no fear of the keen winds in the country of the blue rock.

— translated from Cornish by the author

Pol Hodge
Mab Stenek Veur
(1965 -)

Pol Hodge was born in 1965 in the heart of the Tin mining district of County Kerrier, Cornwall. He was educated at Redruth School, The Polytechnic of the South Bank, London, and The University of Bath where he read Chemical Engineering and became a teacher of Science. Having studied Kernewek, the Cornish Language, at classes in London, Liskeard and his native Camborne, he gained a distinction in the highest Kesva an Taves Kernewek (Cornish Language Board) examination. In 1991 he was made a Language Bard of *Gorsedh Kernow* at An Garrek/Roche and took the bardic name of Mab Stenek Veur (Son of a Great Tin-ground). Pol Hodge teaches Kernewek in evening classes in Grampound Road and St. Austell. He has written and illustrated a number of children's books and translated a series of children's books from Breton to Kernewek. Since being elected to Kesva an Taves Kernewek he has assisted in the production of the latest Cornish dictionary and played an active part in the researches of the Kesedhek Henwyn-tyller (Place-names Committee). In 1994, Hodge translated Alan M. Kent's modern epic poem into Kernewek and in creating a syllable count and rhyme scheme, produced the longest Kernewek/English poem in history. Hodge and Kent then teamed up with Bert Biscoe to form Berdh Arnowydh Kernewek. This radical trio have performed Cornish poetry in Wales, England and their native Cornwall. The accompanying book and tape of *Berdh Arnowydh Kernewek / Modern Cornish Poets* has been published by Lyonesse Press and has sold well throughout Britain. Hodge has also had work published bilingually in *The Celtic Pen* and *Kernow* magazine and without translation in *An Gannas* (the all-Kernewek monthly magazine published by Kowethas an Yeth Kernewek). His newly published *Mewth On Un Like Dolcoath Shaft* is a solo collection of poems with English translations and is set to give his audiences another fiery blast of Cornish nationalism and hope for the future of Kernow. Pol Hodge now lives with his Kernewek-speaking wife, Jane Ninnis, who has been a long serving member of the council of Kowethas an Yeth Kernewek (The Cornish Language Fellowship) and has been made a bard of Cornish Gorsedh for her services to Kernewek. Both are active members of Kesva an Taves Kernewek. They live at Fordh Ponsmeur/ Grampound Road near the Clay mining district of Mid Cornwall.

Pader Agan Taves (Language Prayer)

Agan Yeth ni, eus diworth nev,
Bennigys re bo dres Kernow.
Re dheffo an kernewegor,
Y yeth re bo kewsys yn oll an vro
Kepar hag yn broyow erell.
Ro dhyn ni hedhyw agan kows pub dydh oll
Ha gav dhyn agan trelyans kamm
Dell avyn nyni dhe'n dallethor
Eus ow kammgewsel orthyn ni:
Ha na wra agan gorra yn tewlder
Mes delyv ni diworth sowsnek.
Rag dhiso jy yw an grammasek,
Ha'n erva ha'n Leveryans,
Bys vykken ha bynari.

    Amen

Language Prayer

Our language, that is from heaven,
Hallowed may you be throughout Cornwall.
May come the Cornish speaker,
His language may it be spoken in all of the land
As it is in other lands.
Give us today our daily speech
And forgive us our wrong mutations
As we forgive the beginner
That mis-speaks to us:
And don't put us in silence
But deliver us from English.
For you are the grammar,
The vocabulary and the pronunciation,
For ever and ever.

    Amen

— translated from Cornish by the author

The Queen's English

The Campaign for the Preservation of Rural England,
Lie back and think of England.
This England.

Corner of a foreign field that is forever England.
Land's End – at the very tip of England
England expects every man to do his part.

England's green and pleasant land,
England's dark satanic mills.
There'll always be an England.

Bank of England,
Law of England,
Church of England.

English Lit.,
English Nature,
English Heritage.

I'm not English.
This idn England
An' I dun want to speak
the language a some ol' queen.

Nyns ov vy Sowsnek.
Nyns yw hemma Pow Sows
Ha ny vynnav vy kewsel
an yeth neb myghternes koth.

– translated from Cornish by the author

Edinburgh Castle

Davydh whispers into our ears: "You could travel from Kernow right up through Britain to Northern Scotland and speak just one language. This is before the Gaels, Saxons and Norsemen invaded Britain."

By the left . . . Quick march . . . Drums are beaten. Drones are blown. And the pipes drown the German tourists' chatter. There's no Scots Gaelic in Die Burg von Edinburgh, Le Chateau d'Edinbourg, Il Castello di Edinburgo, something written in Chinese beyond our alphabet or Edinburgh Castle. Only the guide, his voice as clear and as strong as Scotch whiskey, tells this land is Scotland, it's not England, nor Great Britain, nor Europe. And we the Brittonic Celts laughed to ourselves through the six hundred miles, through the thousand years and through the grey Edinburgh mist.

— translated from Cornish by the author

Katrina Waters
(1970 -)

"I was born in Redruth, Cornwall, January 1970. I began writing poetry at around eight years of age, the first was entitled 'Cats' and won a school prize. I continued writing until the age of eighteen, tortured adolescent stuff, at which time I left Cornwall for University despite my real desire (and attempts to persuade those around me that it was a good idea) to go to Art College. My studies for a science degree confirmed my beliefs as I came to realise that I wasn't a 'scientist' in the modern sense of the word and that I was born about two hundred years too late! I began writing again in '94 after attending a poetry reading where the poetry had no 'guts and blood.' At around the same time I began to learn the Cornish tongue, something I had been meaning to do for years, in addition to being involved in the Cornish movement in various guises. I am also interested in psychology, philosophy, herbalism and lots of other wacky stuff. I have recently started work at Falmouth College of Art . . . my work has been published in Cornish in such magazines as *Kernow*."

I Know You Better Than You Think

I know you better than you think.
I listen to what you never say,
to the silence between the jagged lines
that form your fragile words.
Your smiling face, your witty discourse,
betray the inner desolation
that sculpts the wasteland of your dreams,
and pervades your waking hours.

I know you better than I really should.
I have breathed in and entered your mind,
devoured the secret intentions,
that cloud your self-belief.
I have witnessed your wildest desire

during a lapse in your discretion
felt the touch of butterfly's wing –
the possession your passion craves.

This knowledge transcends morality.
The languid hours cannot be stolen
to consume each other's conceptions,
to touch without touching.
Hypnotised by your obsession
you rehearse your sacrificial art
drawn towards your final communion
like an insect to a Venus trap.

– translated from Cornish by the author

Lust

My love lies drowning
    beneath this banal sea.
The wind of promise whips
    the cold, grey desolation
into frenzied lust,
    its spray consuming,
tainting every spirit
    who dallies on its surface.

– translated from Cornish by the author

Muses

Our lives are footprints
in the sand.
The incoming tide
is time
pulled by the moon.

The tide rolls backwards
and our lives
are shape-shifted or lost
as the moon
waxes and then wanes.

– translated from Cornish by the author

(Ellan Vannin)
ISLE OF MAN

MANX

Manx

The native language of the Isle of Man is Manx or Manx Gaelic, which is closely related to Scots Gaelic and Irish. It was not until about 500 AD that Gaelic came to the island, probably with Irish invaders. Assimilation to Gaelic culture was quick, possibly, with Old Irish being the ultimate parent of the modern Manx language. Since the language at that stage must have been identical to that of Ireland and Scotland, it is impossible to identify any writings as being discernibly Manx. Manx is mentioned in the Cormac Glossary, in which Senchan Torpeist, a famous Irish bard of the seventh century, is described as visiting the island and admiring its literary school. The stories and cycles in Gaelic culture, like that of Finn and Ossian, remained popular through oral tradition among the ordinary people well into the nineteenth century. In 1789, Heywood heard a fragment of an Ossianic poem from an old woman in Kirk Michael.

Manx was the majority language in the island until about 1830, but in fact English had been the language of administration, power and prestige for hundreds of years previously. Although the Bible and the Anglican Book of Common Prayer had been translated into Manx, along with a significant number of other religious works, the body of original writing in Manx was not large. This consisted mainly of *carvallyn* (from the English "carols"), religious writings which were popular among the ordinary Manx people until the early years of the nineteenth century. Toward the end of that century, possibly the only creative writer in Manx was Edward Faragher of Cregneash, who wrote stories and anecdotes in the native language. During the nineteenth century, Manx declined disastrously and had disappeared as a community language by about 1910. The 1931 census claimed only 531 speakers.

However, most of the traditional language was preserved in both written and spoken forms: tape recorders came on the scene just in time to record the Manx of the last native speakers of the old language. There were always those who learned to speak Manx fluently as a second language, leading to the current revival and development of what has been called "neo-Manx." The descriptions in many reference books to Manx as being "dead" or "extinct" can therefore be disputed.

There is increasing interest in original writing in Manx in the Isle of Man, an interest which was fostered by the inception of prizes in the 1990s for such writing. Obviously, given the previous lack of cultivation of Manx and the low esteem in which it was held, present writing in the native language generally does not have the degree of sophistication reached by writing in English. By 1991 the number of Manx speakers was as high as 643, a large increase from the 284 Manx speakers recorded in the 1971 census.

For a small country, the amount of cultural activity in the Isle of Man is significant. It is noticeable, however, that it is quite difficult to assess what literary activity is going on in the island, in any language. As with other aspects of Manx life, this is something of a secret world. Because it is a quiet place and taxes are low, there are several relatively well known writers of popular fiction in English based in the island, but their work could hardly be included in a Celtic anthology. Among identifiably Manx writers, the most prominent internationally is Michael Daugherty, who is an established poet and short-story writer. Daugherty does not write in Manx and is irritated by too narrow a focus on things Manx. However, his affiliation may be seen from the titles of two of his books: *Mona My Love & Other Manx Poems* (1979) and *Images of an Underground Manxman* (1984). His latest book of poetry (1996) is entitled *Lines From No-Man's Land*.

> But, here in this bitter kitchen, I bite on
> each word as if it were a bullet. The main thing
> is to survive. This poem is a beach-head.
> I am still alive, despite the sniping,
> my wife's silent propaganda. The fighting
> goes on. My neighbours are foes in friendly beds.

Another poet of note who writes in English in the Isle of Man is Frank Kershaw. Paul Lebiedszinski, who died under tragic circumstances in 1995, was noted for his satirical poems which he recited at festivals and public houses.

Those prominently writing in Manx today include Robert Corteen Carswell, former editor of *Fritlag* (Rag), Colin Jerry, George Broderick and Brian Stowell. Bob Carswell was the first person to be awarded the Allied Irish Bank's prize for writing in Manx Gaelic. This was for a collection of poems.

Manx is now shaking off its label as the Cinderella of the Celtic languages in that more coordinated and determined efforts are now being made to promote it. Manx today is experiencing an unprecedented revival. Government support has been a crucial element in giving a degree of optimism which was previously lacking.

Manx is more in evidence than it used to be. It is used in announcements on Manx Airlines aircraft, it is to be seen on many government vehicles and buildings, and individuals and firms more often feel the need to make Manx visible.

Following the success of its first Feailley Gaelgagh (Manx Language Festival) at the end of 1995, Yn Cheshaght Ghailckagh is committed to making this an annual event. While everyone realizes the enormous tasks facing Manx language activists, great advances have been made and it is increasingly difficult to dismiss Manx as "dead." Top priorities for the language movement are to encourage the emergence of fluent speakers, above all young ones, and to increase the body of original literature in Manx.

— Brian Stowell

Brian Stowell
(1936 –)

Brian Stowell was born in 1936 in Douglas, Isle of Man. He was educated at Douglas High School and Liverpool University, and trained as a physicist. He has worked most of his life as a physics lecturer at what is now Liverpool John Moores University. When he was still at school in Douglas, he started to learn Manx by going around with a group who were recording the speech of the last native speakers of traditional Manx Gaelic. This was the basis for what would be a lifelong passion for Manx and other Celtic languages. He began writing in Manx and recording traditional songs. He edited *Douglas Fargher English-Manx Dictionary* in 1979 and wrote several Manx language courses. In 1992, he returned home to take up the newly created post of Manx Language Officer with the Isle of Man Government. Since then, his main job has been the introduction of optional Manx tuition in schools on the island. He retired from this post in 1996, but continues to be as active as possible in Manx language affairs. He has been married twice and has a grown daughter and son and two young daughters, along with four grandchildren. He lives in Douglas on the Isle of Man.

Stubbin, Gow Kiarail (The Manx Cat)

Ta'n stubbin çheet hood ayns y laa,
Kayt caarjoil, t'ad ooilley gra.
Cha jean eh gobbal strugey meen,
Cree ta bog, jarrood cree reen.
T'eh shirrey graih as treisht ass towse,
Lhieen e chorp dy kiart lesh foays.
Agh eisht t'eh goit ersooyl dy bieau,
Currit stiagh ayns bastag doo.
Atreih, kialgeyrys ren çheet er,
Cosney argid son roosteyr.
As nish t'eh er ny chur ersooyl,
Raipit magh veih thie er-roul,
Ta'n onid echey caillit nish,

Ribbey sollagh fuirraght rish.
Cre fodmayd jannoo, stubbin voght?
Jeeragh lheie ersooyl gyn loght?
Fodmayd shassoo seose as scrabey,
Gobbal goll magh er y vaatey.
Cha nel ansoor ry gheddyn ain,
Agh peeagheree ta faagit dooin.

The Manx Cat

The Manx cat comes to you by day,
A friendly cat, they all say.
He'll not refuse gentle stroking,
A heart that's soft, forget all grudging.
He looks for love that's out of measure,
Filling his body with wholesome treasure.
But then he's taken off so fast,
Into a basket he is cast.
What sad deceit has crept up now,
Earning money for thieves somehow.
Yes, now he's going far from home,
Ripped by force, adrift, alone.
No longer simple, pure and clean,
For him, a trap that's dirty, not serene.
Poor Manx cat, what can we do?
Melt away fast, Manxmen true?
We can stand and scratch and shout
Not for us the boat and out.
Maybe there's no answering,
What's left is caterwauling.

– translated from Manx by the author

Turrys Veih'n Cholloo

Ny veggan, ny veggan, v'ee goll ergooyl,
Yn baatey çheet magh ass ny creggyn,
Yn skimmee foast freayll yn gaue ersooyl
Lesh maidjyn liauyr, aarlit da'n cheayn.

Ersooyl veih ny creggyn, çhyndaa mygeayrt,
Va fys ain dy beagh shin leaystey,
Va'n baatey er-creau myr feanish jeh'n niart
Jeh'n scrodey va cassey sy taailley.

Va'n baatey beg shiaulley noi geay niar-hwoaie,
As paart jeh'n cheayn spreih harrin ayns shen.
Yn cheyllys ren baggyrt er shiolteyryn treih
Lesh strooyn ta scughey ny baatyn.

Yn Burroo, Yn Chlet, Brig Lily, Burroo Ned,
Ny henmyn ta çheet hym sy vaatey.
Shoh enmyn va soit ayns y chione ayd,
Agh nish t'ad ersooyl ass dty aigney.

Yn eaynin ard shen as sleih jeeaghyn neose,
Ny kirp oc, snienganyn beggey.
As foillan ny ghaa va geiyrt orrin heese
Va getlagh er tonnyn ny marrey.

Mygeayrt y keiy liauyr as stiagh ayns y phurt,
Ayns keayn va kiune as rea nish.
Er-ash ayns y teihll jeh argid as niart,
Bee aarloo dy chlamey yn ghreeish.

Turrys Veih'n Cholloo

Little by little she was going backwards,
The boat coming out of the rocks,
The crew still keeping danger away
With long poles, ready for the sea.

Away from the rocks, turning around,
We knew we'd be wallowing.
The boat was shaking, a witness of the strength
Of the screw turning down below.

The little boat was sailing into a north-easterly,
And some of the sea sprayed over us there.
The Sound which menaced miserable sailors
With currents that got rid of boats.

The Burroo, the Clet, Brig Lily, Burroo Ned
Are names which come to me in the boat.
These names which were set in your head,
But now they are out of your mind.

Isle of Man

That high cliff with people looking down,
Their bodies, little ants.
And a seagull or two which followed us below
Flying on the waves of the sea.

Around the long quay and into the harbour,
In a sea which was calm and flat.
Back in the world of money and power,
Be ready to scramble onto the step.

— translated from Manx by the author

Adrian Pilgrim
(1948 –)

Primarily known for his writing of songs and hymns, Adrian Pilgrim also writes poetry in three or more languages including Manx-Gaelic, for which he won the "Poetry in Manx" category of the 1992 Cruinnaght Competition for a poem titled "Sunset" which some say was possibly the first sonnet ever written and published in Manx. Though not a prolific Manx writer, he has contributed much to the language by way of translation over the past thirty years. "I send you my poem 'Lhie ny Greiney' which must be one of my best," he says. He lives still in Baldrine on the Isle of Man.

Lhie Ny Greiney (Sunset)

Ta'n ghrian goll dy lhie er lhiattee Sniaull,
Annoon ec kione e troailtys tess'n y speyr,
E çhiass lane vaarit, t'ee goll fo dy moal,
E gillid aileagh nish ny cruinnag airh.
As s'goan ec oor e baaish t'ee feddyn bree
Dy ghrainnaghey ayns freoagh feïe yn clieau,
Lesh laue neuhickyr, clashyn liauyrey bwee,
Shenn-chowraghyn myr ren ee er dy rieau,
Scrabageyn eiraght roïe er ny treigeil,
E feniee ghaaney 's bardyn mooar ersooyl.
Agh s'kinjagh nish ta'n soilshey faase failleil,
Dy meen goll naardey derrey, er y çhooyl,
Skellys eh roish ayns keeiraght vog ny hoie,
As aagys eh yn thalloo kiune ayns shee.

Sunset

The sun is setting on the side of Snaefell,
Feeble at the end of her journey across the sky,
Her heat now spent, she sinks slowly,
Her fiery brilliance now a golden orb.
And hardly can she find the power at her hour of death
To carve in the wild heather of the mountain,
With uncertain hand, long grooves of yellow,
Ancient marks as she has made from time immemorial,
The scratches of an earlier abandoned heritage,
Its bold heroes and great bards gone.
But all the time now the weak light is failing,
In gentle decay, till finally
It will vanish in the dusk of night
And leave the tranquil earth in peace.

— translated from Manx by the author

Robert Corteen Carswell
(1950 –)

Robert Corteen Carswell works for the Manx Government in the Department of Agriculture, Fisheries and Forestry. He is a fluent Manx speaker who has, for many years, presented the Manx language program "Claare ny Gael" on Manx Radio. In addition, he is very active in many other aspects of Manx culture, including yn Chruinnaght, the annual inter-Celtic festival held on the Isle of Man, and is active in the areas of music and dancing. He founded and is editor of the Manx language magazine *Fritlag*. His book *Shelg yn Drane* was published by Fritlag in 1994. Of his work, he says: "In my process of 'hunting rhymes,' I use a number of methods in my work. First, there are the songs – with rhyming words at the end of the line. Then, there are other poems with rhyming words inside the lines, though there is no rhyme in the final words of these lines. The sounds of vowels and consonants make up the rhyme, or the sound of the words themselves copy meaning. I have also created poems by simply using a syllable count. It's all about the language and finding (new) ways to make it work." He lives in Douglas on the Isle of Man.

Lomman

She lomman creoi ta sheidey veih'n hiar
Harrish ny sleityn rooisht as moanee liauyr.
Agh fo nyn gassyn hene ta mirrilyn dy liooar,
As markiagh er y gheay ta feeagh braew mooar.

Lomman

It's a hard, stripping wind that is blowing from the east
across the bare mountains and long turbaries.
But beneath our feet there are miracles,
and riding on the wind is a great, big raven.

– translated from Manx by the author

Duillagyn Ny Fouyir (The Leaves Of Autumn)

Va duillagyn ny Fouyir nyn lhie;
Lieh-ooir myr v'adsyn nish, va cheet dy ve
Covestit lesh y thalloo mea ren fassaghey ad
Er-feiy nyn laaghyn, voish nyn cheet magh,
As choud's v'ad jiole neese beaghey,
As bishaghey y billey liorish soilshey ny greiney.
As nish v'ad ceaut neose, dy 'assaghey
Duillagyn noa 'sy traa ry-heet.
Ren fer ny ghaa gleashaghey er y gheay veeley.

Ta mish croymmey sheese dy chur my chione
Noi'n thalloo shoh, ta cleayney king
As anmeeyn dy liooar, ayns treisht
Dy 'assaghey my annym's hene.

The Leaves Of Autumn

The leaves of autumn were lying:
half-earth they were now, that were coming to be
mixed with the rich soil which fed them
throughout their days, from their coming out,
and whilst they were sucking up nourishment,
and increasing the tree by the light of the sun.
And now they were thrown down, to feed
new leaves in the time to come.
One or two moved on the gentle wind.

I am bending down to put my head
against this ground, that attracts heads
and bodies enough, in the hope
that it feeds the soul.

— translated from Manx by the author

In The Country

In the country, in the gloaming, a sound comes in the air —
the bleating of the little sheep, caught by the thistles
that grow like a fence: little lambs calling out at each sharp
stalk, whilst they seek a way to walk without wound,
following on each other through the rough wasteland.
Bitter is this world; sad are the complainers
that are bleating to be free: loud of voice but short of wit.
In the morning, the goat will come.

— translated from Manx by the author

The Sound Of Morning

The mist of dawn blew away before the light breeze.
The curtain was being opened to let in
the fresh, new day. The rising of the sun.
A chink of light won its way into the room
through a little gap, going from dust to dust.
The ray caught the spider's web
that was connecting the room's ceiling to the wall.
Suddenly, an alarm clock raised its clarion,
as it threw its noise throughout the house,
in each corner,
but alas, the clock lost heart.
There was not a hand to turn it off,
there was not a voice to swear with hatred at it.
The summons faded away without an answer.
The house was as quiet and still as though it was underground.

— translated from Manx by the author

The Blind Burrowers

Black; cold; silent; far underground; without life.
A split; a drop; a vein of water; wet. Mud,
with blind burrowers in the darkness.
On the seabed, taking in the salty
water, gulping in food that falls from above,
shellfish are lying in the sand.
Scarce is there light in the deep water.
Like morsels from higher water,
a chink or two falls down from the surface.
Transparent shrimps skip about the
shells. Sometimes, they annoy
the flatfish – plaice, sole, turbot – that are hidden,
taking shelter beneath the grains of sand in the bed
of the sea. With a twitch of their tail
fins, they dash all before them away,
leaving behind them clouds like a smoke screen.
Above the spurts of sand, schools
of cod are swimming; and, in the season, will come
a great shoal of herring, to spawn
in the sea on the east coast. Herring
that oil up the surface of the water, and
give a sign to the fishermen that sail out
across the sea. In the air, seabirds are
soaring, while they search for food, hunting fish.
Above them swim the clouds. The sea
echoes the colours that are to be found
in the sky. Up again. The atmosphere thins.
Cold; silent; far above the world; without life.

– translated from Manx by the author

Acknowledgements

Breton/Brittany

"Songs In Springtime," *Al Liamm*, 1959.

"Love For A Country," "Thank You," "My Poems," "Imprison," "Humming," "The Old Mare," "The Dismantling Of Brittany," "The Conquerors," "Elves," *A Modern Breton Political Poet, Anjela Duval* by Lenora A. Timm; Edwin Mellen Press, 1990, by permission of the translator.

"Two Short Tales For May Day," *Ar Majeun*, 1973.

Welsh/Wales

"A Welshless Welshman," "A Poem Of Praise," "Land Of Form," *Selected Poems*, Christopher Davies, 1987, by permission of the author.

"Racing Pigeons," *Asheville Poetry Review*, vol. 3 no. 1, 1996.

"A Funeral In Llŷn," *20th Century Welsh Verse* (1966) and *Poetry of Wales 1930-1970* (1974), by permission of the author.

"For Ewan McLachlan," *Modern Poetry in Translation*, Spring 1995.

"Last Window," "A Density of Light," *Modern Poetry in Translation*, no. 7.

"In Weakness," *The Poetry Book Society Anthology #2*.

"The Coat," *Asheville Poetry Review*, vol. 3 no. 1, 1996.

"Shadows," *Cannwyll yn Olau*, Gomer Press, 1969, by permission of the author.

"A Field of Wheat," *20th Century Welsh Poems*, Gomer Press, 1982, by permission of the author.

"The Welsh Language" and "Memory," *Modern Poetry in Translation*.

"The Horizon-Gazer" and "Llŷn Peninsula," *Asheville Poetry Review*, vol. 3 no. 1, 1996.

"Nunnery," "Double Bed," "Cell Angel," "Wildflowers," *Cell Angel*, Bloodaxe Books, 1996, by permission of the author.

"After The Court Case,""Eucalyptus,""Chinese Lantern" and "Message," *Eucalyptus,* Gomer Press, 1995, by permission of the author.

"As Long . . ." *Far Rockaway,* Gwasg Carreg Gwalch, 1997, by permission of the author.

"Links," *Cyfrif uc ac un yn dri* (One and One Make Three), Barddas Press, 1996; and in translation in *PN Review,* vol. 22 no. 6, 1996, by permission of the author.

"Owl Report," *Barn,* August 1995.

"Silence," first commissioned by the Hay Festival of Literature, 1993.

"Blue," first broadcast on DIM and Celf on S4C Television, Wales, 1992.

Scottish Gaelic / Scotland

"The Language We Know As Scottish-Gaelic . . ." (Preface), *Verse,* vol. II no. 2, 1994.

"Spring Tide," *Reothairt is Contraigh: Taghadh de Dhàin / Spring Tide and Neap Tide, Selected Poems 1932-1972,* Canongate Publishing, by permission of the author.

"Realism in Gaelic Poetry," *Ris a' Bhruthaich. Criticism and Prose Writings,* Acair, 1985.

"The Great Famine," *Somhairle Dàin is Deilbh,* Acair, 1991, by permission of the author.

"A Church Militant," "A Poem When The Gaelic Society of Inverness Was A Hundred Years Old," *From Wood to Ridge,* Vintage/Carcanet, 1991, by permission of the publisher.

"What Compelled You To Write In Gaelic,""Contraband,""Nightmare,""Harper," and "That's Gone And This Has Come," *Making Tracks,* Gordon Wright Publisher, 1988, by permission of the author.

"The Clearances," *Selected Poems,* Carcanet, 1984, by permission of the author.

"Going Home," "Two Songs For A New Ceilidh," "A Young Girl," "For Derick Thomson," "The Letter" and "Oban," *Collected Poems,* Carcanet, 1992, by permission of the author.

"At Callanish Stones,""The Herring Girls,""Budapest" and "Strathnaver," *Collected Poems (Creachadh na Clàrsaich / Plundering the Harp),* MacDonald Publishers, 1982, by permission of the author.

"Thursday Morning In A Glasgow Post Office," *Smeur an Dochais/Bramble of Hope,* Canongate Press, 1992.

"In The Season When Crocuses," *Verse,* vol. II, no. 2, 1994.

"The Contention," "Glen Remote," *The Avoiding,* MacDonald Publishers, 1986, by permission of the author.

"To Any Lewisman," "The Buzzard," *Bailtean,* Gairm, 1987, by permission of the author.

"Language," "Sea Emperor" and "Eagle, Robin, Pine," *Verse,* vol II no. 2, 1995.

"Ghost Dancer," *All My Braided Colours,* Scottish Cultural Press, 1966, by permission of the author.

Irish Gaelic / Ireland

"Winter," *Irish Poetry Now,* Wolfhound Press, 1993, by permission of the author.

"Come Here, I Want To Tell You," *The Flowering Tree,* Wolfhound, 1991, and *Faoi Léigear,* 1980, by permission of the author.

"In A New York Shoe Shop," "Visionary" and "Stranger," *Irish Poetry Now,* Wolfhound, 1993, by permission of the author.

"Sometimes I Am A Phoney Man" and "Ravi Shankar," *The Flowering Tree,* Wolfhound, 1991, by permission of the author.

"Blodewedd," "Poetry" and "Jerusalem," *Pharoah's Daughter,* Gallery Press/Wake Forest University Press, 1990, 1995, by permission of the publisher.

"The Black Train," "Deep Freeze" and "The Voyage," *The Astrakhan Clock,* Wake Forest University Press, 1993, by permission of the publisher.

"Cuair," *Gairdín Pharthais,* Coiscéim, 1988, by permission of the author.

"Release" and "The Grass House," *Deora Nár Caoineadh,* Dedalus Press, 1996, by permission of the author.

"When I Was Three," "Shelter," "Knowledge," "Silence," "Beyond," "A Portrait Of A Blacksmith As A Young Artist," "A Braddy Cow," "To Jack Kerouac" and "Piccadilly," *An Bealach 'Na Bhaile,* Cló Iar-Chonnachta, 1993, by permission of the author.

Cornish / Cornwall

"An Dynas," *The Celtic Pen*.

"Yet I Have Hope," "The Cliff" and "There Is A Shower Threatening," *Delyow Derow*.

"There Was A Young Plumber," "The Shadow," "Old Woman" and "Shadows Of The Soul," *Kernow*, 1995 and 1996.

"Quiberon," "View From The Street" and "Surf," *Gerow (Words)*, 1994.

"The Cornish Society," "Great Heart, Beat By Beat," "My Father" and "In The Country Of Blue Rock," *Selected Poems*, 1994, by permission of the author.

"Language Prayer," "Queen's English" and "Edinburgh Castle," *Mewth On Un Like Dolcoath Shaft*, 1995, by permission of the author.

Manx / Isle of Man

"Sunset," Cruinnaght Competition: Poetry in Manx, 1992.

"Lomman," "Er y Cheer 'Sy Cheeiragh," "Duillagyn ny Fouyir" and "Bun As Baare," *Shelg yn Drave*, Fritlag, 1994.

The Editors

Thomas Rain Crowe is a poet, translator and author of several books of original work and translation including his *Night Sun* trilogy published in 1993, *The Laugharne Poems* (Gwasg Carreg Gwalch, 1997), and *In Wineseller's Street*, the poems of Hafiz, due out in early 1998 by Iranbooks. He is a former editor of such magazines as *Beatitude* and *Katuah Journal,* publisher of New Native Press, and producer of Fern Hill Records. His first book of poems, *The Personified Street,* introduced by Jack Hirschman, was written during his years in San Francisco during the 1970s. He currently lives in the Smoky Mountains of western North Carolina, where he is International Editor-at-large for the *Asheville Poetry Review.*

Gwendal Denez was born in Kemper (Quimper), West Brittany, and is a native Breton speaker. A graduate in English and Linguistics, in 1989 he received a State Doctorate in Breton and Celtic (his thesis was about the Breton writer Fanch Elies-Abeozen), and since 1992 he has taught at Rennes University. He founded, with others, the magazine *Al Lanv* in 1981. Among his published works are: *C'hamsin* (1989), a novel, (1989), *Blues komzett* (1990), a collection of poems (which was awarded the Imram Prize), and *Pesketourien Douarnezez* (1979), a study about the fishermen of his hometown. In addition, he is author of various works about World War I, is a translator, and is editor of the anthology *Skrid.*

Tom Hubbard took his Ph.D. at Aberdeen University and qualified as a librarian at Strathclyde University. In 1984 he became Librarian of the Scottish Poetry Library. He has taught Scottish literature at Edinburgh University and guest-lectured on Scottish poetry in Belgium, Germany, Poland, Hungary, Italy and the United States. His articles, essays, reviews and Scots poems have appeared in a wide range of magazines and books in Scotland and mainland Europe. He is one of the *Four Fife Poets: Fower Brigs ti a Kinrik* (AUP, 1988), and has read his work on Scottish Television's *In Verse* series. His collection, *The Lane an Luveless Leddy Turandot,* is a grotesque theatre-piece in Scots verse. He is the editor of the Scots language anthology, *The New Makars* (Mercat Press, 1991), author of *Seeking Mr. Hyde* (Peter Lang, Frankfurt-am-Main, 1995), and *The Integrative Vision: Poetry and the Visual Arts in Baudelaire, Rilke and MacDiarmid* due out from AKOS Press in Edinburgh in 1997.

Text set in Bembo and Humanist.
Composed at allpoints, Asheville, North Carolina.
Designed by Irwin Graphics, Asheville, North Carolina.
Printed on recycled paper and bound by
Thomson-Shore, Dexter, Michigan.
Made in the United States of America.